Toolful Coach

SPARKLE Coaching Model
with 150 Useful Tools and Case Studies

Laura Komócsin
Coach Editor: Zita Delevic, PhD

Toolful Coach

SPARKLE Coaching Model
with 150 Useful Tools and Case Studies

Laura Komócsin

Coach Editor: Zita Delevic, PhD

Copyright 2012 by Laura Komócsin

All rights reserved. No part of this book may be used or reproduced in any manner whatsoever without the written permission of the Publisher.

Author: © Laura Komócsin
Translation: © Rita Gallen
　　　　　　© Andrea Szabados
Coach Editor: © Zita Delevic, PhD
Cover Design: Imre Arany

ISBN-13: 978-1478106449
ISBN-10: 1478106441

Contents

Foreword 11
Acknowledgement 13
Introduction 15

A Few Thoughts about Coaching 19

A) Coaching Process Models 23
    1. GROW Model 23
    2. Vogelauer's Model 24
    3. RAMM Model 25
    4. PACE Model 26
    5. FLOW Model 27
    6. LASER Model 28
    7. CLEAR Model 29
    8. Magic Lamp Model 29
    9. RAVE Model 30
    10 STAR Model 30
    11. The 'Six Thinking Hats' framework 31
    12. Seven Cs Model 32
    13. SPARKLE Model 33

B) Coaching Tools – an Overview 37
I. Tools of the Situation Stage 47
    1. TRUST Model 47
    2. Shadow Map 49
    3. Square of Trust 51
    4. Process Strategy 52

5. Johari Window 53
6. 5D – Opening Tool 55
7. Door Openers 56
8. Nodders 56
9. Model T 56
10. Icebreakers 57
11. SWOT Analysis 58
12. Assessment Center and Development Center 59
13. Work Style Analysis 60
14. Van der Meer's Model 62
15. BCG Matrix 63
16. Montage 63
17. Onion Model 64
18. Shadow Coaching 65
19. Stakeholder Analysis 69
20. Iacocca's 9C' Model 70
21. Social Atom 71
22. MPH Client Mapping 75
23. Confrontation, Holding up a Mirror 76
24. ACE FIRST Model 79
25. 3-Column Thought Record 80
26. 5-Column Thought Record 81
27. 7-Column Thought Record 81
28. Document Analysis 83
29. Behavioral Window 83
30. Problem Window 84
31. Pie Chart 84
32. Change of Perspective 86
33. Outsider Input 87
34. 180/360 Degree Assessment 88
35. Tests 89
36. MBTI – Myers–Briggs Type Indicator 90
37. GPOP – Golden Personality Profile 91
38. Diary 92
39. Happiness and Success Curve 93
40. Activity Records 96

41. Old House – New House 96
42. Coat-of-arms 99
43. Reverse Job Advertisement 100
44. Analogue Environment 100
45. Free Association 101
46. Fantasy Ladder 102
47. Fantasy Domains 103
48. Wisdom Cards 103
49. Task Lists 105
50. Creative Writing: Fairy Tale 109
51. Creative Writing: Map 109
52. Creative Writing: Funeral Eulogy 109
53. Mind Mapping 109

II. Tools of the Positioning Stage 113

54. SMART Goals 114
55. Integrity Coaching 115
56. PURE Goals 115
57. CLEAR Goals 116
58. MbO – KPI 116
59. Balanced Scorecard 117
60. Benchmark 119
61. Specification 120
62. Let Us Complete the Sentence 121
63. Mercedes Symbol 122
64. Miracle Mountain Metaphor – 5P 124
65. ABCDEF Method 125
66. Positive Visualization 126
67. Post-it 128
68. Role Models 128
69. Attribute Card 129
70. Choosing an Object or Animal 130
71. Positive Feedback 130
72. Rubber Band 130
73. Wheel of Life 132
74. Drawing a Tree 133

- 75. Training Courses 134
- 76. Creative Writing: Ideal Day 134
- 77. Creative Writing: Letter 135

III. Tools of the Alternatives Stage 137

- 78. CREATE Model 138
- 79. Paper Clip 139
- 80. Illogical Ideas 139
- 81. Film and Book Recommendations 139
- 82. Parable 143
- 83. 'What if...?' questions 144
- 84. Stepping Out of One-to-One Coaching 144
- 85. The Coach's Ideas 145
- 86. 10+10 Minutes 145
- 87. Change in Emotions 146
- 88. Consulting the Encyclopedia 146
- 89. Reverse 147
- 90. Combining 147
- 91. Grouping 148
- 92. Adaptation 148
- 93. Magnification 149
- 94. Reduction 149
- 95. Ideal People 150
- 96. Consultant 150

IV. Tools of the Route Stage 153

- 97. Pros and Cons Analysis 153
- 98. Pros and Cons Analysis with the Time Dimension 154
- 99. Pros and Cons Aanalysis with Post-its 155
- 100. Win-Win 155
- 101. Adenauer Cross 156
- 102. Musts and Nice to Haves 156
- 103. Labeling 158
- 104. PMI Map 158
- 105. Walt Disney Model 158
- 106. Autonomy Triangle 158

107. Simulation 159
108. Black-White, Yes-No 159
109. Decision-Making List 160
110. CHOICE Model 161
111. Fishbone Diagram 162
112. Action Plan 163
113. Flowchart 165
114. Gradual Task-Growing 165

V. Tools of the Key Obstacles stage 171

115. Measuring Trust and Faith 171
116. Creative Writing: Saboteur 172
117. Learning from Our Own Mistakes 172
118. Helpmate 173
119. Magic Shop 174
120. Profit-Loss 175
121. Victory List 175
122. Role-Play 175
123. Sailing Ship 177
124. List of Self-Limiting Beliefs 178
125. Drama Triangle 179
126. Y Curve 180
127. Cockpit Confirmation 180
128. Deferring Games 181
129. Buckets and Balloons 181
130. eMAP (Russel) 182

VI. Tools of the Leverage Stage 185

131. Grades of Transfer 185
132. Ready - Stepping Ahead - Obstruction - New Challenge 186
133. Behavioral Tests 186
134. Positive Self-Talk 188
135. Distracting and Refocusing Attention 188
136. Confrontational, Provocative Coaching 188
137. Punishment 191
138. Reactive/Proactive Conditioning 193

    139. Pause Point Model 193
    140. CHANGE Framework 195

VII. Tools of the Evaluation Stage 199
    141. Summary Pattern 199
    142. Controlling the Client's Prosperity 201
    143. Drawing Conclusions 202
    144. Celebration 202

VIII. Tools of Questioning Techniques and Active Listening 203
    145. Meta-Model 205
    146. Repetition 206
    147. Summary 207
    148. Describing With Other Words 207
    149. Silence 208
    150. Good, Better, the Best Question 208

C) Sample Questions of the SPARKLE Model 211

D) Reconstruction of a Real Business Coaching Conversation ... 214

References 219

About the Author 221

About the Coach Editor 222

Foreword

Coaching has come of age. The past two decades has seen a growth in popularity of coaching as an organisational intervention to help support learning and drive performance. Over this period coaching has spread into the world of health services, education and personal coaching. Individuals can now select from a wide array of specialists including career coaches, life coaches, executive coaches or business coaches. Each of these offers specialist services to meet the variety of challenges we all experience in life.

Over this period coaching books too have changed. Early titles often focused on a single model and simple tools reflecting the immaturity of the coaching market and the emerging nature of coaching. There was little research about coaching or its impact. Most of the studies were personal accounts, case studies or used small qualitative samples. Since 2000 the number of research studies has mushroomed and good quality research has demonstrated that coaching can make a significant contribution to personal development and have positive impacts on organisational life and wider performance. Research has also started to help explore what is it that coaches do which makes a difference for their clients. Key facts in this seem to be the importance of the relationship, particularly empathy, combined with respectful and insightful challenge. Further good coaches have a diverse range of frameworks, tools and techniques to drawn upon which help them to meet their client where the client is, as opposed to expecting the client to fit the model or technique which the coach always uses.

Toolful Coach is part of the new generation of coaching books which reflects the complexity of coaching and the need for diversity in the tools, techniques and models which the coach uses. This book provides coaches with the opportunity to develop their knowledge about different approaches and frames of reference. However the truly master coach is not only knowledge about a diverse range of approaches and understands when to use them, they are also highly skilled in how these approaches are used with clients. This book is thus an encouragement to continually challenge our own practice and to explore new and refresh ways of working with clients to help them to fulfil their potential.

Professor Jonathan Passmore
Evora University, Portugal
Bestselling Author of *Excellence in Coaching*

Acknowledgements

Relationships are instrumental in life and in business success. I am fortunate to have wonderful people around me who encourage me and support me. I would like to express my thanks to Nikoletta Benedek and Anikó Uj to help me finalize the SPARKLE Model, and to Rita Gallen and Andrea Szabados for their work to translate the Hungarian edition into English.

The editor, Zita Delevic has been invaluable in the creation of this book. She demonstrated a unique ability to position this project to suit the needs of the English speaking readers. I appreciate her support and collaboration during the whole process even when I got into the "Key Obstacles" stage.

My acknowledgment and gratitude also go to those coaching and management gurus who inspired me either when we met personally or through their books. I am grateful for their selfless work in reading my book and writing the foreword and recommendations.

I am so fortunate to have a father like Mihály, who is my role model in knowledge sharing as an author of several books. As always, with all my work and publishing, I wish to show some good examples to my children as well.

Finally, I would like to dedicate this book to my husband, who encouraged me to "go for it and show that a Hungarian woman can also bring some SPARKLE to the coaching world!"

Introduction to the English Edition

With this book, you will discover new horizons in the coaching field, whether your focus is executive or leadership coaching, business coaching, career coaching or life coaching- a world founded on a methodical approach and well-defined processes. This book offers an in-depth presentation of 13 model frameworks and 150 tools that you can instantly place into your active toolbox and that will enable you to approach coaching with clearly defined processes and methods suitable for almost any coaching scenario.

This book is unique in many respects:
1. The author gathered in one place 13 coaching frameworks and 150 coaching tools from a variety of disciplines, including professional coaching, psychology, training, and business management.
2. It introduces a new model for the coaching process (SPARKLE Coaching Model), organizes and leads the reader through available tools in accordance with different phases of this model.
3. It combines theory and practice, providing not only a list and description of coaching tools but also valuable illustrations by way of many insightful "one-minute" case studies. Both the tools and case studies are tangible, the latter demonstrating practical application with real-life examples.
4. To facilitate implementation by the reader, four categories (life coaching, career coaching, business coaching and executive coaching) are set forth, with each tool listed in the Table of Contents falling where it fits best.

This book was first published in Hungarian in 2009. Laura Komócsin ACC is the CO-founder and leading faculty member at the Executive Coaching and Mentoring Academy run by KPMG-BME Academy (a management school, established by KPMG in Hungary and the Budapest University of Technology and Economics/BME). In addition to serving as a coach and coaching instructor for many years at the Academy, she was the Founder and first President of the International Coach Federation's (ICF) Hungarian chapter from 2008 to 2010. She is currently ranked as the No. 1 Coach in Hungary. Thus far, she has published three best-selling coaching books in Hungary. When her first book *A Guide for Coaches and Managers Who Utilize Coaching Tools, Vol.1 – 150 Coaching Tools With Case Studies* was published she received several requests from abroad (US, Canada, Singapore, Austria, and Germany) to translate it into English. While there are a substantial number of coaching books in the international market, the feedback she received was that her book, which contains an extensive overview of coaching models and tools, is unique in its kind and would be valuable to a larger, international audience.

Laura Komócsin goes beyond simply compiling the numerous methodologies and coaching examples. In **Part A** of the book, she presents 13 coaching frameworks, including the SPARKLE Coaching Model which she created and teaches at the Executive Coaching and Mentoring Academy. Her model consists of assisting the coach in following the natural flow and stages of a typical coaching process. SPARKLE is an acronym comprised of seven stages whereby each letter represents a step in the coaching process.

S – Situation
P – Positioning Yourself
A – Alternatives
R – Route
K – Key Obstacles
L – Leverage
E – Evaluation

In **Part B,** she presents the 150 coaching tools, each of which is assigned to the corresponding stages of the aforementioned SPARKLE Model. The reader will recognize the ease and practicality of identifying the right tools when searching for a specifically-tailored solution to a given phase (tools for assessing the situation at the onset of coaching or for experimenting with a new method of setting goals). All the coaching tools are assigned accordingly to the various steps of coaching, such as Situation – Positioning (yourself) – Alternatives – Route – Key Obstacles – Leverage – Evaluation.

Part C sets forth sample questions of the SPARKLE Model, while in **Part D,** namely the reconstruction of a real-life conversation, provides greater insight into business and executive coaching.

The English edition is an improved and updated version of the first edition. The language and content have been adapted for the English-speaking audience, and the book contains even more case studies to demonstrate more effectively for the readers the coaching tools in question. They are now marked by a symbol in the table of contents and classified into four categories. These symbolize the four most common coaching fields, namely: life coaching ♀ , career coaching ☿ , business coaching ∠ , and executive coaching ✻ . Many coaching tools are not exclusive to one particular domain and may serve a purpose in the other coaching fields as well in a wide range of situations. However, the small symbols provide guidance by indicating a tool's primary use. We, coaches, know how various techniques can serve multiple purposes and be applied to a multitude of scenarios. Therefore, a single tool is not confined to its originally intended use but instead may have numerous applications.

To further demonstrate the coaching tools' versatility, let us examine a specific example. You will find an unusual case study excerpt under MBTI (Tool # 36). One might think the Myers-Briggs Type Indicator is only used in organizations to support a host of different functions and business situations such as those involving the management of others, leadership development, conflict management, executive coaching, and change management. The beauty of this tool (and that of others) is its applicability to life coaching as well, as shown by the case study of a scenario involving a family. While extroverted and introverted personalities clash in this family, through coaching and the utilization of MBTI which facilitates the understanding and acceptance of individual differences, – parents and children found a "modus vivendi" that smoothed out the "family wrinkles".

According to findings from the most recent study on coaching (Global Coaching Survey 2011 by PWC), there are currently 47,500 professional coaches worldwide, and that number is growing each month. This book is dedicated to assist them and others who are seeking to learn new ways of helping to improve themselves, their clients or their work teams. In view of the generous selection of theoretical and practical examples the author provides in her manuscript, this book can be unquestionably valuable for anyone looking for a helpful set of tools in his or her coaching or even in the practice of management ingeneralor self-coaching. New and seasoned coaches alike will find practical models and tips, irrespective of the coaching school from which they graduated. It is also an invaluable resource for managers, leaders, and executives who are committed to the continuous improvement of their team as well as for others who are simply interested in adding some coaching tools to their existing profession. With 150 tools from which to choose in this book, you will always have a valuable resource at your disposal.

Zita Delevic, PhD
Coach Editor
Executive Coach and Consultant
www.pebblejam.com
President, ICF South Florida Chapter

A Few Thoughts about Coaching

The aim of this book is not to cover all aspects of coaching since it could be quite voluminous. We will solely focus on tools and case studies illustrating the latter. Notwithstanding this, it is necessary to provide a brief overview of coaching in general.

A professional coach (executive, business, career or life coach) is an individual who is typically in the business field but also in other areas; a coach who helps the client exploit his or her potential (in this case, the latter being not an athlete but rather a leader in his or her professional and personal life). It is not the coach who runs; he or she only enables success. It is the runner who has to run and consequently, who wins the award. Professional coaches are personalized "developers", in case of an executive or leadership engagement for example they are "executive developers"; they focus on the clients' existing issues rather than deliver an across-the-board presentation. For instance, when working with executives, their clients are key figures in their organizations from a specific aspect. Coaches are "developers" because they are remunerated for contributing to the executives' betterment. Essentially, a good coach does not teach but inspires.

A coach is not a trainer because he or she
• customizes the message for each client (does not sell ready-made, but tailor-made clothes);
• does not discuss general matters and theory but addresses the client's specific issues, thereby attaining more general lessons;
• does not work with a group of 10 to 12 individuals but rather one partner (in the case of 1-on-1 coaching).

A coach is not a therapist because
• his or her clients are not ill or injured but healthy individuals seeking to improve their skills;
• he or she does not examine the past but focuses on the future;
• he or she does not focus on mistakes, but possibilities and solutions.

A coach is not a consultant because
• he or she does not provide ready solutions but utilizes skillful questions to further the exploration of alternatives and catalysts. In the implementation phase, participants cannot be replaced. If a consultant or his or her client becomes ill, a substitute may resume the process the following day. In coaching, however, the session would be rescheduled in such an event.
• in corporate coaching, for instance, the focus is primarily not on the organization but on the executive who is being coached. It is the executive who will develop, which in turn will positively impact the organization.

One of my clients summarized this for me the following way: "If I want to "sweat" for my success, I will recruit a coach. If I want someone else to "sweat", I call a consultant, even though I know I will have to call them again when I am faced with a similar problem."

A coach is not a mentor because[1]
- he or she and the client are not employed by the same organization;
- he or she does not suffer from "work myopia";
- a mentor is expected to possess leadership experience, whereas a coach is expected to demonstrate coaching knowledge and experience;
- a coaching engagement lasts for a contracted term, generally 3 to 12 months, while the duration of a mentoring engagement is longer, lasting even until both parties are employed by the company, sometimes 3 to 5 years;
- coaching centers on performance (except for career coaching) while mentoring focuses usually on careers.

Coaching is not a conversation with a friend due to the fact that:
- only the coachee's issues are addressed;
- it is structured (Situation – Positioning (yourself)–Alternatives – Route – Key Obstacles – Leverage – Evaluation); specific coaching tools are employed.

Anthony M. Grant illustrates the essence of the aforementioned in the following diagram:

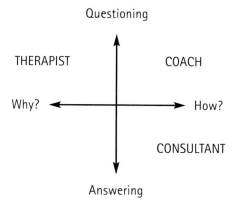

An effective coach does not focus on "why" but "how", and his or her tool does not consist in providing answers but questioning.

As far as the comparison between consulting and coaching is concerned, another illustration comes to mind. If a client is sitting with his or her back to a rose and asks his or her consultant facing him or her what color the rose is, then the consultant will respond in a split second that it is red. If the client wants to know whether the rose has thorns, then he or she again asks the consultant who promptly responds, and so on. The client has to rely continuously on the consultant's help each time he or she needs new information.

If the client asks his or her coach about the rose's color, then the coach will not even inform whether or not the latter sees it. Instead, he or she guides the client by proposing that he or she turn around. While it also takes the client one second to turn around, henceforth he or she will not depend on the coach because of the additional information he or she has acquired through personal experience than simply from the color or the thorns of the rose. For instance, the client can also observe how long its stem is, how many leaves it has, whether it is in a vase or not, and so on. I find this elementary and yet very expressive illustration to be very useful.

I have a strong and sincere devotion to this profession, partly because I have always enjoyed assisting others and also because it is personally rewarding to engage in an undertaking that is progressive. This explains my appreciation for the following maxim by John Whitmore:[2] "Coaching focuses on future possibilities, not past mistakes."

I was often asked in radio interviews why a successful executive would need a coach. When answering this question, I always draw on an example from sports: only the really good athletes have their own coaches; it is not worth investing in a coach for also-rans. An individual who is offered a coach should not feel there is something is amiss with him or her but instead view it as a token of appreciation from their company that is willing to invest time and resources towards their betterment. It is not the workhorse but the racehorse that needs a coach.

In the fall of 2008, I had the honor of giving a presentation at an international coaching conference immediately following John Whitmore, with whom I had an opportunity to speak afterwards. He pointed out: "Quality coaching has the profit of the coachee exceeding the limits of the coach's knowledge."[3] The same applies to sports, in that a coach is not superior to the athlete (otherwise, the coach would be a world champion), but he or she is more capable of bringing out the most out of the athlete. A highly-qualified coach accepts an assignment if he or she knows that they can achieve this.

CASE STUDY (EXCERPT)

I once had a client who was an executive in a large corporation. After the third session, the principal- the company's deputy CEO- called me and informed me he had been dissatisfied with my client for years but pointed out that it was not my fault. He was cognizant of the fact that one could not work a miracle in three sessions even if he witnessed an improvement on the executive's part. Nevertheless, he decided to discharge him. He asked me to facilitate the situation for both of them and to initiate a conversation concerning the employee's goals in life, his view of an ideal job, etc...Clearly, he was aware that my client was not comfortable in that situation either. I too felt terrible and as if I had been taken in. I had been asked to enable my client to become a better leader, and the plan was modified along the way. I harbored the suspicion that this action had been premeditated, and that their intent was for me to conclude that my partner was not developable. I was having sleepless nights. Having worked with many executives before, I found my client to be anything but a poor leader. On the contrary, I felt that it was the deputy CEO who committed an error – recruiting a coach for an employee and then laying him off three weeks later.

After a few months, my coachee left the company with a generous severance pay. The HR director later called me and said: "I am sorry about what happened. The deputy CEO was not a very good leader. He kept blaming the executive and made a scapegoat out of him. The deputy CEO will be dismissed next month. Could you help us convince our former executive to return to the company?" I was very pleased that I had accurately perceived the situation- that the flaw did not in my client, who was reinstated in the company as a deputy CEO...

Every coaching session is followed by homework. Unlike high school, however, the deadline for the latter is set by the "student", as opposed to the teacher. Several of my clients observed that coaching was beneficial to them because it forced them to examine tasks that they had procrastinated prior to each session (which serves their interest because they are well aware that they continued postponing them), and, that owing to the mental pressure, accomplished more of those than they had ever done in preceding. There are clients, of course, who fail to do this even in the last moment, and if it repeats several times then we address it in a coaching session, particularly if the classic excuse "I didn't have the time for it" is given.

I do deploy all the tools presented in this book. There are some that I prefer to use more frequently and some that I rarely use. However, I believe it is better for a new coach to have a broader set of tools from which he or she can select than to resort to the same one or two at all the times.

As John Whitmore states, "We are more like an acorn, which contains within it all the potential to be a magnificent oak tree. We need nourishment, encouragement and light to reach towards, but the oak-treeness is already within."[4]

A similar quote from André Louf reads: "The key to your internal life is within you. However, there is a need for an external person, a word, a gesture, the density of the relationship to make the harmony hiding in you deeply resound by a touch."[5]

For their children, people are able to make herculean efforts, even those which they would never have imagined themselves capable. Individuals are able to deploy superhuman efforts in a critical situation when their child's life is at risk. Why should we always experience crises to achieve the most? A coach helps to maximize a client's potential, even such things that they would have regarded as impossible beforehand.

Finally, I would like to reassure executives, leaders, managers that it is worthwhile to support their employees through coaching and will do so by quoting Harvey S. Firestone: "It is only as we develop others that we permanently succeed."[6]

J. D. Batten also said: "A good leader is aware of the fact that the most exciting experience and the greatest challenge in life is to make average people perform above average."

Laura Komócsin, ACC

Notes

1 This list was drawn from *Excellence in Coaching* by Jonathan Passmore, Kogan Page, 2006
2 John Whitmore: *Coaching for Performance*. N. Brealey, 1996
3 Ibid.
4 Ibid.
5 Andre Louf: *Grace Can Do More: Spiritual Companionship & Spiritual Growth*. Cistercian Publications, 2002
6 http://thinkexist.com

A) Coaching Process Models

> "Vision without action is a dream.
> Action without vision is simply passing the time.
> Vision with action is making a positive difference."
> Joel Arthur Barker[1]

Coaching process models are in overabundance these days. The list of models outlined here is not intended to be exhaustive. A part of the coaching process models included in this book was created specifically for this purpose. Another part was adapted to coaching from another field.

The process model to be employed and the timing of its use depends on many factors, such as the client's current dilemma, his or her personality (for instance, whether or not he or she likes to celebrate his or her successes) and the corporate culture.

1. GROW Model[2]

The word GROW perfectly matches the objective of coaching, which is to enable the client to make progress, grow, and develop. It is a four-stage goal setting tool in which the coach follows the client with a Socratic approach, without any psychological background. The coach assists the coachee in making progress through the use of open questions. They focus on what accomplishment is needed to achieve the goal that was fixed at the inception.

The model (see figure below), originates from Graham Alexander, Alan Fine, and Sir John Whitmore who had further developed and popularized it, is perhaps the most prevalent process model among coaches today.

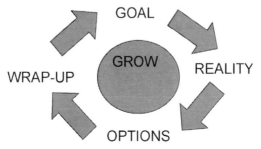

G – Goal – Defining the goal
R – Reality – Assessing the current situation
   Do you know what you want to change – what is the starting-point? The coach should aid in exploring the client's present situation, by relying on facts and focusing on the situation at hand, and eliminate desire and prejudice. This stage includes the objective and detailed exploration of the point of departure as well as the current conditions of the goal to be achieved.
O – Options – Consider the possibilities
   Identify the possibilities – no decisions have to be made yet. The coach assists in brainstorming and, above all, in including unfeasible considerations on the list so that nothing is omitted due to biases and assumptions.
W – Wrap-up, What will you do?
   Planning the path for attainment of your goal.
   In the final stage, you must decide what tasks are required and create a plan of action. The coach should raise many clarifying questions concerning specific steps and consequences, e.g. deadlines, obstacles, support. How satisfied will the client be upon reaching his or her goal? The client should rank the level of satisfaction on a scale from 1 to 10. If it falls below 10, a new plan of action must be devised.

2. Vogelauer's Model[3]

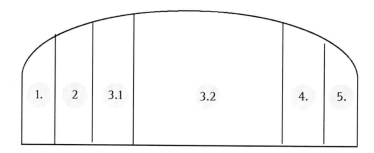

1. Entry and contact phase.
   As the author describes in his book: "This conversation serves for exchanging information and getting to know each other. It provides a mutual opportunity without any commitment for starting joint work, but also for either party to quit the process and not to begin coaching ... It is essential that an atmosphere of mutual and acceptance be established, the issue raised be appropriate for coaching and the client be visibly committed."
2. Agreement and contracting.
   "It is important that the starting situation and the ideas about the goal be put in writing, and that the client accepts the terms and conditions."
3. Work on the coaching focus – it can be divided into two sub phases.
   3.1. Assessment of situation and diagnosis: The coach's objective is to be as informed as possible about the client's situation.
   3.2. Problem solving, creating a plan. Generally, this is the longest phase; therefore, the author provides a structure for the stages of a coaching session (see the following diagram):

A – Warming up/Current issues. What issues is the client currently concerned about? Those must be tackled even if they are not very pertinent to the goal of coaching because they might block the work needed to accomplish the goal.
B – Transfer Connection. How is the client progressing towards realization? What positive and negative experiences has he or she had since the previous coaching session?
C – Working on Goals and Problems. New goals can be set, and existing ones can be altered.
D – Translating plans into how the parties define what the client is going to do and when and how it is going to be accomplished.
E – Feedback and Outlook. Summary of the coaching session.

4. Conclusion and feedback.
"The coaching process has successfully come to the finish line. It is advisable to look back on the process as a closing step when we have reached our goals, processed problems and found solutions."
5. Evaluation.
Practicing its execution in the workplace; sharing experience, providing inspiration and encouragement.

3. RAMM Model[4]

Mitchell Axelrod dubs the process, comprised of the following stages "the recipe for success":
Result – Action – Measure – Modify.
He calls this model a tool that helps people become successful and supports the process of success-oriented action. To get from A to B, you must complete four steps:

R – Result
To attain a destination; you have to know where you are heading and your point of departure, as well as how you can proceed from A to B. You have to be aware of your outcome and destination. It is as important to know your starting point as the final destination.
Where are you now? Where do you want to arrive?
A – Action
If you know where your finish line is, then you have to take action. After finding the optimal manner of attaining your destination, you must begin the journey even if you make a mistake. You will never arrive anywhere if you do not take any action.
What is your plan? What will you do? What are you doing NOW to get to B?
M – Measure
You have to measure your progress to B both qualitatively and quantitatively. For instance, if the plan sets forth that a plane has to fly from A to B, and then the flying height will be known. These measuring and evaluating efforts aid in ascertaining whether you are on the right course. Constant reflection on your steps.

M – Modify
A desire for change: you can only complete the first three steps if you have an intention, a desire for change, the capacity to reconsider your actions, flexibility, a receptive attitude, and the capacity to adapt to the specific situation.
What is that you could change? To what should you adapt?

This model begins with goal-setting rather than assessment and progresses iteratively, i.e. exploring various options to achieve the goal and finding a new one if they fail. This model has its place in corporate cultures where some risk-taking is embraced. Companies where many ideas are implemented annually, with the risk that some of them might fail, could benefit from this model. In other companies where decisions need to be safe and where action is preceded by extensive analysis (e.g. nuclear power plant) should probably not choose this model.

4. PACE Model[5]

This model, which is associated with Lynn I Ward, has been adapted to coaching. The word PACE refers to the notion that achieving one's goal is also possible in small paces. On the other hand, it refers to the idea that paces and actions are needed to achieve goals you would never attained before if you stay where you are and do not leave your comfort zone.

Originally it served as a model for a self-revealing process. The author suggested that one should retire to a quiet place with a pen and a piece of paper and carry out the following tasks. This may be accomplished effectively with a supportive partner or a coach; moreover, a partner or a coach can make this process even more effective.

1. Specify your dreams.
• Ask yourself the following questions:
– If I knew I could not fail, what would I do?
– What have I always wanted to do, but have not?
– What are the benefits of realizing my dream? To myself? To others?
– What has it cost me thus far to delay realization of my dream?
– What will it cost me to put off my dream even longer?
– What makes my life meaningful?
– What do I want to accomplish in the next 10, 20, 30 years?
– What legacy do I want to leave?
• Prepare a list of your dreams. This is the first step to realize them, making sure to include all sorts of eccentric ideas on the list.
• Prioritize your dreams upon compilation of your list. Select your top 10, write them on a separate sheet of paper and place the list in an area where you can read it daily.
• The following step: Determine the resources you need to achieve your dreams. (Note: These may be people, tools, money, skills, attitude, and objects.) List your dreams in the first column and write the requisite resources next to each dream.

2. Build a team of committed individuals who will offer you understanding, support and encouragement. Create a Dream Journal and include the following lines:
My dream is: ....

The people supporting me in making my dreams a reality, mentors and coaches are: ....
....
....
....

3. PACE.

How do you actually turn your dream into reality? How to be successful? For this, you will need a tool for planning specific steps.

- P – Plan – Plan and list the Action Steps needed to reach your destination and plan backwards. Jot down every step and set a deadline for each one.
- A – Act – Take daily action steps. Doing something each day means making progress. Every night, write three things you will perform the following day. Remind yourself every day that you can only be successful if you are consistent.
- C – Celebrate – Celebrate all the small steps and accomplishments along the way. Plan how you will celebrate in advance.
- E – Energize – Take the necessary breaks to revitalize yourself.

4. Prepare for the fear obstacles.

Endeavor to understand your fears- why they are there, what they tell you, which of them poses a real threat and which do not. Identify fears that are old familiar patterns and that do not pose any actual threat. Ask yourself these questions:

- Do I experience fear whenever I undertake a new project? If yes, what are my fears? To what can I trace my fears?
- What form do my fears take? Are they physical in nature? A voice in my head telling me that I cannot do something?
- Some common fears include: fear of failure, fear of success, fear of change, fear that it will be "too hard", fear that I will not do it perfectly. Which ones can you relate to?
  – Compile a list of your fears. Mark the fears in one column and write down when they manifest themselves most potently.
  – Make a list of actions you could take to offset your fears. These should be arranged in two columns (fears and remedies).

This model devotes a separate stage for celebrating and recharging one's batteries. The step called "Energize" is unique in coaching models but could be very useful. It might be interesting to try this model in a corporate culture with a client who is not accustomed to celebrating, who moves on right after each accomplishment he or she made. The coaching process itself may induce a change in the client that might entail benefits even in other areas of their life.

5. FLOW Model[6]

Yes, I imagine that this headline likely evoked 'Flow' by Mihály Csíkszentmihályi (1991). This should not pose a problem since the most gratifying fruit of coaching is achievement of this state by the client or coach. However, this is another FLOW model consisting of the initial letters of the following words:

- Fast
- Linked
- Outcome
- Worthwhile

This is a model designed for following the coaching process. It enables tracking the progress of the latter as well as the understanding of what is happening and how questions follow each other. The word refers to the notion that the coaching process should also be implemented as a flow.

It is worth examining a coaching process retrospectively from this aspect – even together with the client or the coach's supervisor or coach.

Each of the words making up the model's acronym may be resolved by a question, making it possible to evaluate an interactive dialogue from the aspect of effectiveness. In fact, it is akin to a checklist for the coach.

F – Fast   Question: Did we make maximum use of the time available?
L – Linked   Question: Were our questions coherent, i.e. did they follow a logical process?
O – Outcome   Question: Have we made progress through the questions?
W – Worthwhile   Question: Is the outcome valuable for the client?

6. LASER Model[7]

This model of the coaching process was published by Graham Lee in his book *Leadership Coaching*.

L – Learning – in this stage, the learning space should be established and maintained.
A – Assessing – in this phase, the coach should focus on gathering and reviewing data. This should include all requisite information, regardless of its source, i.e. information obtained from the client, feedback and insights of the coach, data acquired from third parties (for instance, data from 360-degree assessments) and various tests.
S – Story-making – this is the step where the information gathered is used to construct useful stories about the client's developmental need, goal and journey.
E – Enabling – in this stage, the factors that can promote or limit development are considered.
R – Reframing – this is when interactions promoting development and change occur.

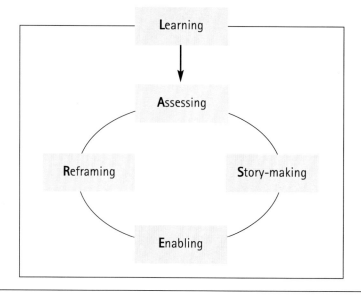

7. CLEAR Model[8]

Although this five-stage model was originally designed specifically for the supervision of coaches, it can be used as a coaching process model as well.

The word CLEAR refers to the importance of a clear coaching – the client should be aware of its beginning, ending and what they can expect. This is fostered by various coaching process models that provide further clarification of the coaching process for both parties.

C – Contract
As a first step, define your tasks, your areas of focus on, and boundaries.

L – Listening
In the next stage, listen to what your partner wants to address, what issue is he or she raising, etc. In addition to the content, you should also pay attention to emotions, small signs during story-telling and the client's behavior. Before making advances in the process, it is important to reassure the client that you understand the situation and that not only did you comprehend the information but are also aware of the circumstances and feelings.

E – Explore
In this stage, you should focus on a deep understanding of the situation, the relationships between the players involved in the process and the relationship between client and coach. Upon reviewing these processes, the parties can move forward…

A – Action
…to determine the new direction. Here, the coach should facilitate new actions.

R – Review
The parties review and summarize the entire process.

Nomen est omen, it's a quite CLEAR coaching model.

8. Magic Lamp Model[9]

The same issue is addressed by the Magic Lamp Model developed by Keith Ellis. His goal-setting book titled *The Magic Lamp* is recommended for people who resist having to set goals.

L – Lock on – Decide which wish you would like to make and do not lose sight of it. Hold on to it! Do not simply state what your goal is but take full possession of it: Set up a plan how you seek to accomplish it, divide the process into mini-steps and set a deadline for each of them.

A – Act – Make the leap from thinking to executing. Do not postpone steps; take action today rather than tomorrow. The more time elapses between your resolution and the first steps, the more unlikely you will accomplish your goal. If you take only a single tiny step to reach your goal (for example, you call a friend to ask for his or her advice or tell him or her that you have found your path), then it will be easier for you to take the second step because of the reluctance of feeling that the first step was futile and a waste of effort. The law of inertia states that a body in motion tends to remain in motion, and a body at rest tends to remain at rest. Taking one small step toward your goal each day is useful, even if it is a very tiny step; it will not be inconsequential. (In the case of my book, I wrote at least one paragraph every day because it is a volume that you can draft even if you are very busy and tired. While this is not much, I was at least able to maintain my momentum.) As an old Chinese proverb states, "A journey of a thousand miles begins with one small step."

Finish today what you regret having put off yesterday and complete also what you would regret failing to do tomorrow. Every minute allocated towards the accomplishment of your goal (instead of sitting in front of the TV and internet) brings you closer to the latter.

M – Manage your process – Track the causes you have set in motion to produce the desired effects and adjust your strategy if necessary. You should not feel ashamed if you reach your goal by following a different route than initially planned – there are always new pieces of information and experiences that force you to modify instead of pursue your original plan.

P – Persist – Finish what you start. Hold on and don't give up!

Belief feeds persistence – which leads to success. When you begin to feel that your belief is weakening, try to strengthen it by asking yourself the following questions: "Do I believe this wish is worth the effort?" and "Do I really want to give up?" The author offers specific tips in his book:
- Keep your goal in front of you – taped to the mirror, refrigerator, or computer monitor.
- Repeat your goal to yourself over and over again every day.
- Never go to bed without doing something to accomplish your goal, even if it is a very small step.
- Keep a weekly progress report.

When people complain about not reaping from life what they want, the reason is usually that they lack a notion of what it is that they in fact desire and blame fate instead of themselves.

There are a vast number of goal-setting techniques; in order to select the appropriate one, the personalities of both coach and client have to be considered.

9. RAVE Model[10]

Dale Carnegie offers a model that was originally recommended for performance assessment that is when a leader furthers an employee's development as an internal coach. However, there are also independent external coaches who utilize model. The acronym RAVE consists of the initials of the following four words:

R – Review – Review the situation.
A – Analyze – Analyze performance and identify potential areas of improvement.
V – Vision – A vision of the individual's future development, reaching the next level.
E – Encourage – The coach encourages the client.

10. STAR Model[11]

While this process model was not specifically conceived for coaching, it is often referred to by coaches. This is very similar to other coaching models but many coaches and clients prefer this one because it is easy to remember and easy to explain to others.

S – Situation – Assessment of the specific situation.
T – Target – Target setting.
A – Action – Actions that enable progress.
R – Result

11. 'The Six Thinking Hats' framework[12]

Created by Edward de Bono, originally this model was not designed for coaching. Still, it can be employed both in team and individual coaching. A great advantage of this framework is that it directs flashing thoughts in one direction so that problem-solving becomes more time-efficient.

As stated in De Bono's book *The Six Thinking Hats*:

"Confusion is the greatest enemy to effective thinking. We try to do too many things at the same time. We look for information. We are affected by feelings. We seek new ideas and options. We have to be cautious. We want to find benefits. Those are a lot of things that need doing.

Juggling with the six balls at the same time is rather difficult. Tossing up one ball at a time is much easier.

With the Six Hats method, we try to engage in only one activity at a time. (...)

There are two main purposes of the Six Thinking Hats concept. The first purpose is to simplify thinking by allowing an individual to address one thing at a time. Instead of having to tackle emotions, logic, information, hope and creativity all at once, the thinker is able to deal with them separately. ...

The second key aim of the Six Thinking Hats concept is to allow a *switch* in thinking. If a person at a meeting has been persistently negative, he or she can be asked to remove the black thinking hat. ... Alternatively, the person may also be asked to put on the yellow thinking hat, which would constitute a direct request to be positive. In this way, the six hats provide an idiom that is definite without being offensive. ... The hats become a sort of shorthand of instruction."

There are no strict rules for which hat should follow another. You can also step back, but there are a few recommendations on the sequence of hats.

- White Hat: neutral, objective, addresses facts and data as if you were a computer with no emotions (diagnosis).
- Red Hat: signifies feelings. In this stage, you do not have to explain or justify your emotions; you should only express your own feelings. The goal is not to get personal. This hat validates feelings, the message being that you should not stifle them because that could lead to frustration. (If there are strong emotions surrounding a particular issue, then it is recommended to wear this hat immediately after diagnosis so that it would not obscure sight.)
- Green Hat: focuses on creativity and new ideas (collecting alternatives; however, it might be worth putting it on again after the black hat to find creative solutions for overcoming the identified obstacles).
- Yellow Hat: symbolizes brightness and optimism. It is much more difficult to wear it than the black one because, as Bono explains, in the latter case, there is a natural mechanism in human brain that helps avoid threats but there is no such mechanism where the yellow hat is concerned.
- Black Hat: judgment. You wear it when you spot difficulties and dangers. It represents critical thinking, helping to assess whether a specific idea corresponds with your values, strategy and current possibilities. (It can serve as an effective Provocative Coaching tool.)
- Blue Hat: management and control (decision and conclusions).

"The hats are there for you to use at your discretion as a formal means to ask for a certain type of thinking. ... Instead of the general and vague request to 'think about this', there is now a precise way to ask for a particular mode of thinking."

If the coach explains Edward de Bono's 'Six thinking hats' framework well (if this tool is relied upon in coaching, then it is advisable to offer a copy of the book to the coachee for homework purposes), coach and coachee can speak the same language throughout the process.

It is a valuable tool because it compels even very optimistic clients to put on the black hat and examine the dark side of an issue, and it also forces very pessimistic people – the devil's advocates – to wear the yellow hat and be constructive and positive.

It is important to set a time limit for wearing each hat so that you can separate the individual stages and prevent them from blending.

12. Seven Cs Model[13]

Mick Cope discussed this framework in this book The Seven Cs of Coaching as follows:

C – Client: What do you want to accomplish? Why do you need external help?
C – Clarify: What has prevented you from accomplishing it so far?
C – Create: Do you have any ideas about the solution?
C – Change: Are you able to effectuate the change?
C – Confirm: Do others agree that there is something wrong?
C – Continue: What factors might draw you back and which ones could enable the new solution to become permanent?
C – Close: What additional value does the new solution bring to your life?

Not only does Mick Cope describe the Seven Cs framework in his book, but he also offers tools for each stage:

Stage	Tools
1. Client	MPH mapping tool
2. Clarity	Fantasy ladder, Shadow Map
3. Create	CREATE model, CHOICE model
4. Change	Y-curve, CHANGE framework
5. Confirm	Cockpit confirmation, F-games model
6. Continue	Buckets and Balloons, Miracle Mountain
7. Close	Look Back and Learn, Fly Solo

Here are some illustrations of thoughts or sentences in each stage:

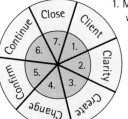

7. If manage to get that promotion then I will ask his or her help in getting the next one as soon as possible.

6. Change does not present a problem for me.

5. I believe that success is measured only by a high salary.

1. My spouse thinks I need to get a promotion so that we can move into a new home.

2. I have no idea why I haven't been promoted thus far – I think executives just don't understand me.

3. Yes, I have tried to work with several coaches but somehow it is of no use.

4. I think I need to attend additional trainings – I believe it is the key to my appointment.

13. SPARKLE Model

Having read the chapter on coaching models, you could discern that the most coaching frameworks emanate from the English-speaking world. People are often keen on acronyms, especially if every word has the same initial (see the 7C framework) or if the initials form a relevant and positive word. The framework we have created in Hungary is called the " SPARKLE Model". This model demonstrates the typical stages of a coaching process.

I studied and worked in the Netherlands for a few years. In Amsterdam I have seen how enthusiaticly diamond polishers work and realized how similar it is to the coaches' job. They start out with a piece of diamond in the rough and we all know how beuatiful the end result is; the diamond sparkles like nothing else. We also „polish" our clients to reach their goals and really sparkle…That is the reason why our model is called: SPARKLE.

Naturally, as we say, "Nobody coaches the way I do."[14] No coaching model should be viewed too rigidly, and neither should the SPARKLE Model. This framework was designed only to assist in understanding and constructing the stages of the process and to serve as a reference on what a coach can do and what tools can used in each stage, as well as what the client can expect. The GROW Model employs four stages and the 7C framework uses seven stages, our SPARKLE Model divides the process into seven stages as well but a bit differently:

1. Situation
2. Positioning (yourself)
3. Alternatives
4. Route
5. Key Obstacles
6. Leverage
7. Evaluation

S – Situation: in this stage, the coach and the coachee assess the starting point, the time for initiating the coaching process, the challenges faced by the client. To properly evaluate the current situation, you can choose from among multiple methods and a vast number of tools. First of all, however, it is essential to win the client's confidence so that he or she knows that he or she is not being badgered with questions (Questioning Technique), "spied upon" (Shadow Coaching), "investigated" (360 Degree Assessment) out of sheer curiosity, but rather this is all done to help him or her.

The Situation stage should include assessing the coachee's openness and secret zones that are best avoided (for example, in business coaching, the coachee may stipulate that no personal issues will be covered). If you are aware of taboos, then you can employ opening methods and then perform detailed research based on this. Coaching tools coupled with some psychological background as well as different creative writing techniques may be utilized in this stage. With all means at his or her disposal, the coach will effectively use the tools of Active Listening and Questioning Techniques.

P – Positioning (yourself): In the next stage, the client, assisted by the coach, defines his or her desired vision, dictates the direction and the aim. Here, the coach basically helps the client decide upon a reasonable objective that can be achieved (a SMART goal). Tools used in this stage can be divided into two large groups depending on how visual the client is. For instance, resuming the previous stage, Montage, Wheel of Life, Old House - New House techniques or Coat-of-Arms may be used. However, there are clients who bring to the first coaching session their individual SMART goal summarized in a few words.

A – Alternatives: In this stage, you focus on identifying and drafting options and possibilities to be able to determine how the aim could be accomplished. The importance of this stage lies in consideration. Instead of jumping to make a decision, the client should be able to consider several options and make a well-informed decision and Route in the next stage. The coach can inspire brainstorming using various tools such as Magnification, Consulting the Encyclopaedia, Ideal People, Action Plan, or the CREATE Model, although he or she might also achieve a satisfactory result using spontaneous Questioning Technique.

R – Route: In this stage, the coach will support his or her client in making a choice from among the available alternatives. The best way to help may be to use a Pros and Cons Analysis, but other options in the coach's toolkit should be also offered. You can deploy the Mercedes Symbol or the CHOICE Model if you have not used them in a previous stage, but it might be sufficient to project yourself as a challenging and/or "confrontative" coach. At the end of this phase the coachee will have an action plan describing what to do, when and how.

K – Key Obstacles: In this stage, the coach supports the client in going the distance on the selected route to ensure that he or she would accomplish his or her goal instead of retreating upon meeting the first obstacle. Until this point, clients usually enjoy the coaching sessions. In general, neither the diagnosis (Situation), the goal-setting (Positioning), the working out of alternatives, nor the decision making (Route) are "painful" for them. No later than at this point, however, the client is required to leave his or her comfort zone. He or she may even start cancelling regular appointments. In this case, a coach should not take offense. It is a completely natural process, and it is advisable to make the coachee aware of it. To do so, a skilled coach has his or her tools, such as the Sailing ship, Magic Shop, Rubber Band, Buckets and Balloons provided they were not already deployed in the Positioning stage.

L – Leverage: In this phase coaches support their clients taming self-defeating behaviors. There are plenty of useful tricks and tools to utilize when clients start thinking about giving up but there is no excuse they have to go on if they want to reach their desired outcome.

E – Evaluation: Coaching engagements ideally come to an end when clients have accomplished their goal. In this case, the coach celebrates the accomplishment together with the client, and this is the point where (in a corporate coaching situation) they both report to the client's manager on the joint efforts taken.

Notes

1 http://www.famous-quotes.com
2 G. Alexander, B. Renshaw: *Super Coaching*. Random House Business Books, 2005
3 Werner Vogelauer: *Methoden-ABC im Coaching*. Luchterhand Verlag GmbH, 2011
4 Mitchell Axelrod: *The New Game of Business*. thenewgame.com, 2004
5 Lynn I Ward: *4 Keys to Being a Million Dollar Dreamer*. www.FinfingYourselfAfter50.com, 2005
6 G. Alexander, B. Renshaw: *Super Coaching*. Random House Business Books, 2005
7 Graham Lee: *Leadership coaching*. Chartered Institute of Personnel and Development, 2003
8 Hawkins P., Shohet R.: *Supervision in the helping profession*. Open University Press, 1989
9 Keith Ellis: *The Magic Lamp. Goal Setting for People Who Hate Setting Goals*. Three Rivers Press; Updated edition, 1998
10 www.dalecarnegie.com
11 http://en.wikipedia.org/wiki/Situation,_Task,_Action,_Result
12 Edward de Bono: *The Six Thinking Hats*. Penguin Books, 2002
13 Mick Cope: *The Seven Cs of Coaching*. Pearson Education Ltd., 2004
14 A motto of the Hungarian Organizational Development Society, see www.szmt.hu

B) Coaching Tools – an Overview

Coaching tools can be classified in several ways. You can carve out categories according to the source of the tools. Of course, there are tools whose original purpose is not evident, i.e. they are used in coaching, as a management tool, in training and in psychology. However, we are able to distinguish the following categories.

Management tools include ones like the Fishbone Diagram, MbO, and the Balanced Scorecard or SWOT analysis. Example of tool with psychological base includes the 3-5-7 Column Thought Record. Other adopted coaching tools include the TRUST Model and the 5D Opening Tool. Another example of this type of adoption are the icebreaker tools which originate from training.

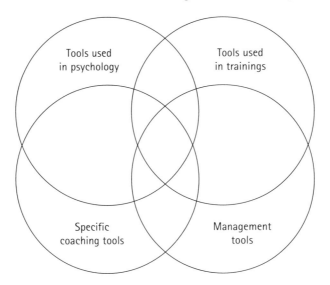

The 150 coaching tools in this book are classified into four categories that represent the four most common coaching fields, namely: executive coaching ✦, business coaching ∠, career coaching ☾, life coaching ♀. Many coaching tools are not exclusive to one particular domain and may serve a purpose in the other coaching fields as well in a wide range of situations. However, the small symbols provide guidance by indicating a tool's primary use. We, coaches, know how various techniques can serve multiple purposes and be applied to a multitude of scenarios. Therefore, a single tool is not confined to its originally intended use but instead may have numerous applications.

Summary of tools by coaching fields

TOOLS	Executive Coaching	Business Coaching	Career Coaching	Life Coaching
1. TRUST Model				X
2. Shadow Map				X
3. Square of Trust		X		
4. Process Strategy				X
5. Johari Window			X	
6. 5D Opening Tool	X			
7. Door Openers				X
8. Nodders				X
9. Model T			X	
10. Icebreakers		X		
11. SWOT Analysis		X		
12. Assessment Center and Development Center		X		
13. Work Style Analysis		X		
14. Van der Meer's Model			X	
15. BCG Matrix			X	
16. Montage				X
17. Onion Model	X			
18. Shadow Coaching		X		
19. Stakeholder Analysis			X	
20. Iacocca's 9C's Model	X			
21. Social Atom		X		
22. MPH Client Mapping				X
23. Confrontation, Holding Up a Mirror				X
24. ACE FIRST Model				X
25. 3-Column Thought Record			X	
26. 5-Column Thought Record			X	
27. 7-Column Thought record			X	
28. Document Analysis		X		
29. Behavioral Window				X
30. Problem Rectangle	X			
31. Pie Chart	X			
32. Change of Perspective	X			
33. Outsider Input	X			
34. 180/360 Degree Assessment	X			
35. Tests			X	
36. MBTI			X	
37. GPOP	X			
38. Diary	X			
39. Happiness and Success Curve			X	

TOOLS	Executive Coaching	Business Coaching	Career Coaching	Life Coaching
40. Activity Records			X	
41. Old House - New House	X			
42. Coat-of-Arms			X	
43. Reverse Job Advertisement			X	
44. Analogue Environment	X			
45. Free Association			X	
46. Fantasy Ladder		X		
47. Fantasy Domains		X		
48. Wisdom Cards	X			
49. Task Lists		X		
50. Creative Writing: Fairy Tale				X
51. Creative Writing: Map			X	
52. Creative Writing: Funeral Eulogy				X
53. Mind Mapping		X		
54. SMART Goal				X
55. Integrity Coaching				X
56. PURE goals		X		
57. CLEAR goals	X			
58. MbO-KPI	X			
59. Balanced Scorecard	X			
60. Benchmark	X			
61. Specification	X			
62. Let Us Complete the Sentence				X
63. Mercedes Symbol			X	
64. The Miracle Mountain Metaphor - 5P	X			
65. ABCDEF Method				X
66. Positive Visualization			X	
67. Post-it				X
68. Role Models			X	
69. Attribute Card			X	
70. Choosing an Object or Animal				X
71. Positive Feedback	X			
72. Rubber Band	X			
73. Wheel of Life				X
74. Drawing a Tree				X
75. Training Courses			X	
76. Creative Writing: Ideal Day			X	
77. Creative Writing: Writing a Letter		X		
78. CREATE Model		X		
79. Paper Clip		X		
80. Illogical Ideas	X			
81. Film and Book Recommendations			X	
82. Parable	X			

TOOLS	Executive Coaching	Business Coaching	Career Coaching	Life Coaching
83. 'What if...?' questions		X		
84. Stepping Out of One-on-One Coaching	X			
85. The Coach's Ideas				X
86. 10 + 10 Minutes			X	
87. Change in Emotions	X			
88. Consulting the Encyclopedia			X	
89. Reverse	X			
90. Combining				X
91. Grouping			X	
92. Adaptation	X			
93. Magnification		X		
94. Reduction		X		
95. Ideal people				X
96. Consultant	X			
97. Pros and Cons Analysis	X			
98. Pros and Cons Analysis with the Time Dimension	X			
99. Pros and Cons Analysis with Post-its		X		
100. Win-win			X	
101. Adenauer Cross		X		
102. Musts and Nice to Haves	X			
103. Labeling		X		
104. PMI Map	X			
105. Walt Disney Model		X		
106. Autonomy Triangle	X			
107. Simulation	X			
108. Black-White, Yes-No				X
109. Decision-Making List		X		
110. CHOICE Model	X			
111. Fishbone Diagram			X	
112. Action Plan	X			
113. Flowchart	X			
114. Gradual Task-Growing		X		
115. Measuring Trust and Faith			X	
116. Creative Writing: Saboteur			X	
117. Learning from Our Own Mistakes	X			
118. Helpmate		X		
119. Magic Shop		X		
120. Profit-Loss				X
121. Victory List		X		

TOOLS	Executive Coaching	Business Coaching	Career Coaching	Life Coaching
122. Role-play	X			
123. Sailing Ship			X	
124. List of Self-Limiting Beliefs			X	
125. Drama Triangle				X
126. Y curve			X	
127. Cockpit Confirmation	X			
128. Deferring Games		X		
129. Buckets and Balloons			X	
130. EMap (Russel)	X			
131. Grades of Transfer		X		
132. Ready - Stepping Ahead - Obstruction - New Challenge	X			
133. Behavioral tests	X			
134. Positive Self-Talk			X	
135. Distracting and Refocusing Attention				X
136. Confrontational, Provocative Coaching	X			
137. Punishment	X			
138. Reactive/Proactive Conditioning	X			
139. PAUSE Point Model				X
140. CHANGE Framework	X			
141. Summary Pattern	X			
142. Controlling the Client's Prosperity				X
143. Drawing Conclusions	X			
144. Celebration				X
145. Meta-Model			X	
146. Repetition	X			
147. Summary				X
148. Describing with Other Words	X			
149. Silence				X
150. Good, Better, the Best Question				X

Alternatively, tools can be classified by the stage of the coaching process in which they are applied, i.e. they are matched with stages of the SPARKLE model. As displayed in the table below, most tools can be utilized in several phases.

Summary of tools by coaching stages

TOOLS	Situation Stage	Positioning Stage	Alternatives Stage	Route Stage	Key Obstacles Stage	Leverage Stage	Evaluation Stage
1. TRUST Model	X	X	X	X	X		X
2. Shadow Map	X				X		X
3. Square of Trust	X						
4. Process Strategy	X	X	X	X	X	X	X
5. Johari Window	X						X
6. 5D Opening Tool	X						
7. Door Openers	X	X	X	X	X		X
8. Nodders	X	X	X	X	X	X	X
9. Model T	X	X	X	X	X	X	X
10. Icebreakers	X	X	X				
11. SWOT Analysis	X						X
12. Assessment Center and Development Center	X	X					
13. Work Style Analysis	X	X					X
14. Van der Meer's Model	X	X					
15. BCG Matrix	X	X					
16. Montage	X	X					
17. Onion Model	X						
18. Shadow Coaching	X				X		X
19. Stakeholder Analysis	X	X	X	X			
20. Iacocca's 9C's Model	X						
21. Social Atom	X	X					
22. MPH Client Mapping	X						
23. Confrontation, Holding Up a Mirror	X				X	X	X
24. ACE FIRST Model	X	X			X	X	X
25. 3-Column Thought Record	X						
26. 5-Column Thought Record	X	X	X				
27. 7-Column Thought Record	X	X	X				
28. Document Analysis	X				X	X	X
29. Behavioral Window	X						
30. Problem Rectangle	X						
31. Pie Chart	X						
32. Change of Perspective	X						
33. Outsider Input	X						X
34. 180/360 Degree Assessment	X						X
35. Tests	X						X

TOOLS	Situation Stage	Positioning Stage	Alternatives Stage	Route Stage	Key Obstacles Stage	Leverage Stage	Evaluation Stage
36. MBTI	X						
37. GPOP	X						
38. Diary	X				X		
39. Happiness and Success Curve	X						
40. Activity Records	X				X		
41. Old House - New House	X	X					
42. Coat-of-Arms	X	X					
43. Reverse Job Advertisement	X						
44. Analogue Environment	X	X					
45. Free Association	X						
46. Fantasy Ladder	X						
47. Fantasy Domains	X						
48. Wisdom Cards	X	X					
49. Task Lists	X						
50. Creative Writing: Fairy Tale	X	X					
51. Creative Writing: Map	X	X					
52. Creative Writing: Funeral Eulogy	X	X	X				
53. Mind Mapping	X	X	X				
54. SMART Goal		X					
55. Integrity Coaching		X					
56. PURE goals		X					
57. CLEAR goals		X					
58. MbO-KPI		x					
59. Balanced Scorecard		X					
60. Benchmark		X					
61. Specification		X					
62. Let Us Complete the Sentence		X					
63. Mercedes Symbol		X		X			
64. The Miracle Mountain Metaphor - 5P		X					
65. ABCDEF Method		X					
66. Positive Visualization		X			X	X	
67. Post-it		X	X				
68. Role Models		X					
69. Attribute Card		X					
70. Choosing an Object or Animal		X					
71. Positive Feedback		X			X	X	

TOOLS	Situation Stage	Positioning Stage	Alternatives Stage	Route Stage	Key Obstacles Stage	Leverage Stage	Evaluation Stage
72. Rubber Band		X				X	
73. Wheel of Life		X					
74. Drawing a Tree		X					
75. Training Courses		X					
76. Creative Writing: Ideal Day		X					
77. Creative Writing: Letter		X					
78. CREATE Model			X				
79. Paper Clip			X				
80. Illogical Ideas			X				
81. Film and Book Recommendations			X				
82. Parable			X				
83. 'What if…?' questions			X				
84. Stepping Out of One-on-One Coaching			X				
85. The Coach's Ideas			X				
86. 10 + 10 Minutes			X				
87. Change in Emotions			X				
88. Consulting the Encyclopedia			X				
89. Reverse			X				
90. Combining			X				
91. Grouping			X				
92. Adaptation			X				
93. Magnification			X				
94. Reduction			X				
95. Ideal people			X				
96. Consultant			X				
97. Pros and Cons Analysis				X			
98. Pros and Cons Analysis with the Time Dimension				X			
99. Pros and Cons Analysis with Post-its				X			
100. Win-win							
101. Adenauer Cross				X			
102. Musts and Nice to Haves				X			
103. Labeling				X			
104. PMI Map				X			

TOOLS	Situation Stage	Positioning Stage	Alternatives Stage	Route Stage	Key Obstacles Stage	Leverage Stage	Evaluation Stage
105. Walt Disney Model				X			
106. Autonomy Triangle				X			
107. Simulation				X			
108. Black-White, Yes-No				X			
109. Decision-Making List				X			
110. CHOICE Model				X			
111. Fishbone Diagram				X			
112. Action Plan				X			
113. Flowchart				X			
114. Gradual Task-Growing				X			
115. Measuring Trust and Faith	X		X	X	X		
116. Creative Writing: Saboteur					X		
117. Learning from Our Own Mistakes					X		
118. Helpmate					X		
119. Magic Shop		X			X		
120. Profit-Loss					X		
121. Victory List					X		
122. Role-Play					X		
123. Sailing Ship		X			X		
124. List of Self-Limiting Beliefs	X			X			
125. Drama Triangle					X		
126. Y curve					X		
127. Cockpit Confirmation					X		
128. Deferring Games	X	X		X	X		
129. Buckets and Balloons		X			X		
130. EMap (Russel)		X			X		
131. Grades of Transfer						X	
132. Ready – Stepping Ahead – Obstruction -New Challenge		X				X	
133. Behavioral tests						X	
134. Positive Self-Talk						X	
135. Distracting and Refocusing Attention						X	
136. Confrontational, Provocative Coaching	X	X		X		X	
137. Punishment						X	
138. Reactive/Proactive Conditioning		X				X	
139. PAUSE Point Model		X				X	
140. CHANGE Framework						X	

TOOLS	Situation Stage	Positioning Stage	Alternatives Stage	Route Stage	Key Obstacles Stage	Leverage Stage	Evaluation Stage
141. Summary Pattern							X
142. Controlling the Client's Prosperity							X
143. Drawing Conclusions							X
144. Celebration							X
145. Meta-Model	X	X	X	X	X	X	X
146. Repetition	X	X	X	X	X	X	X
147. Summary	X	X	X	X	X	X	X
148. Describing with Other Words	X	X	X	X	X	X	X
149. Silence	X	X	X	X	X	X	X
150. Good, Better, the Best Question	X	X	X	X	X	X	X

I worked as a management consultant with a large global consulting firm for years. Many people assume that now I do the same without being employed. To a certain extent, they are right. When I was a consultant, I tried to get my own way using coaching instead of resorting to autocracy. However, it is different in numerous respects. A consultant gives advice, whereas a coach makes the most out of the client. I will demonstrate the distinction by using a very simple example: When I was a consultant and a client asked me what color of tie he should wear, I advised him to wear one that was navy and wine-red striped. Today, I would ask questions instead (in brackets you can see the stages of the SPARKLE Coaching Model the questions relate to).

• What is the occasion? Is he attending a ball, a business meeting, an interview or... *(Situation)*
• What is his objective? To present a professional image, to project himself as an irresistible male, to be trendy or... *(Positioning)*
• What color can the tie be? After he has listed all the colors of ties hanging in his closet, I would suggest for him to purchase a new one, even a purple spotted orange tie... *(Alternatives)*
• Which one will he choose among the available options, in this specific situation, to achieve the specific goal? *(Route)*
• What is stopping him to make a final decision? (*Key Obstacles*)
• The television interview is in 2 hours. How can the coach help to get over this difficulty? *(Leverage)*
• Finally, he made a choice to wear a navy and wine-red striped tie...and he received compliments from me and others as well. *(Evaluation)*

I. TOOLS OF THE SITUATION STAGE

> *"When you confront a problem, you begin to solve it."*
> Rudy Giuliani[1]

> *"The manager who comes up with the right solution to the wrong problem is more dangerous than the manager who comes with the wrong solution to the right problem."*
> Peter Drucker[2]

> *"The ship is safest when it is in port, but that's not what ships are built for."*
> Coelho[3]

In the Situation stage, coach and coachee undertake to map the reality, namely, striving for objectivity in order to draw the most realistic picture. They must, at all costs, filter beliefs, biases, opinions, concerns and hopes that would hinder an objective assessment.

To accurately evaluate the present situation, you may select from a vast array of methods and tools. First, however, as noted earlier, it is imperative to gain the client's confidence so that he or she knows that he or she is not being bombarded with questions (Questioning technique), "spied upon" (Shadow Coaching), "investigated" (360 degree assessment) out of sheer curiosity, but rather for his or her benefit.

Thus, the Situation stage should include ascertaining the coachee's openness and the areas where secret zones are best avoided (for example, in business coaching, the coachee may stipulate that no personal issues will be covered). If you are aware of any taboos, then you can use opening methods and then carry out a detailed assessment premised on the former.

Sometimes clients say that they do not want to waste money and time for this phase and jump to the next one. Our experience is that if we skip this one, later on we have to return and do it anyway.

1. TRUST Model[4]

Another English acronym comprised of the initials of the following words is:
T – Truthful
R – Responsive
U – Uniform
S – Safe
T – Trained

The word TRUST refers to a key factor in the coaching process; it serves as a base for honest communication that is required for each step.

This model as a tool helps manage and gauge the relationship based on trust.

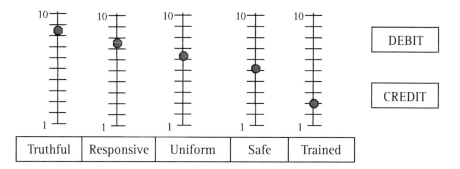

The problem with trust is that although you are aware of whom you trust, it is hard to define the specific factors. If you trust someone, then you know that you do so. But why? What triggers your trust in him or her? Trust is a pivotal factor in the coaching process since it serves as a foundation for joint efforts. A coach should grasp how trust works because he or she invests valuable time and energy into the process and the former's work should rest on a firm base.

T – Truthful: Both parties have a responsibility to be honest with each other. When entering into a collaborative partnership, it is very easy to yield to temptation and tell the other person what he or she wants to hear. However, a coach should instead be honest. The coachee is also expected to be frank because an effective cooperation demands mutual sincerity.
If you intend to score higher on this scale, consider acknowledging your mistakes with honesty. For instance, communicate the reason for your tardiness instead of waffling and avoid excessive praise.

R – Responsive: A coach has a demanding job: he or she will not only listen to the coachee but be present with latter in a holistic fashion. In practice, responsiveness can be demonstrated both verbally and non-verbally through body language, eye contact, and validation of the client's emotions via a smile or a few words of affirmation and support vis-à-vis the coachee. The coach should also determine when to take notes and when to refrain from doing so. A good coach is open, cooperative and ready to freely share ideas and information.
This parameter can be mastered by disregarding the outside world (avoiding to look at one's watch and turning off one's mobile phone) and by preparing for upcoming meetings by reviewing notes from the earlier session.

U – Uniform: A good coach is consistent. The coachee knows from one session to the next what to expect and need not apprehend any surprises. You can learn a lot from repetition. It is important for the coach to be consistent at all times and in his or her content, behavior and language so that both parties know what to expect, thereby strengthening the mutual trust between them.
The criterion of uniformity advises coaches to withhold personal emotions, utilize a consistent language and keep regular notes.

S – Safe: A credible coach is well-intentioned and helpful. It is useful to understand what makes a client feel safe. For some, safety means emotional support; for others, it might be associated with a specific type of environment or a formal and black-letter contract that stipulates, at the outset, all terms, including non-disclosure, agreed to by both parties. The client must feel that it is a safe space for him or her and that he or she can share any information with the coach without fearing that the latter would impose on him or her. An external coach can often achieve more progress with a client than an internal one due to the fact that the former has no contact with colleagues of his or her client, enabling the latter to feel safer.

This parameter may be improved by not discussing other clients' issues or defaming other coaches. You must unequivocally avoid any semblance of dependability, such as by never losing your notes and so on.

T – Trained: A good coach is competent and equipped with the necessary skills and abilities.

This attribute may be enhanced through active listening, demonstration of prior coaching experience or appropriate and timely questioning.

The coach can ask the following questions:
- How was the session?
- Is there anything you feel worried about?
- What would you like to cover during the session?
- Is there any issue concerning the last session that you would like to raise?
- Is there anything I could do to make the sessions more effective for you?

Sometimes, a coach's tardiness and justification for the latter is sufficient to lose a client's confidence. Similarly, if a coach fails to provide the assistance expected, then the client will not consider him or her responsive. If a coach invariably approaches the same issue in a different manner, then the picture presented will no longer be coherent and uniform. To make a client feel safe, you must be prudent when sharing personal information about third parties– he or she might suspect that you would be indiscreet about him or her as well. Conscious communication and self-control on the coach's part can improve the parameters of the TRUST model as a tool.

2. Shadow Map[5]

This tool also originates from Mick Cope's book. It helps the client explore any problem area that are not amenable to discussion and tackle issues freely hat he or she is reluctant to share with others.

Below is a list of typical surface (discussable) and shadow (secret) topics.

Surface	Shadow
Positive aspect of performance appraisal	Feelings about the coach
	True personal goals
Personal goals	Personal fears
Family goals	Family problems
Responsibility	Politics
Personal values	Rigid habits
Personal successes	Knee-jerk reactions
Planned career	Gut-feel decision making
Espoused ideals	Failed efforts to change

The assessment can be somewhat more sophisticated, such that instead of classifying issues into two categories, you can create several levels and set up shadow steps.

CASE STUDY (EXCERPT)

A trainer used a microphone in a training that she held because she "had lost her voice."
- The surface that she would share with anyone was that she had laryngitis.
- Since the training focused on establishing stress management, she only informed a few individuals from the company that her laryngitis had been brought on by shouting.
- She only shared the information that she was shouting at her husband with a few people.
- She did not disclose to anyone that she was shouting at her husband because she had learned that he had a lover and was frustrated about it.
- And she did not even admit to herself, but rather suppressed – that he loved his paramour so much that the latter would get divorced if she knew that he would certainly marry her.

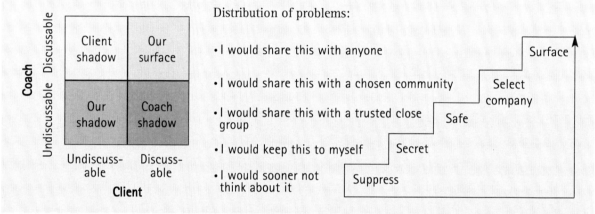

The first time I saw the aforementioned diagram, I must concede that I did not understand it. To begin with, I could not fathom why the discussable issues of the coach have any importance, and furthermore could not determine what issues could be included here. Since then, I have met many coaches so that my list has grown to encompass issues that might pose a problem for others. For example, some coaches dislike discussing the coaching fee and hence utilize coach agency services. A client selects an affordable coaching rate for purposes of remunerating the coach, and the agency recommends on the basis of that information.

The meeting should cover only coaching instead of price negotiations. There is another delicate issue that can be also avoided by enlisting the services of an agency: Generally, coaches are eager to know whether their client was satisfied, but prefer that a third party solicit the feedback and to obtain it in an indirect way, as by an e-mail sent to the agency. In this manner, if the client was satisfied then he or she does not have to promote themselves with the agency to obtain new assignments. Conversely, if any area necessitating improvement is identified, the client can immediately find a coach or supervisor through the agency to focus on it.

The two above-mentioned issues can be considerably limited since they arise at the beginning and end of the coaching engagement. However, sometimes there are issues that coaches prefer to skirt during the coaching process: e.g., there are executive and business coaches who prefer to focus mostly on the client's professional and business challenges and not so much on their personal life. Faced with this predicament, such coaches go blank immediately and recommend another coach as a replacement. This is a topic that should be clarified in advance, ideally at the introductory session. (*Introductory session* is used througout this book as the meeting where the potential client is introduced to both the coach and the coaching process to see if there is chemistry and alignment of mission, goals and process. Should they decide to work together the coach and the client schedule the first session where coach and coachee start the work by designing the coaching alliance.) Sometimes a coach can help explore areas that are seemingly off-limits for the client both by acknowledging that they can identify with the situation (see above) and by citing examples from their previous coaching experience about taboo topics other clients had grappled with.

3. Square of Trust[6]

A typical application of this tool is in the Situation stage when attempting to map the category that the client thinks he or she belongs to since this furnishes information to the coach relating to subsequent steps. It is advisable to encourage your client to cite a specific example where he or she placed his or her confidence in someone and why; if their confidence in that individual was called into question and the reason for it, etc. This is all useful information for the coach during the process.

Suspicious still	Trust until
Suspicious until	Trust still

CASE STUDY (EXCERPT)

As mentioned earlier, we normally employ this tool in the Situation stage. However, I had a case when I deployed this tool much later, in the Route stage. My client worked as a Head of Department with a renowned financial institution. Although he was young, dynamic and brimming with ideas, a sizable number of the latter failed to reach the implementation phase due to lack of time. As a homework, he kept a diary for one week, taking notes on his actions every 15 minutes. We analyzed his notes, and he informed me that he was monitoring himself when logging his actions and realized that of all his activities, his Achilles' heel was e-mailing. He wished for a fairy to eliminate this electronic medium. While he was accustomed to work when he only received letters and phone calls, he is not able to do that anymore. I asked him how his wish would sound if there was a fairy but that she could not eliminate e-mailing completely because there are many who are fond of it. How could the fairy compensate him?

Client: OK. Dear Fairy, if you cannot eliminate e-mail entirely, then please cast a spell over the e-mailing software in my computer and incorporate it into your laptop, read all the mails and answer as many as possible and come into my office at 11:00 am every day and offer me a synopsis.
Coach: You know that it's not impossible...
Client: Oh yes, it is.
Coach: Such a fairy is called a secretary...
Client: I will never have one.

At first, I thought he deemed it unrealistic because he "only" led a department with sixty employees. I considered citing examples from other companies where even a team of ten people had a secretary, but it turned out that he had trust issues.

In connection with the Square of Trust name, we were debating into which cell to classify the people around him. He had no wife and no children; the only person in the "Trust still" section was his mother. Most people were rated as "Suspicious until". Upon discovering the latter, we did not return to the beginning of the Situation stage but proceeded to the Route phase as he succeeded in suggesting two alternatives:

He would either employ his mother, who was living on disability, as a secretary (because he trusts her completely), or attempt to work with the other department head's secretary by sharing her time 50-50%. If she proves her aptitude during the probationary period, he would entrust her with managing his e-mails.

4. Process Strategy[7]

This concept, which was devised by Vogelauer, grew out of the core theme of Hans von Sassen and Don Binsted/Robin Snell.

It is highly suggested that the proceeding strategy be discussed at the outset of the Situation stage to ensure that it is acceptable for both the client and the coach. This avoids the risk for both parties of realizing in the middle of the process that each had in mind different proceeding strategies and different expectations.

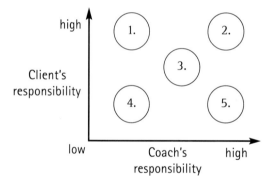

The five potential strategies are:
1. – Independence strategy
2. – Strategy of compromise
3. – Protecting strategy
4. – Reciprocal strategy
5. – Floating strategy

active	Resisting	Doubtful	Cooperative
	Changing		Follower
	Full of constraints	Ambivalent	Needs assistance

Client's involvement (vertical, active to passive) — Client's willingness (horizontal, to high)

"The proceeding strategy created based on your observations and assessment of the situation determines the measures to be taken. Considering that you intend to support the client's actions towards problem-solving and his or her development, it is imperative to apply a fighting or negotiating strategy. An effective choice could be the implementation of the "cooperative strategy". Within this category, Binsted and Snell distinguish additional strategies depending on the level of responsibility: (1) independence strategy, (2) strategy of compromise, (3) protecting strategy, (4) reciprocal strategy and (5) floating strategy.

Since the client and the coach are responsible for the content and the process, respectively, the parties will most likely agree on a strategy of switching influence, namely the reciprocal strategy, independence strategy or strategy of compromise.

The degree of the client's willingness in participating in the coaching process is a key factor during strategic planning. Another major criterion is the client's attitude- active or passive- towards the coaching situation and the issues to be discussed. The above diagram illustrates the potential strategic aspects correlating to the client's attitude.

If the client's attitude is characterized by trust, partnership and openness, then the first phase of the discussion can be relatively short. Otherwise, more time and energy will need to be expended to increase the client's willingness and his or her level of involvement.

The client's style also plays a role in planning the content and schedule of the work. The length of his sentences and the manner he or she expresses himself or herself, i.e. in a verbose and complex manner- ought to be taken into account.

Other elements that should be considered when planning strategic proceeding include safety, thorough knowledge, operability and the enhancement of measures.

The proceeding is also impacted by the client's ability to quickly seize ideas, specify and implement his or her own intentions or conversely, his or her tendency to react slowly, with excuses, resistance and "games" to the questions.

To effectuate a solid and effective coaching process, it is worth investing time in establishing awareness and raising its level. This may be achieved via any of the following tools: situational or background analysis, diagnosis, finding realizations as well as assessment and learning processes.

In a later phase of strategic proceeding, time should be allocated to decision-making and judgment, filtering and assessing multiple methods and possible solutions. Dependencies also play a central role in this stage and must be considered from the standpoint of timing.

It is important that, during the discussion, the client has sufficient time to communicate, think aloud, contemplate and generate his or her own ideas and proposals." (Vogelauer)[8]

5. Johari Window[9]

Published by psychologists Joseph Luft and Harry Ingham in 1955, this tool is intended for the assessment of positive attributes. (The so-called Nohari-window is used for assessing negative attributes.) The name of the model is a hybrid of the names (Joe and Harry – Johari). Initially, this model was designed to measure individual effectiveness.

	Known to self	*Unbeknownst to self*
Known to others	Arena	Blind spot
Unknown to others	Facade	Unknown

Making Sense of the Johari Window

To understand the "self", two dimensions are delineated- the behavioral features that are known to self and those concerning the person known to others. The areas vary in size. Thus, for instance, when a child is born, the "unknown" area covers almost the entire diagram. As life progresses and a person gains self-knowledge and the people around him or her become acquainted with him or her, the "Blind spot" area continuously shrinks and the size of the other three areas grows correspondingly.

Arena – Illustrating the public "self", this quadrant represents traits of subjects of which both they and their peers are aware. The "arena" quadrant contains information such as name, physical appearance, family, corporate, political or other open affiliations, etc.

Blind spot – The "Blind spot" quadrant presents data to which others, but not the subject, are privy. For example, a person can be flamboyant, bumptious or mannered without realizing it and he or she might be surprised and skeptical when hearing a remark about this aspect of his or her personality of which he or she is unaware. This is a field where coaching plays a significant role in that the coach, who holds up a mirror and provides objective feedback, helps to reduce the Blind spot.

Hidden – The so-called "Hidden" quadrant represents information about individuals of which their peers are unaware, that is to say, secret information. For example, an employee might feel uncomfortable about not being offered a seat by his or her boss at an office meeting but would withhold their opinion and accept the situation. A substantial segment of the "Hidden" quadrant contains suppressed remarks for the purpose of maintain a good relationship.

Unknown – The "Unknown" area is unapproachable for both the "self" and "others" who are in contact with them. Some psychologists describe it as a very large area consisting of attributes and actions coming to light only under certain special circumstances (accident, emergency, a special life stage, or other very rare and exceptional cases). For example if someone asks me whether I could swim in an icy river I would say no. But if my child fell in, I am sure I would be able to.

An interactive version of the Johari Window is available on the Internet. There is a great tool which can help improve self-awareness and is recommended to readers and clients. It is based on a simple system consisting of a window containing 25 attribute types (extroverted, introverted, helpful, friendly, etc.). After being asked to select the five words that best described the individual, you have to enter a unique ID and send it to five friends, asking them to provide their input about your personality traits. You will then receive a link that features your own personal Johari window, with the attributes that you feel describes you and the ones that other people view you as manifesting. In other words, the traits displayed will be those known to you but not known to others and those that others think describe you the best but of which you are unaware. It can be a very valuable lesson.

Case Study (Excerpt)

One of the coach's main tasks is to hold up a mirror to the client. There are some who will allow this with little objection while others with greater resistance. Prior to performing this step, it is imperative for you to furnish a reason for your feedback since a coach's goal is to develop the client and to also communicate to the latter how you intend to help him or her to develop. To help them realize this, you can also create a Johari window so that they will know with certainty that they are not being singled out, but that everyone has a "Blind spot."

No matter how tactful a coach is, there are coachees who still will feel offended by the coach's feedback. While some might go as far as refuse to meet with the coach again, sooner or later they will likely be grateful for the sincerity that they might never experience with anyone else. It is also possible that the client will not believe the feedback and needs more tangible evidence, in which case you can resort to document analysis (re-reading, past e-mails) or even confrontation with a video recording. An illustration of the latter is as follows: After recording a salesman's negotiations, we watched the videos together and he easily realized how cynical his behavior was.

6. 5D Opening Tool

The following 5D-tool is a modified version of the tool published by Mick Cope[10] and designed for "opening up" the coachees.

Disclosure: Open up to the coachee and share your "secrets" with him or her.

Deflection: Speak as if you had a friend with the same problem or seen it in a movie: What would you suggest? As an outsider, what new ideas do you propose? (Example: If I were John, I would have married Helen. (In the movie "Analyze This", Robert de Niro portrays a gangster with phobia/distress. It is easier for him to say to the therapist:" I have a good friend, who is a gangster and he has phobia/distress".)

Detachment: Communicate in the third person singular or as a detached observer any new ideas you have. (John would have married Helen.)

Direct: If your relationship is strong enough, then you simply have to ask it directly.

Drink: It does not have to be alcohol; sometimes it is enough to take the client out of the work environment by inviting him or her for coffee.

CASE STUDY (EXCERPT)

Each client requires different tools – choose one from the above list, or use any combination of them. When hired by an executive, I asked him to tell me a few words about my future coachee, a department head in the company. Regrettably, he informed me that she was extremely reserved. The only information he knew was personal data from her resume that is her mother's name, place and date of birth, etc.

However, he knew nothing about her personal life (this posed no problem for him; he only mentioned it because normally everyone knew everything about everyone else in the company, and therefore, she was an exception to the rule). More importantly, however, he did not know how she felt about working for the company and whether he could depend on her in the long term.

We held the introductory meeting in one of the upscale cafés in town and surprisingly, the new setting worked wonders in that it enabled the coachee to open up. Taken out of the professional context, she talked the hind legs off a donkey for two and a half hours. When she looked at her watch, she was dumbfounded that she could talk so much about herself. She shared a lot of information with me about herself including secrets that I have kept confidential ever since.

In most cases, however, clients do not open up for the first time as easily as the woman in the aforementioned scenario, not even in a new environment. Therefore, an established practice involves initiating the introduction ourselves to make the client get a sense of the level of openness we expect from them.

7. Door Openers[11]

To open up the client, Gordon suggested the followings in his book *L.E.T.:*
"When someone conveys a brief message disclosing his or her feelings, it is a signal for the listener about the probable existence of a problem. At this point, the coach has not yet set in motion the problem-solving process. This takes place only when the listener encourages the client to do so and opens the door to the person who needs help. The person who is listening to the speaker can say the following:
- Is there anything I could be of assistance in this matter?
- I care about what you feel.
- Would it help you if we talked about it?
- Sometimes it helps if you can discharge the load.
- I would really like to help you if I can.

These answers clearly demonstrate how close the receiver is to the person communicating the message; not only does he or she listen but also undertakes listening."

8 Nodders[12]

The following finding was also published by Dr. Thomas Gordon in his book:
"Most people need something more than absolute silence when they constantly grapple with their problems in thought. They want evidence that the listener is with them instead of mooning around or occupied with their own thoughts." From time to time, speakers expect feedback to their messages, such as:
- Eye contact. • Nodding. • "I see." • "I understand." • "Interesting."

9. Model T[13]

In his book *Effective Coaching*, Myles Downey published this model as a coaching tool.

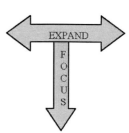

It enables the coach to focus on allowing the client to discuss issues that are important to him or her, possibly, new ones they had confronted between two coaching sessions. The coach's task is to open up the coachee as much as possible in order to elicit a lot of pertinent information – this is referred to as "Expand". However, the coach must also help the coachee focus on the contracted goal when the latter digresses and introduces many new elements to a session.

CASE STUDY (EXCERPT)

Coach: You have provided me one option to delegate the project to Jamie. What other options are there? (EXPANDing question)
Partner (Coachee): I could assign the operational part to Jamie but still supervise the strategic issues myself.

C: Anything else? (EXPANDing question)
P: I could do it myself.
C: Anything else? (EXPANDing)
P: I cannot think of anything.
C: OK. But let us see if there are any other options. Tell me what you would really like to do, regardless of consequences. (EXPANDing)
P: Actually, I am interested in this project and can perform it on my own but in three weeks when my current project will be completed since I cannot take on two projects simultaneously.
C: I see; therefore, four options are available:
- Delegate it to Jamie in its entirety.
- Assign the operational tasks to Jamie.
- Perform it yourself now.
- Perform it later.

Which of those is the most interesting? (FOCUSing question)

10. Icebreakers

As illustrated in the diagram demonstrating the origin of coaching tools, coaches can also use training tools. Icebreakers might be necessary, particularly at the beginning of the session, to "warm up" the client but can also be deployed at a later stage, such as for goal-setting in the Positioning stage. Introduce an icebreaker when you feel that the coachee fears presenting objectives that pose real challenges or when you need to encourage your client to identify alternative solutions or unconventional ideas. When using any icebreaker, you must ensure that it does not consume more than five to ten minutes and explain to the client the purpose of it so they do not consider utilizing it a waste of time.

Team coaching provides an ideal context for applying icebreakers, which are used in a way that is similar to trainings. The toolset is unlimited, bound only by the coach's imagination in introducing new exercises. Notwithstanding this, I only present two icebreakers in this book, one for individual coaching and another for team coaching.

In *individual coaching,* you can ask a few (tricky) questions in the first meeting when you and the coachee are debating on the nature of coaching and the power of questions:
- How many species of animals did Moses embark on his Ark? (None – it was Noah, not Moses.)
- In a running contest, you pass the one who is in second place. What place are you on now? (2nd of course)
- If an archeologist tells you he excavated a gold coin with a legend which states "made in 46 B.C.", then why should you assume that he is lying? (Because they did not know at the time that they were Before Christ.)
- Is there a law governing whether a man can marry his widow's sister? (If he has a widow, then he is already deceased.)

At the same time, you encourage the coachee to think instead of searching for a ready answer, which in turn renders the coaching process effective.

In *team coaching,* participants already know each other. They are taking part in the coaching process together because they work as a team. You can still use the following icebreaker successfully at the outset of the process. Each participant is given a handout with the following list:

- My favorite book.
- My favorite holiday destination.
- My favorite restaurant.
- My favorite food.
- My favorite sport.
- My favorite music, etc.

Team members are asked to answer the questions in writing and then search for a person in the team with the same answer. The winner is the one who finds the most identical answers with his or her own list. The whole exercise should not take more than five to six minutes.

11. SWOT Analysis[14]

SWOT analysis is commonly known to anyone who has studied economics in college or at a university. It is often used in work and is a substantial aid in coaching as well. You can apply it in the Situation stage and for Positioning. In addition being applicable in two stages, it can be used both in team coaching and individual coaching settings. The analysis aims at mapping the company's/team's/individual's internal resources and the possibilities of the external environment.

Strengths: What is the company's strengths/assets (technology, workforce management, financial balance sheet, product, corporate culture, etc.)?
Weaknesses: What is the company's developmental need and where can it be improved (organization, human resources, culture, processes, systems, etc.)?
Opportunities: Where does the company have attractive opportunities and what are the leading trends (market environment, political/financial relations, economic conditions of the industry, consumer needs, commercial opportunities, etc.)?
Threats: What external hardships will be faced and what actions are undertaken by competitors?

After exploring SWOT, the following questions must be addressed:
- What strengths could help in exploiting the opportunities?
- What weaknesses prevent you from exploiting the opportunities?
- What strengths do you have that enable you to cope with threats?
- What weaknesses prevent you from coping with threats?
- What internal weaknesses do your competitors have?
- Which strengths of your competitors should be avoided?
- What are the areas where the company is weak as well as exposed and therefore ill-advised to consider withdrawal from the market?

CASE STUDY (EXCERPT)

An apparel company faces organizational development challenges. In addition to reviewing their vision and strategic goals, it should carry out a SWOT analysis prior to specifying organizational development tasks.

	Positive	Negative
Internal	**Strengths** • qualified workforce, • competitive product, • nationwide retail coverage.	**Weaknesses** • vague work processes, • unclear scopes of authority, • employees are uncertain about the shareholder's future intentions.
External	**Opportunities** • favorable changes in legal environment for regional expansion, • a significant competitor is leaving the market.	**Threats** • economic recession, • ne competitor is launching a new online service.

12. Assessment Center and Development Center

An *Assessment Center (AC)* is a tool applied in external or internal hiring processes which assesses the aptitude for fulfilling the specific position and overall skills.

Although an AC normally takes one to three days, there is also a shorter version that lasts half a day.

The number of participants is in the range of 5 to 12; their performance and behavior is observed and evaluated by qualified raters.

In an AC, individual and team tasks have to be solved, compiled based on the competencies to be assessed by the former. Some tasks mimic fictitious situations simulating certain aspects of the work environment for the position to be executed. Ideally, actual company problems are also included in the tasks.

Typical tasks in an AC:
• Tests (verbal and numerical skills, IQ, personality)
• role-play (e.g. various executive positions are assumed by candidates in an executive meeting, and they are required to articulate their points)
• presentation task
• case study
• processing and prioritizing documents
• discussing a specific issue in a team.

A *Development Center (DC)* is a tool that is very similar to an AC. It differs from the latter in that it is not applied in a selection process but rather in career planning, assessing managerial skills and identifying areas for improvement.

The assessments created using ACs and DCs do not only inform employers but are also useful for candidates in that they serve as self-awareness exercises. The results can be used effectively in coaching as well. It is expedient to review the results of AC's and DC's with the client in the Situation and in the Positioning stages of the SPARKLE framework.

13. Work Style Analysis[15]

Developed by Vogelauer, this is a great tool that can be applied both in the Situation and Positioning stage.

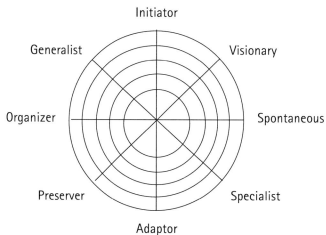

Along the outline of the circle, pairs of opposites can be found. The client reads the description of each style and evaluates themselves accordingly. The extreme values in parentheses at the end of the definitions will be indicated by marking the outline of the circle. For example, in the case of the generalist/specialist pair, the client should place a mark by the outline of the circle at the point labeled "specialist" if he or she is very meticulous and immerses himself or herself in details. Conversely, if he or she is quite balanced in this area, i.e. he or she is as much specialist and generalist as required by the specific position or situation, then he or she can put a mark in the middle of the circle.

Definition of Work Styles (by Vogelauer)

INITIATOR	ADAPTOR
Actively approaches things, decides individually how to resolve the upcoming task, view himself or herself as independent, paves the way and defines measures, seizes opportunities. (A **dictator** acts egoistically, disregards others and seeks to dictate.)	Takes one's own time, adapts to the existing structures/instructions. He or she is reactive, acts upon request, adjusts and allows others to make decisions. (A **passive** person might be overly adaptable, dependent; does not do anything by himself or herself and feels being controlled by others.)

VISIONARY

Is attentive to what is occurring or what might happen in the future, focuses on goals and future opportunities, and looks ahead. He or she is open to new things.

(A **utopian** fantasizes about the future and what might happen tomorrow. He or she is preoccupied solely with innovations.)

PRESERVER

Draws on achievements, focuses on events that took place, likes looking back, views past achievements and events as benchmarks, wants to preserve and maintain the things created.

(A **traditionalist** is focused strictly on the past and strives to keep things as they are, would not change anything; views norms and rules as benchmarks.)

SPONTANEOUS

Follows and monitors situations, evolves with the changing times. He or she is creative and flexible, needs free space, acts spontaneously and emotionally.

(A **chaotic** person confuses everything, becomes tedious. He or she is disorderly and impulsive.)

ORGANIZER

Strives for order, draws up tables, schemes and checklists to ensure more efficient work. Adjusts to structures, draws on logics. He or she is accurate and exact.

(A **perfectionist** is petty-minded interested only in logics, has overly-precise plans, and he or she believes that nothing works without order.)

SPECIALIST

He or she is preoccupied with details, devotes much time and energy to beginning and completing an activity, specifies things and identifies mistakes buried in the details.

(A **meticulous** person finds himself or herself submerged in details, refines them endlessly, does not get to the point, and is identified by a substantial gap between his or her level of commitment and the importance of the task.)

GENERALIST

Displays a comprehensive understanding (task, period of time, situation...), strives for clarity and transparency, focuses on inherencies, thinks big. He or she is able to create chains of thought.

(An **abstract** person builds complex structures of thought, acts too theoretically, and gets entangled in theories.)

The author also proposes an idea for a step towards progress and suggests involving the client's colleagues or staff by asking them to describe him or her. Thus, the self-portrait can be contrasted with the image presented by others.

14. Van der Meer's Model[16]

This is a great tool because it enables the client to see the contrasting poles of his or her own behavioral patterns. It helps them better analyze their current context and set the direction of development more effectively. It also provides considerable guidance to the coach when he or she thinks that the client overstates certain parameters.

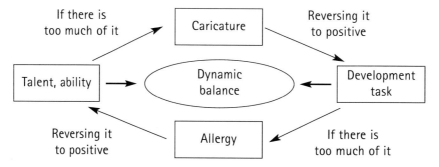

The following questions can be found in each of the four boxes:

Caricature: Which of your attributes might irritate or annoy others and would be included in a caricature of you? You may follow the arrows in the diagram above, finding a positive reversal for this attribute that will be your development task.

Development task: Here you can also ask yourself what your role models' areas of expertise are in this field and what you could learn from them.

Allergy: What is the antithesis of your caricature, e.g. that you find irritating in others' behavior? For example, you might be hasty but be annoyed by persons who are always fidgeting. This represents the inverse of what you would like to achieve.

Talent, ability: What are its rewarding aspects? (i.e. this attribute of yours) For example, it enables you to complete tasks in an expeditious manner.

After the coach has explained the model, the coachee fills the boxes with content to avoid that the coach dictates the words to him or her. Below you can find a specific example:

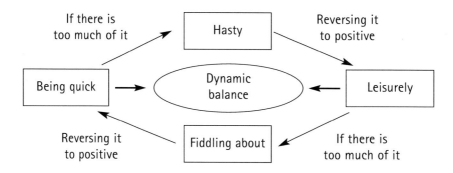

Upon completing the diagram, the client will examine the latter and the new insights gained from this task and determine how he or she can apply it in his or her life and situation.

15. BCG Matrix[17]

This tool may be applied in both individual and team coaching at the Situation and Positioning stage.

Developed by the Boston Consulting Group, this matrix helps identify the level of commitment and motivation of the coachee (or that of his or her colleagues) and provides an opportunity to discuss the components.

	COMPLIANT • following orders • disengaged	ENGAGED • high performing • loyal, enthusiastic, • "owner/entrepreneur minded"
Discipline	AIMLESS • lethargic • disorganized	UNGUIDED MISSILES • engaged, enthusiastic • unfocused and uncontrolled • not too concerned with rules

Motivation ⟶

The coach asks the client to mark in the matrix where he or she, his or her boss and colleagues would be situated:
- What is the current state of things and how would he or she envision the future?
- How can he or she or they achieve that?

16. Montage

Montage as a tool is ideal when working with creative clients with a preference for visual techniques. The coach asks the coachee to compile a montage of pictures describing him or her, his or her family, or his or her workplace, depending on the focus of the coaching. You can use glossy magazines, but some people prefer to take photos from their own family album.

This is an optimal tool for tackling work-life balance or assertiveness issues. It is often hard to face up to the fact that your current situation may not be in conformity with the goal or values that are valuable to you. It might occur that the coachee is not aware of the price he or she has to pay to achieve a goal. In such cases, it often helps if he or she, instead of sharing his or her story with consciousness, views the montage as a projection of him/herself. He or she might be astonished to see which fields of life he or she is neglecting (e.g. he or she only has pictures taken at work and with his or her kids and completely omit the "self" and his or her own needs). The montage might clearly illustrate what needs and expectations the coachee wants to fulfill, those being either his or her own expectations or external pressure (e.g. includes pictures that matter to him or her or ones that his or her spouse likes).

Evidently, the montage technique can also be used creatively in discussing many other issues where the coach feels that there is something that the client does not want to realize, although it is obvious to an impartial observer. For example, instead of using his or her own photos, the coachee can compile a magazine montage about what they want to achieve and how they want to be. Alternatively, the client can prepare a work montage illustrating the current and the desired situation. Or the montage can demonstrate how the client's home looks like at this moment and how he or she wants is to look. The montage provides a substantial amount of information. Only the coach's imagination sets the limit for potential issues to be raised and, as already mentioned above, this tool can be applied not only in the Situation stage but in the Positioning stage as well.

Case Study (excerpt)

One of my clients, a young lady, arrived at the coaching session full of complaints. I felt it necessary to allow her to vent her sorrow and waiting patiently for her to do so. I learned that she and her husband had planned to have two children, but following the birth of their first child, twins were born. This meant that she had to take care of her children 24/7, feed them, clean the house and cook. Her former intellectual life became virtually inexistent and the situation took on a toll on the intimacy with her husband, as all of their discussions centered around the children- i.e. the number of times she had to change their clothes, and which child threw a temper tantrum most of the day.

While sensing that it would be beneficial to exit this discussion, we nevertheless remained stuck on the level of words. It was in vain to ask her to describe a perfect day, what she would like to do in a different way, or what an ideal situation would look like. She repeatedly remarked: 'Not this way' while failing to mention something specific. I realized that if we could not make a breakthrough verbally, we should utilize the montage. I asked her to create a montage of the current situation and one of her desired life. To describe the present situation, she cut out extremely shocking photos from magazines, including a prison with lattice windows, a deserted island, Cinderella selecting lentils, and a slave in irons. In the other montage, aimed at illustrating the desired future, there were lavender fields, a library, a desk, a rocking chair, elegant fountain pens, books, and a candlelit dinner… While glancing at the pictures she fixed her goal, namely the re-integration of her intellectual life for at least one day per week.

She took the two montages home and showed them to her husband in the evening after putting the kids to sleep. He was extremely surprised because he thought that his wife had been happy at home with their three children, and naturally he planned to wait patiently for the return of his intellectual wife. As he acknowledged that this situation was no good to either of them, they immediately started to find a solution. As a first step, they introduced a lunch together once a week where they could talk as adults and without the children, in lieu of the candlelit dinner listed on the montage, as they did not want to leave bedtime to a babysitter. Every week, she started visiting the library again and writing short stories about a woman wearing lavender dress.

17. Onion Model

Everyone may be compared to an onion. The "external skin" containing the most visible signs of your behavior is recognizable to anyone (see also Johari window). By venturing inside an individual's personality, we will find an increasing number of hidden features that are more difficult to recognize and, at the same time, play a more important role and have an effect over a longer term. The innermost part of a personality can be reached by peeling off external "skins." Just as we can get teary peeling an onion in the kitchen, a coaching session can bring tears to the clients' eyes when learning more and more about themselves, especially in emotionally sensitive areas.

Ask the coachee to draw their five characteristic layers describing who he or she actually is. (It can take about 15 minutes.)

Case Study (excerpt)

A top-level executive of a large company presented me with this case and consequently, tool. He peeled off the following onion skins of his personality, proceeding inwards from the outside:
- a jolly good fellow, helpful and calm;
- a reliable and credible employee and a recognized leader;
- a big child longing for professional and human esteem;
- an anguished man full of self-condemnation who is constantly dissatisfied with himself, strives for self-actualization and freedom;
- an ambitious soul who wants to change the world.

18. Shadow Coaching

Shadow coaching is a very popular tool. There are coaches who begin and close each coaching process with this tool. While it can be very effective since the coach can learn what the coachee really is like (not only by listening to the latter), it is regrettably one of the most expensive solutions.

The idea behind shadow coaching is that the coach follows the coachee like a shadow for a certain period of time, generally for one whole day. The coach participates in meetings, listens to phone conversations, takes notes, but does not offer any feedback immediately. Notes are taken in a structured form using a template (see next page). Clearly, points that are not clear during the day will be marked with "N/A". The coach draws up a summary of the shadow coaching on the next working day and instead of emailing the synopsis, sets up an appointment with the coachee in order to discuss the results of the shadowing.

Preparations for shadow coaching: The day prior to the session, the coach and the coachee discuss the schedule for the day so that the coach will know what to expect (who else will be present, when and where), and the client shares his or her specific expectations (e.g. asks the coach to be circumspect in his or her communication with the supervisor).

The following template was designed for a simple general shadowing. Clearly, the template to be filled out may change subject to the fields to be observed. This template was prepared by a colleague of mine. It is quite detailed since the client's explicit request was to receive an in-depth feedback since until then; he had only received general information that proved to be worthless for him. He also asked the coach to add specific proposals to the observations. Of course, every summary is written in a different style and length, but typically, the following common categories are covered.

The template must contain the following information:
- the client's identifying data;
- date of shadow coaching;
- a list of the fields observed, which, based upon his or her experience, are rated as good or susceptible of improvement by the coach;

- the coach may add proposals for development to the fields evaluated as susceptible to improvement. Here you can list the latter fields that can be addressed using coaching, the ones that can be developed by attending trainings, or, if there is a specific field of key importance that could not be observed during the day, then organize a specific mini shadow coaching devoted to that field, etc.;
- summary.

The coach can choose from a wide range of fields to be observed. The following are the ones most frequently covered:
- communication:
  - with managers,
  - with staff,
  - with colleagues,
  - with suppliers or customers;
- appearance and image;
- time management, punctuality, keeping deadlines;
- visible stress;
- conflict-management;
- motivation;
- negative or positive feedback.

Template for Shadow Coaching

Shadow coaching: Name (Date)				
Communication	with staff	with clients	with colleagues	with managers
Written/E-mail	keeps to the point	very good	coarse	N/A
Verbal/Phone	quick and objective	very good	coarse	good
Other	dry sense of humor	–	–	–

Time management	Good	To Improve	Comments and specific examples
The daily schedule was realized as planned in 90%	X	X	good at daily tasks but in case of tasks received, mainly acts ad hoc
There was only a minor number of ad hoc tasks		X	many tasks received from customers and staff
The majority of the tasks completed was in fact managerial, i.e. cannot be delegated		X	10 to 20%
Tasks were completed by deadline	X		if it depended on him
Usage of tools (electronic calendar)		X	only if sitting in front of the computer
To do list prioritized		X	tries to carry out every incoming task as soon as possible

Time management	Good	To Improve	Comments and specific examples
Socializing	X	X	good with staff but not with others
Key strategic tasks (ensuring place/time)	X		
Arrives and leaves on time to/from meetings	X		arrives even earlier
Organization		X	
Administrative tasks			N/A
Answers only important phone calls		X	
Manages phone calls efficiently and with good timing	X		sometimes uses inappropriate style

Other	Good	To Improve	Comments and specific examples
Meals (quantity, quality, venue, snacks...)		X	Coca-Cola, carbohydrate; sitting in front of the computer
Personal life (number/duration/content of phone conversations)	X		hardly any
Conflicts (winner/loser/compromise)	X	X	clients: flexible; peer executives: fight, winner; staff: compromise
Praise		X	None
Calling to account, negative feedback	X		
Professional knowledge, credibility	X		to the depths
Dynamism, optimism, motivation	X		encourages his team
Control of emotions	X	X	good towards clients, not as good vis-a-vis his team
Decision-making skills	X		
Politeness and humor	X	X	has a dry sense of humor, often at the expense of his staff
Negotiation technique	X		
Presentational technique			N/A
Visible stress	X		
Externals (office, appearance)		X	lacks very high standards

Summary:
- **Communication**: effective, fast, keeps to the point, logical; employs simple sentences. No chit-chat or small talk. He often makes jokes at the expense of others.
- **Time management**: the daily schedule is partly planned in advance and partly ad hoc (clients and staff members regularly send requests). This is also thrown off balance/thrown into disarray when an application for tender will be prepared with a time limit. He often carries out non-managerial tasks (in 80 to 90% of the time!), which is primarily explained by his own two ongoing projects. All 18 members of his staff turn directly to him with any ideas, questions or doubts; thus, his work is interrupted frequently. This is also enhanced by the open space office. He tends not to wait until someone completes a task even if it progresses slowly or not so well; instead, he resolves it alone. He devotes hardly any time to socializing. He respects deadlines (if it depends on him) and is never late to meetings. He replies to e-mails almost immediately and always returns phone calls (does not prioritize).
- **Other**: His professional entourage is characterized by team spirit, efficiency and communication. However, he should set an example with regards to meals and appearance. He does not bring his personal life to the company. The individual in question is flexible in team debates on professional issues but dauntlessly confronts other teams and is uncompromising. In his view, motivation necessitates the setting of an example (and it does work with selected individuals). He never praises. He assigns tasks in a clear manner, sets deadlines and calls team members to be accountable. He makes decisions quickly and firmly.

Areas to Improve:
- Delegating (to achieve this, his staff will improve – hopefully he can complete by the end of the year the two projects he currently oversees).
- Communication.
- Time management.
- Socializing.
- He will progress from an executing leader to a coordinating leader.
- Appearance.
- Praise.
- Healthier lifestyle, starting with energizing meals.

Proposal:
- Delegating:
  – Supply him with relevant literature to read;
  – Provide proper training or coaching to his staff.
- Communication:
  – a mini shadow coaching, specifically at an in-house meeting at the company where other team leaders are also present.
- Time management: the coach is pleased to offer him with pertinent literature to read and serve a pragmatic purpose afterwards.
- Socializing:
  – staff: he should have lunch with each team member at least once quarterly;
  – team: eating in front of the computer should be prohibited (instead, all meals will be consumed in the common dining room; furthermore, everyone can benefit from twenty minutes of daily relaxation and engaging in private time and conversations, otherwise their working capacity and health can be undermined);

– team leaders: discuss issues other than work for a few minutes each time they meet or converse on the phone.
- Evolution from an executing manager to a coordinating leader: to achieve this, organizational development is also required (increase in staff, improvement of current staff, delegation of projects).
- Appearance:
  – wardrobe, haircut, using folder and pen with company logo when meeting clients;
  – it is advisable to create a dress code for the team;
  – the coach is ready to assist in both, even with a specific shopping tour or a consultation;
  – office walls could be decorated a bit.
- Praise: praise a staff member daily, both in the morning and in the afternoon (prepare a list for the next coaching session).
- Healthier lifestyle, meals:
  – although now it may be irrelevant for him what he eats and when, he should pay more attention to his diet for the sake of his health and his work performance as well;
  – consult a nutritionist about a healthy diet (in the first round, the coach is pleased to assist);
  – order a special menu (that contains little sugar and is rich in fiber and vitamins).

19. Stakeholder Analysis[18]

A stakeholder can be anyone who influences your actions or work or is influenced by you. Since a person's stakeholders can be identified in every field of life, this type of analysis can help in evaluating the environment and in setting goals as well as prove to be useful during implementation.

The following key questions will be answered:
- Who are your stakeholders? (employer/manager, peers/colleagues, staff, trade union, wife, children, friends, etc.) What are their interests?
- How much do they affect you?
- How do you influence them?
- How do you handle them?

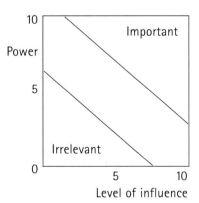

It is one of the tools that can be both applied in business and life coaching. In business settings, I used it as a management consultant for several projects. In a life coaching context, for instance, a colleague of mine utilized it when the coachee wanted to resolve a dilemma involving a choice between obtaining a divorce or staying together.

20. Iacocca's 9C's Model[19]

The name of Iacocca's 9C's framework is another acronym. Employed as a tool, it facilitates the understanding of true leadership values more. Originally, it was developed by Iacocca for the recruitment of executives and young leadership talent. In such cases, a person rates the candidates on nine different parameters. However, it can be applied as a self-assessment tool, in which case an individual rates himself or herself using a scale of 1 (poor) to 5 (excellent). Self-assessment is as valuable as assessment by others, but the executive can also request feedback on these parameters. 9C's can be used as a tool in both cases.

The nine parameters are:

Curiosity – A leader must ask questions and listen to the answers. No one is so perfect that there is nothing to learn for him or her. It is always enlightening to understand how others function.

Creativity – A leader has to be creative and keen on trying something different. A leader has to think out of the box.

Communication – A leader has to communicate and converse with others. Bill Clinton once said, "It is silly not to talk to people you disagree with. There is hope as long as you are talking."

Character – A leader must distinguish between right and wrong and have the courage to do the right thing. Abraham Lincoln once said, "If you want to test a man's character, give him power."

Courage – Swagger is not courage; neither is force. Courage is a commitment to sit at the negotiating table and communicate. A good leader does not simply talk the talk but also walks it, stands up for justice and assumes personal liability.

Conviction – To be a competent leader, you must have ardor, passion and the drive to succeed. You should have a desire to accomplish what you set your mind on.

Charisma – Charisma is the ability to persuade others to stand up for something. It is the capacity to inspire them to act in accordance with the good things in their hearts instead of acting in conformity with bad things in others' hearts. For a charismatic leader, others' well-being is more important than one's own image.

Competence – A good leader does not only talk but can demonstrate achievements and resolve problems. A competent leader makes decisions and assumes responsibility for them. –

Common Sense – As Charlie Beacham observed, "The only thing you've got going for you as a human being is your ability to reason and your common sense."

Instructions:
1. Write the names of the candidates for a given position.
2. Rate each candidate on each C, using a scale of 1 to 5, where 1 is poor and 5 is excellent and then add each row in the last column. If any of the parameters is more relevant than the others for the given position in the specific corporate culture, then you can also weigh the parameters.

Candidates	Curiosity	Creativity	Communication	Character	Courage	Conviction	Charisma	Competence	Common Sense	Total
1.										
2.										
3.										

It can be utilized as a self-assessment tool in the Situation stage and can also help elicit feedback about the client from individuals deemed influential.

21. Social Atom[20]

These days, network research is a trendy topic. It is used by national security authorities and large banks as well as by those consulting someone's network on Facebook. It can be useful to check the friends you have in common with another because a good friend of yours might know him and her. It will help you prepare for a business meeting.

According to Jacob Levy Moreno's personality theory, an individual's personality develops through their relationships, roles and interactions and can be understood together with their social microenvironment.

A social atom is the conglomeration of an individual's relationships and connections that have emotional meanings attached to them in the social universe.

Basically, there are three potential solutions for application of this tool. Each of them can be enhanced to various levels of depths:
1. In a drawing.
2. Using objects (chess pieces, pebbles, stuffed toys, coins, etc.)
2. Using people.

In individual coaching, of course, the first two versions are the easiest ones to carry out, and the third version can be used in team or group coaching.

The solution involving drawing has two advantages. First, it can be kept, and you can view it a few months later (in the case of objects, you can do the same by taking a picture using your mobile phone; nevertheless, a drawing is better) to compare it with a new one. Also, more information can be included, e.g. it is easier to highlight the negative or positive nature of a relationship or the sequence in which each individual was drawn. Secondly, the coachee's creativity is not limited by the set of objects; he or she is free to draw any symbol he or she wishes.

Instructions to the coachee:
1. a) Draw yourself on the paper using a symbol;
   b) Also using symbols, draw the people who are dear to you (they do not have to be alive), the objects that are valuable for you (e.g. the following have already been included: laptop, TV, car, etc.), animals that are important for you (e.g. their pets), values that you deem important (knowledge, loyalty, religion, family, etc.);
   c) Indicate the number of each object in the sequence they were drawn;
   d) Mark positive relationships with a continuous line, negative ones with a broken line and ambivalent ones with a wavy line;
   e) In the same way, also mark the relationships between others;
   f) In case of each character, the distance from your symbol should indicate the closeness of your relationship with them. Draw a circle around your symbol. The ones with whom you have close relationships will be within the circle and acquaintances should be outside the circle.
2. Choose an object that represents you. Place it somewhere on the board/table. Then select objects for each of the relevant individuals and place them too.
3. Determine where you are located and stand there. Instruct the other team members on where and how they should stand.

Analysis:
When the drawing/set-up is completed, ask the coachee whether he or she can see anything that he or she has not considered or that has not been relevant for him or her thus far.

It is expedient to study the following:
- What did the coachee use to represent himself or herself and the others?
- How many symbols are there within the circle and outside the circle? E.g. if there are hardly any symbols or there is no symbol, then it is worth discussing it – it can be an early sign of burn-out. Alternatively, it is also interesting if there are too many symbols within the circle in that they might be superficial relationships.
- Is the diagram balanced? Where is the symbol of the coachee located (in the center, on the edge)?
- Homogeneity. E.g. most of the symbols are of the same gender, of similar age, or from the same circle: there are only workplace relationships, strictly family members, or only objects represented.
- Are there any negative relationships? If yes, why doesn't the coachee terminate his or her relationship with them? If not, aren't there any suppressed feelings? Isn't he or she a conflict-avoider to an overly extent?
- Does the coachee want to change anything in the social network? If yes, what?

Application:
This tool is frequently used with people who solicit a coach's assistance with a time management problem because it can help explore neglected areas and stifling factors (for example, work and family suppress relationships with friends or sporting partners).

Also, it is often applied in the case of coachees facing initial burn-out problems: if there is only a very small number of symbols in the internal circle, then you have to discuss whether relationships with those situated in the external circle can be restored, i.e. is it enough to contact them again, or is there a need for a more significant change, e.g. to select a new hobby.

We had a client who was not burned out, and yet this tool was used in his case: he told us that everything around him was OK but he still was not content. In his case, it was useful to set up a model of his social network because he could observe that the majority of his relationships derive from the same source.

This tool can be further elaborated. If applied in a business setting (e.g. development of business communication), then you can instruct the coachee to draw only his or her work relationships. Therefore, more individuals will be included in the drawing, and at the same time, it will become more important to illustrate the relationships amongst others.

CASE STUDIES (EXCERPT)

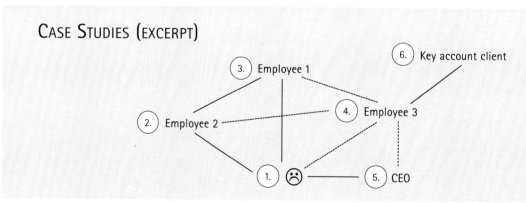

I once had a coachee who came to the session with the conviction that she was an ineffective leader because she really disliked one of her employees and wanted to change this.

She started but did not finish her drawing as she soon realized what the roadblock was. As illustrated in her drawing, she first cast herself on the sheet (the numbers in the top left corner indicate the order in which others were added) as a sad face, which indicated the toll that the situation was taking on her and then her three teammates. She then drew the relationships between them, which revealed that she would get along very well with the first two employees and that the third one was the odd one out. She then continued drawing the relationships of the disliked colleague, from which it transpired that he did not have a good rapport with anyone-team members or bosses, only with one key account client (whom nobody else knew). This was a good starting point for her to scrutinize the situation further. As a result, she was no longer angry with or blaming herself for being unable to embrace this individual and so, the coaching also started to take another direction.

The division director of a market leading service-providing company was seeking a coach to improve his relationship capital. He knew very few people because he had been working for the same company for over ten years, was married and his wife preferred to have him at home in the evenings. Therefore, he lost contact with his university friends and had fewer than 30 numbers saved on his cellular phone. He made a drawing of the current situation, which was really very surprising. Actually, his wife used to restrict him in building relationships while their children were small. Presently, she did not mind if he went out occasionally, except there was no longer anyone with whom to go out. Along with his coach, they designed an action plan which called for him to explore additional networking tools between coaching sessions He also brought back the original drawing to each session and added the individuals who joined his network in the last two or three weeks.

These included old university buddies and former colleagues who had left the company a long time ago, but there were also many new names added. For example, he made a very conscious effort to attend conferences and took advantage of the coffee breaks. He also wrote an article for the company newsletter, which prompted many readers who were unaware that he worked for the company to contact him. Also, as sport became a part of his life again, this meant new names added to his drawing.

The outcome of the coaching was not only the single success with networking, but the coachee also drew the conclusion that it is very important for him to have new contacts (since he spent a considerable amount on the coaching), and not to neglect the existing ones. Furthermore, in just a few months he also mastered some very useful networking techniques.

The chief operating officer of a big corporation was appointed as the CEO. At one of our sessions, we spoke about the former CEO. What are the mistakes that he should avoid? Then we moved on to discuss the skills and fields in which the former CEO excelled and concluded that he did not quite measure up yet. Citing one of these shortcomings, he mentioned that she did not yet have much of a relationship capital in the media world as her predecessor did, and she considered this to be a major drawback. I informed her about the coaching tool known as social atom and asked her whether she would be interested in trying it. As I was beginning to explain it to her, she was already pulling out a sheet of paper and displayed a great deal of enthusiasm. She drew herself in the middle of the sheet and then added all the people in the media world that the ex-CEO knew and with whom she would also like to acquaint herself. Unfortunately, there were really quite a few individuals on the list who she did not know and therefore, this appeared a tough challenge indeed. We then proceeded as if we were using Facebook. One by one, we verified whether there was anyone in her group of acquaintances who knew the given person. The company's marketing and commercial directors and her employees knew nearly two-thirds of them. Therefore, these could be checked off the list easily, and already she was assigning herself as homework the task of asking the two directors to attend the upcoming meeting and introduce her to these media personalities. As for the remaining one-third, she began to lose heart as only the former CEO knew them, and they were so inaccessible. Clearly, she thought, she could not ask him for help. She then made a passing remark:

Coachee: How interesting it is that my husband knows these people!

Coach: Really? We never talked about your personal life since we focus on business topics, not life ones, but may I ask you what your husband does?

Coachee: Sure. He works in PR.

Coach: That sounds promising.

Coachee: Maybe I could meet some media personalities through him.

Coach: Is he supportive of your efforts?

Coachee: Yes, he is very pleased that I was appointed and assured me that he would support me in this. I don't want to take advantage of him, but I think he would actually be glad that I could attend the business dinners and concerts whereas up to this point, I was not very keen on accompanying him.

This proved to be a win-win situation and beneficial for both the client's personal and the professional life.

A second successful task that we performed in the course of a team coaching session and following the warm-up or icebreaker was one based on the concept of the social atom.

I began the exercise by asking the department head to leave the room. It was his deputy's responsibility to put together a team for the exercise.

He asked who would be willing to play the role of the department head in the exercise, but no one volunteered, so they drew lots. This intermezzo in itself spurred the coach to further ponder the matter.

The deputy department head then had to instruct the one who had the dubious honor of impersonating their boss to stand on a chair in front of the window and facing the door. Next, he asked all the staff members to squat and look in the direction of the "boss." None of the team members seemed surprised or resisted, but all squatted down and were looking up to the "big leader" standing on the chair – that is, their co-worker chosen for the task.

Then one of them said that while all of this is fine, the boss should not even look at them. He noted that it would be much more symbolic if the employer turned his back toward them and gazed straight ahead, leading the way but not looking back at his employees to see if they can keep up the pace.

It was bewildering how very subordinated a position they put themselves in.

The department head later entered, and the coach asked him if he has any idea what this scene was supposed to depict, and he replied in the negative.

The coach gradually made him realize that this was a department at their company. He then said it was impossible since they have absolute democracy in the company, and such a relationship of superiority and subordination between a leader and his or her team could never exist. His remark was followed by silence.

He was a tough, "macho" type of man. Finally, he began to realize who it really was standing on the chair. If he had been a sensitive type, he might very likely have started to cry. He did not utter a word but simply walked out...

A few terrifying minutes elapsed, with countless questions raised and concerns articulated.

"Is he offended?"

"What if he does something stupid?"
"Do you think he is going to fire us all?"

It was only minutes but really felt like hours. The coach also started to wonder about the potential consequences. Perhaps they will never ask him to do team coaching for this multinational company.

The department head then entered with two bottles of champagne. He offered one to the coach and congratulated him for holding up a mirror to him, as a result of which he learned more in two hours than in the four years since he was appointed department head. He offered the other bottle of champagne to his team.

This was not the intended topic of the coaching, but since this was the second task immediately following the icebreaker exercise, the topic previously agreed upon was taken off the agenda. The team members were talking and drinking, while the department head was making notes on a large flipchart about the things that he should do to avoid being an autocratic leader, and what truly constitutes a democratic leader. He did not critique the ideas but continued taking notes. When his team took a lunch break, he did not accompany them but put a deadline next to each task and started the afternoon session by making a commitment to change.

Following the half-day team session, the coach continued to work one-on-one with the department head, who mentioned many times afterwards this "game," since it was such a cathartic experience for him to see himself from the outside. He observed that this could not have been brought to the surface solely with the use of words.

A Chief Executive Officer had three vice presidents; that is to say, there were four of them on the management board. He had been on bad terms with one of them for a long time: he was satisfied with him professionally but he "inherited" him. They had very different views on certain matters, which often complicated the daily professional collaboration with him. Although the coach was aware of this situation from the beginning of the coaching process, she also knew that the CEO was able to work very efficiently with his other two managers and therefore overlooking his poor relationship with the third.

At this point, however, some important new information surfaced: he found out that his two right-hand men accepted money from a supplier. It was no trivial change either. He knew for certain that they had accepted a kickback but had no evidence in his possession. Therefore, he came to the coaching session stating that he could see three options: a) firing the two thereby setting an example, b) letting them know privately that he is conscious of the situation but is willing to give them another chance or c) turning a blind eye to the whole thing.

He drew the social atom, which reiterated that he could not rely on the third manager, and that if he had a disagreement with the other two or even terminated them, he would be very much left to his own devices. The coach could not render advice in this situation; he had to make the decision by himself. They reviewed the SPARKLE Model and pondered over the situation. The CEO's phone rang and he found out that the two deputy general managers had told the supplier that he was also "in," and that they need so much money because the three of them share it. This was precisely the information he needed to make his decision.

22. MPH Client Mapping[21]

This is another tool described by Mick Cope in his book *The Seven C's of Coaching*. It helps to extract the whole story and not solely those aspects the client prefers to share. The letters included in the acronym are:

Magnitude (Meta – Macro – Micro)
Periodicity (Past – Present – Projected)
Holistic dimension (**Heart** – Head – Hand)

The aim is to provide information in each of the nine boxes. People tend to approach a situation only from three aspects:

	META Describe in general terms	MACRO Provide an example	MICRO Desribe in greater
M			
P	PAST Looking back...	PRESENT At the present time...	PROJECTED In the future...
H	HEART How do you feel?	HEAD What do you think?	HAND What are you doing?

For example, if the client has a preference for 'Meta, Past, Head', i.e. describes in general terms his former thinking style, the following questions can help map each of the remaining boxes.

- MACRO: I understand that it is a general problem that occurs to you frequently. Can you cite me a specific example?
- MICRO: I see. Still I would appreciate if you could offer me some specific details so that I could better visualize every aspect.
- PRESENT: What you told me happened in the past. Can you describe what is happening at the present time? Is there any change?
- PROJECTED: What do you think was the reason for the improvement? Do you think it will continue to get better? How do you imagine the situation to be in a year?
- HEART: You mentioned that such cases make you lose it. Can you tell me exactly how you feel then?
- HAND: Although I understand what you feel and think in such cases, is there anything you actually do? How do you act?

23. Confrontation, Holding Up a Mirror

Most leaders consider an impartial observer's sincere feedback to be of tremendous value. The higher a leader's position, the less feedback he or she receives (e.g. an executive at the highest level of an organization cannot receive feedback from his or her boss). However, it is not simply the quantity that matters, but also the quality. You should emphasize the word *sincere*. The sincerity of the feedback received from staff members can be questionable in some cases. Also, feedback received from peers may be distorted because there might be fear that the other will be awarded a promotion first and therefore, they avoid offering feedback that would enable the other leader to improve. This is another way that a professional coach can assist a leader: he or she knows that in the long run, in addition to praising, it is also worth providing constructive feedback to the client.

There are several types of mirrors, each with its own unique role and function. We can draw a distinction between flat, convex and concave mirrors, each one reflecting a different picture of the same object. It is the coach's duty to select the appropriate mirror in the given situation.

A flat mirror reflects objective feedback. In some cases, it is also necessary to display the problem of the environment, or diminish the given problem and display the whole "big picture" as reflected by a convex mirror. Conversely, in other cases, you have to focus on a single object, detail or area susceptible of improvement, and magnify it when the coachee fails to notice it or wants to downplay it – in which case, you can hold a concave mirror.

The mirror as an object reflects solely your outward appearance. A coach as a living mirror reflects your inner world – or a part of it that is visible from outside. Many people usually lack the courage to look in the mirror because they do not want to face themselves. This is even more applicable to the inner world. This could partly explain why sometimes it is not easy to sell coaching services, and why a relationship based on trust between coach and coachee is a key factor.

Effective feedback can be provided under the following conditions:
• the client is interested in it (e.g. specifically asks the coach to provide feedback of his or her work because he or she never receives any or it is inconsistent);
• it is descriptive, not evaluative;
• it is specific, not general.

A large multinational company requested a proposal from us and listed the pre-requisites that a coach working for by the former must meet. The list included knowledge of the industry, business and life experience, three years of coaching experience, references (as objective criteria), but also boldness on the coach's part to take the risk of illuminating the client's blind spots. Indeed, the act of offering objective feedback requires courage, and many coaches who "coach for a living" do not assume this risk because they fear being replaced. The professional community where I work advocates the following practice: the introductory meeting will be devoted to discussing what the client expects from the coach, and if it includes offering sincere feedback, then you can test immediately whether he or she truly means it or is simply making a routine statement.

A coach can be of considerable help by providing as much descriptive, rather than evaluative feedback as possible. Another important point: the more specific the feedback in question is, the more efficient it is.

Instead of saying:
"You made a poor presentation." – It is preferable to list specific details:
• The structure was good, but your tone was monotonous.
• It included a lot of technical information in a well-structured form, but next time it is expedient to illustrate it with specific cases.

Case Study (excerpt)

The shareholder of a trading company employing 500 people decided to fund coaching for the firm's top management. Prior to the commencement of the process, the shareholder invited the coach to share his expectations with the employees. He articulated two requests:
• They will not address more than three areas susceptible of improvement at a time because that would be overwhelming
• If the coach identifies a field susceptible of improvement, then he or she will praise at least two aspects in which coachee excels since it is commonplace to his or her corporate culture. As he explained, "You have to praise in a sandwich". This is an acceptable requirement as well because when giving objective feedback, a coach will cite not only negative features but also emphasize positive observations to reassure the coachee.

John Whitmore[22] presents a good example in his book on distinguishing the levels of feedback.

1. Personal judgment:
You are useless!
The reasons why this is not a good feedback from the coach:
• It refers to the person instead of the given task or activity.
• It is absolutely general.
• It expresses no intention to help, i.e. does not focus on how the client should enhance his or her performance next time.

You can see that a coach does not have to use forceful language or raise his voice to undermine the client's self-confidence.

2. Qualifying statement:
This report is useless!
This statement is more desirable because it does not describe the person but his or her performance, and yet it is still very powerful and lacks a good intention to help.

3. Your report is well-structured but the language is inappropriate for the target audience.
This statement is not judgmental but descriptive, and it is more specific, although it still lacks support for the next step.

4. How do you feel your report is? In which area could it be improved? How do you think I could ameliorate it even further?
This will certainly not disappoint the client, but he or she he will feel that the report is still not perfect. You only have to provide guidance on "how to do it", which in turn helps him or her learn and improve significantly.

Whereas in the first three cases the client might react out of sheer spite by furnishing explanations, excuses or trying to retort in the fourth scenario, the client has to consider and express what he or she can observe and how he or she views his or her performance.

Clients often evoke questions in the coach with their statements or behavior. In such cases, it is prudent to interrogate, and you should not fear that the client would perceive it as an attack. Examples are classic statements such as:

Coachee: This problem is not of great concern to me. I am not really concerned by this situation, and it does not really matter; I just thought I would tell you that...
Coach: Could you tell me why you mentioned this problem if it was not very important for you?

Coachee: The truth of the matter is that there is nothing I could do in this situation.
Coach: Is there really nothing you can do in this situation?

Coachee: Anyway, I will never change.
Coach: Did you not turn to a coach precisely because you wanted to improve/make progress in this field?

Coachee: I would like to express myself clearly without beating around the bush... (And then he or she talks in very obscure and long-winded sentences).
Coach: You told me you wanted to express yourself clearly... Could you sum it up in one sentence?

Coachee: I have complete trust in you because I know that you mean well... (However, the coach has a feeling that this is not completely the case).
Coach: You stated that you trust me completely, yet I still sense that it does not add up to 100%. What could I do to deliver the missing few percent?

As mentioned above, feedback should not be exclusively negative, not at all. A good mirror-holder does not only reflect negative aspects. To form an objective picture, positive features should be also incorporated. A coach should not lavish praise sparingly but must be careful to remain realistic: the client does not need any unjustified praise but rather genuine objective feedback from an impartial observer. Heaping praises on the coachee simply to retain him/her as a client is unethical and counter-productive in the long run. The image of the individual providing sincere feedback can be undermined by a single slip of the tongue and ultimately ruin confidence in the coach.

24. ACE FIRST Model[23]

Graham Lee introduced this model in his book *Leadership Coaching*. The acronym ACE is comprised of the initials of the words Actions, Cognitions and Emotions. 'FIRST' is an acronym created using the initials of Focus, Intentions, Results, System and Tension.

This is a valuable tool in the Situation stage when the client evaluates the state of affairs – what he or she does, thinks or feels in the given situation, but can also prove to be helpful in later stages of the coaching process. Upon setting a goal (Positioning phase), you can ask the client what he or she wants to do, think or feel when he or she achieves the goal. It can be applied equally in every case during the coaching process when you look back and determine whether any change in the actions, thoughts or feelings have occurred. For instance, it can be useful in the Key Obstacles/Leverage stage, or even in the Evaluation stage to ascertain whether that the coachee has accomplished the goal in each of the three fields.

This ACE model has also been presented with a different name by other authors. For example, Mick Cope[24] introduced the same model using the names of three bodily parts that begin with the letter 'H':

H – *Hand* – Action • H – *Head* – Cognition • H – *Heart* – Emotions

ACE and FIRST complement one another because while ACE describes the goal of the coaching process, FIRST addresses the content of the coaching work.

ACE can also enable the coachee to attain the same state (acts, thinks, feels the same) as when he was facing the given problem or difficulty. The coachee may have to close his or her eyes and search his or her soul... Also, the coach may adopt the same body posture as that of the coachee (e.g. sitting with his or her hands clasped behind him or her or with his or her shoulders in a relaxed pose, or even knitting his or her brows) to better understand how the coachee might have felt.

Action:
- What did you do?
- What did you say?
- How do others describe what you did?
- What physical manifestations did it result in?

Cognitions:
- What thoughts did you have?
- How did you perceive the situation?
- What did you think of yourself and others?

Emotions:
- What did you feel?
- How powerful were your emotions?
- How hidden were they?
- How conscious were you with regard to your emotions?

Questions to the stages of FIRST:

Focus:
- What did you focus on?
- What was conscious?
- What might have been unconscious, subconscious or instinctive?

Intentions:
- What did you want to achieve?
- How do you know you have achieved it?

Results:
- What did your behavior result in?
- To what extent did you follow through on your intention?

System:
- What external influences impacted your behavior?
- What internal influences impacted your behavior?

Tension:
- What physical manifestations did your behavior produce?
- Did you experience any physical tension?

25. 3-Column Thought Record[25]

This tool also originates from the toolset of cognitive therapy and features two advanced versions- five- and seven-column thought records. It applies to each of these tools whose aim is reduction rather than absolute deletion, and the coachee has to keep records both in the coaching session and at home.

Its aim is similar to that in cognitive therapy. It often occurs in coaching also that otherwise healthy clients are hindered by the same cognitive distortions and negative automatic thoughts (NAT) when performing certain actions. The goal is to enable the client to identify by himself or herself negative automatic thoughts typical for him or her, and isolate the event, emotions triggered by the latter and the specific negative automatic thought.

Objective description of the situation, event	Emotion triggered by the event	Negative automatic thought (NAT)

When can you apply this tool in coaching? It is an optimal tool in the case of clients with a low self-esteem (e.g.: I'm stupid, I could never achieve it anyway; I'm useless) in the Situation stage. As a part of assessing the situation, you can define the mindset typical for the client as a starting base. It is important to teach the client in the session first how to use this tool and complete the template together with a few illustrations, and assign it for homework only afterwards. You can achieve very good results in identifying mindsets even in the time between two sessions.

Furthermore, this tool can prove to be useful in cases where the client's sight is clouded by emotions, e.g. when he or she looks at a problem only from an emotional standpoint.

26. 5-Column Thought Record[26]

This is an advanced version of the 3-column thought record.

Case Study (excerpt)

The coachee had to choose three or four situations when she felt that she did not achieve her objective, or believed that others achieved much more than her. The five columns are labeled as follows: situation, negative automatic thought (NAT), how she felt; what would have been a more reasonable thought and how she would feel then.

Objective description of the situation	Negative automatic thoughts (NAT)	Moods, %	Alternative thoughts (brainstorming)	Re-evaluation of moods, %
Husband is late	He had an accident 5% He does not love me and is being unfaithful 95%	Fear 80% Worry 10% Anger 10%	The meeting was long Traffic jam Flat tire He is buying a surprise	Fear 70% Worry 10% Anger 10% Optimism 10%

27. 7-Column Thought Record[27]

This advanced version of the 5-column thought record helps question the rationality of NATs and seek more reasonable (alternative) thoughts to replace distorted thoughts. Hence, this tool aids the client in revising his or her subjective thoughts, thereby enabling him or her, for example, to boost self-confidence. When applying this tool, it is important that you first complete the template together during the session with the client and then that he or she observes himself or herself between sessions like using the previous tool. In addition to the Situation stage, this tool can be integrated in other phases (Positioning and Alternatives) since it helps restructure the client's mindset and achieve an outcome that is tangible and noticeable even to the environment.

Case Study (excerpt)

A multinational company was seeking a coach for one of its employees, a young woman who had just completed the two-year-long management training program funded by the company. She was soon to be promoted to a management position. The coach found out as early as during the introductory session that, despite the positive appraisals she had received, she lacked confidence and was riddled self-doubt. As she put it, "I'll never succeed in anything"; "I'm stupid". In the first session, they began discussing the contexts in which these feelings arise, and found that that they manifested themselves both in her work and private life. Therefore, the coach taught her how to use the 7-column thought record, and they agreed that she would keep a log of the events throughout the coming two weeks when she experienced similar emotions. The following table contains a few events she recorded:

Objective description of the situation	Moods, %	Negative automatic thought (NAT)	Supporting evidence	Opposing evidence	More realistic thought	Reevaluation of moods, %
I cannot cope with capacity planning.	Anxious 80%	I am incapable and not good at anything.	The work is not completed	I have worked on it a lot. I already have a great deal of information. So far, I have managed every task.	I am not silly; I am on the right track. I have to keep working because it is a complex task. I still have to interview X.Y.	Nervous 30%
Out of the tasks on the language proficiency exam, I am deficient at providing a summary	Tense 90%	I am stupid.	I have already looked up unfamiliar words in the dictionary and am still not ready with the summary.	I passed the oral exam. I understood everything on it. / My teacher is encouraging me	I am not stupid; I simply have to learn how to do this.	Tense 50%
It is Friday, and I am sitting at home alone. I do not have anyone to go out with.	Lonely 80%	Nobody needs me.	I am at home alone.	I haven't even tried to seek company. I didn't call anyone.	I was tired from work. I am too exhausted to go anywhere.	Lonely 60%

The two weeks of self-observation and manifestation of a more conscious mindset helped the client approach situations and challenges more calmly. Furthermore, this tool will remain constantly at her disposal; she can resort to it anytime in the future to help herself.

28. Document Analysis

If the client has a dilemma that is supported by written evidence, then he or she brings written documentation with him or her. For instance, if he or she wants to improve his or her style in written communication, then the coach will read it aloud. This is not aimed at satisfying the coach's curiosity. Rather, when the coach reads the document out loud and word by word, the client must simply listen to what he or she wrote. Consequently, this enables him or her to view it from a new perspective and it will evoke different impressions in him or her. It will also enable him or her to notice what he or she had overlooked up to now.

CASE STUDY (EXCERPT)

Many executives are unable to control their emotions well. For most of them, this manifests itself in a raised voice, which is undoubtedly an attitude that their staff resents. However, what is more detrimental than shouting is when a leader responds with cynicism and a condescending attitude. In most cases, people are not even cognizant of others' perception of their own behavior, and are surprised when they obtain this feedback as part of their performance evaluation. One of my coachees was astonished when he heard what his boss had said about him. So, he requested my assistance. In his personal life, he was not as cynical as in his work, since in the former, he sought to be in the company of the right kind of persons. By contrast, in his professional life he was unable to do so. I saw two potential solutions: shadow coaching, which is a more complex and costly technique, and document analysis. Being that the latter was the simpler one, we started with it and eventually the shadowing was no longer necessary. I asked the coachee to print out his e-mail correspondence from the previous week and read it to him as if the messages were addressed to him. There were moments when he almost raised his hand to question my audacity in speaking to him in that manner, even though I was only reading to him what he wrote to his employees. He felt ashamed. What he had failed to regard as offensive when he wrote it took on a different meaning now, and he realized what his boss meant.

The following week, he asked me to check every e-mail intended for his team, but one week later, it sufficed to save his emails as drafts and then quickly re-read and revise them, once he was able to overcome emotional roadblocks, prior to clicking only the "Send" button. This meant that he was no longer dependent on me and my review of his correspondence, and a few weeks later his boss even expressed his satisfaction that his employees no longer complained about him.

29. Behavioral Window[28]

A method of Thomas Gordon, this is a tool that can be employed in the Situation or Positioning stage. The client will verify "through a window" which employees demonstrate behavior that is acceptable or unacceptable to him or her. This useful tool helps the client be cognizant of his or her feelings about a specific behav-

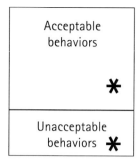

ior and reveals what presents an issue to the client. Clearly, this is a tool that can be applied not only in business settings but also in life coaching: A client can not only check through the window which category his or her staff belongs to, but, in the life coaching context, he or she can also ascertain what is applicable to the people around him or her (family, friends, etc.). It is expedient to compare the proportion of acceptable to unacceptable areas within a specific diagram.

Gordon warns about to be aware that the line dividing the behavior window into two areas is not static. It often moves upwards or downwards:

1. because of the things happening within you (how I am feeling: when I have a good day and I am relaxed, then the acceptable area is larger within the rectangle);

2. because of the environment (where that specific behavior is demonstrated and who is present: for example, it is completely acceptable for employees to be loud after consuming a few drinks at the company's Christmas party; the same behavior would pose an issue if it were occurring during business hours);

3. depending on who the other person is (you tend to accept some people more easily than others: you might more easily tolerate the whims of a colleague who has been with the company for a long time than those of a new hire).[29]

❀ 30. Problem Rectangle[30]

This is an advanced version of the behavior window. Also a method of Thomas Gordon, it enables clients to identify the owner of the problem very effectively and apply a tool that is appropriate for the case. In every organization, there are behavioral patterns that could raise an issue for the leader or staff, and there is a problem-free zone where productive work is performed. The leader's objective is to enlarge the problem-free zone, thereby assisting employees in resolving their problems (tools: Door Openers, Active Listening, Questioning), and also themselves.

	Behavioral patterns pointing employees' problems
Problem-free zone	Mutually-satisfactory needs, Productive work
	Behavioral patterns causing problems for the leader - leader's problem

❀ 31. Pie Chart[31]

This cognitive therapy technique assists clients in exploring other possible reasons for a certain outcome. For example, if an individual feels that he or she was the sole cause of something which in fact he or she was not the only responsible one, then this tool can be of use. It can be also used effectively by the coach when a client attributes success solely to himself or herself although it is well-known to be a team effort and also a result of circumstance.

CASE STUDIES (EXCERPT)

A client who was a project manager had experienced difficulty with making presentations and considered himself to be incompetent for the task. He was 100% certain that he would not succeed in making a presentation at the upcoming Steering Committee meeting because he lacked the competence to do so. We then considered the idea of using a pie chart to ascertain/to identify other potential explanations for an unsuccessful presentation. The chart reads as follows:

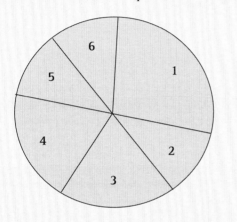

1 I am inadequate

2 The team does not inform me about every key issue

3 The projector does not work

4 The members of the Steering Committee will not be present

5 The support provided by the sponsor is insufficient

6 The team will not be ready with all deliverables

This tool assisted my client not only in boosting his self-confidence in relation to the presentation and modifying his NAT that he was inadequate for making a presentation, but also in taking into consideration all the factors to be considered prior to the presentation to ensure that it will be successful.

"Swinging to the other extreme", the same tool was used with a very talented managing director who did not lack self-confidence. Upon attending a successful roundtable discussion, he claimed all of the success for himself. However, when we analyzed the situation using a pie chart, he realized that a number of other factors had also contributed to the success. He expressed his appreciation for presently becoming aware of the fact that, in the event of similar future milestones, he must ensure that all these conditions are in place (for instance, that questions will be discussed in advance with the moderator, capable fellow participants, proper marketing material).

As an illustration of another "anti-case": a young executive attributed all of his success strictly to himself, although the almost one million dollars contributed by his father to build his enterprise played a key role. Furthermore, the economy and particularly his industry were prospering so that the business would have been profitable anyway unless he performed extremely poorly. Consequently, in times of a financial crisis, he had to evaluate the degree to which his achievements and leadership abilities contributed to success in recent years as well as the percentage in case of other factors. When he drew up a pie chart, he became slightly discouraged; it was evident that it was difficult for him to face the reality. He needed a few seconds to cope with it, after which he ordered a coffee and stated: "Thank you. Initially I was planning to devote thirty minutes to our meeting but now, I would like to ask you if we could stay a little longer, perhaps two hours. That way, we can start working immediately because I consider it worthwhile to cancel a meeting with one of our suppliers so that I may begin to enhance my leadership skills now as opposed to two weeks from now."

32. Change of Perspective

Most leaders tend to forget quickly how it was to work as a beginner.

Case Study (Excerpt)

One of my clients, a CEO and owner of an IT company with nearly one hundred employees, had never undertaken formal studies of management theory or practice. Everything that he had learned was at his own cost. One day, he approached me with the following dilemma: He could not make sense of why his staff would not follow his directions and why he had to spoon-feed them. Although we debated this issue and discussed effective delegation and empowerment, it became clear that we needed some form of confrontation since, as the proverb states, "words fly away writings remain". I took a sheet of paper and a few color pencils from my bag (this is another reason why it pays for a coach to have small kids) and tried the exercise referred to as "The three castles". It proceeds as follows: the coach instructs the client to draw a castle. He or she does so but seemingly does not understand the purpose behind it and why he or she has to draw during a coaching session. Thus, he or she tries to complete the task with as little effort as possible and draws only a few lines to be done with it.

The coach berates the client for drawing such a castle without windows or a gate, points out that it does not resemble what he or she originally imagined and tears the drawing to pieces.

The coach repeats the task of drawing a castle and while the client is beginning to do so, he or she continuously provides instructions on where to draw a line, how to perfect it, etc. This results in the client not generating a single original thought in his or her mind. Because the client is a leader and is not accustomed to being instructed on what to do and how to perform it, he feels frustrated.

The coach once again presents the client with a blank sheet of paper again and says: "OK, let's try it again."

The coach explains why the client should draw a castle (it is a birthday present for his or her son), i.e. offers the big picture. With the understanding of why he had to draw and without being instructed, the client tapped into his creativity, took out coloring pencils and drew even a tree and a flag although they were not included in the task. After asking the coach for his son's name, he writes in the caption on the lawn in front of the castle "Happy Birthday Timothy!"

When the client had completed the drawing, the coach asked which version he liked the best:
1. assignment of the task with minimal instruction,
2. assignment of the task and continuous instruction, control or
3. empowerment?

They then gathered the tools of effective delegation. Since, the executive client has substituted weekly status reports for continuous control of the company so that both the leader and the staff have become more balanced, resulting in a win–win situation. Sometimes it is advisable for employers to re-experience what it is like to be a beginner because they tend to forget after many years of leadership.

33. Outsider Input

Outsider input occurs when the hiring manager informs the coach in which area the coachee should improve. In such cases, the coach has to be fully present because there is a high risk that the client is only "assigned" to coaching. If the coachee does not agree on the goals set, then the engagement can involve a number of risks.

Each company's corporate culture is unique and therefore demands which entails a different approach to coaching.

1. I have clients who do not disclose that they have a coach, i.e. pay me from their own pocket.
2. There are some clients whose corporate culture supports coaching but who believe that the ideal solution is for both the hiring manager (e.g. the Director of Human Resources or the client's manager) and the coach to assign the task of elevating the client's performance to a new level.
3. The next level occurs when this meeting is conducted together with the coachee so that the coach is not a messenger stating "dear executive, although you haven't been informed, you'll have to improve in...". In this case, the client is part of the alignment meeting where the parties discuss the desired outcome of the coaching engagement. Any questions or concerns may be addressed straight away.
4. And there are executives who display confidence in both the coach and the coachee and trust that they will spend the time constructively. Such executives allow the coachee to determine the specific theme of the coaching.

Clearly, there is no direct outsider input in the first and the fourth cases cited above. Nevertheless, it will still be apparent indirectly, as for instance, if the client brings a previous appraisal of his or hers. However, the approach to areas of improvement is vastly different than in the other two cases.

Versions No. 2 and 3 can also lead to the same initial situation if it is an autocratic organization, and the coachee dares only to keep nodding in the meeting attended by three participants.

If the coachee lacks even confidence in his or her coach, then it will be only a masquerade. This will frustrate the coach because as a general rule, coaches strive for success. It will also frustrate the coachee because 90 minutes of his or her time is lost every week when he or she is also going through the motions. Finally, the client's manager will also experience disappointment because he or she does not receive the benefit of his or her bargain.

A competent coach is mindful of this, and unless he or she is desperate to keep the client, it is ethical to offer sincere feedback or recommend a replacement for him or her. In the latter case, if the hiring manager is very autocratic, it is a substantial achievement if he or she allows at least the client to select his or her own coach – someone in whom he or she can place complete faith and who would not make him or her feel coerced that what he or she does is strictly by command but rather that improvement is being effectuated for his or her sake.

34. 180/360 Degree Assessment

With a 180/360 degree assessment, the client is rated by colleagues working on the same level as well as on the level above and below him or her in the organizational hierarchy. This is a mapping tool that helps identify the specific fields in which the client wants to improve. Within multi-national corporations, there is a culture for multi-rater assessments. In most cases, coachees working for a multinational company bring their assessments with them. If no multi-rater assessment is performed within a company and the coachee would like to know others' perceptions of him or her, then an assessment can precede the coaching.

Normally, raters are supervisors/bosses, subordinates, peers and clients. 180/360 degree assessments available in the market are extremely sophisticated and use advanced technologies. Ranging between $200 and several thousand dollars, they offer a detailed feedback to the client. In all honesty, sometimes it is completely unnecessary. There are circumstances where two simple questions will suffice: "What can you learn from him or her? At what does he or she have to improve?"

If employees and colleagues must complete a long questionnaire, then it is useful to add a few questions that are not included on the standard list but target a specific field where the client especially needs feedback because he or she lacks sufficient competence. I once had a client who was a new leader with a very casual style at work. It was important to include the following question: "On a scale from 1 to 5, indicate how appropriate you think he is dressed for the given executive level in question."

Case Study (excerpt)

A top-level corporate executive enlisted the services of a coach for a middle-level manager because the latter employed an improper tone. Their dialogue went like this:
Coachee: My boss is wrong. I don't yell at all, he must have a sensitive ear!
Coach: Will we perform a 360 degree assessment? Would you like to know what your colleagues, staff and peers like and what they don't appreciate about you?
Coachee: Sure.
Upon reviewing the feedback forms, he realized that there was room for improvement. Since, he has been controlling his temper which has led to an improvement in the overall corporate climate.

35. Tests

The timing and types of tests that should be utilized depend on a number of factors. Tests can be applied in the Situation stage or in the Evaluation stage to measure the success of the coaching. Furthermore, if a new issue arises in any of the sessions and is worth examining, then tests can serve as a valuable tool.

Some clients are particularly keen on completing tests while others freeze when they see one. This means that it is expedient to first become acquainted with the coachee and avoid opening a session with a test.

Some clients receive a 180/360 degree assessment at work. There are cases when coaching begins with an outsider input, i.e. the coachee's supervisor directs his or her attention to an area susceptible of improvement. In such cases, the coachee might prefer a more objective picture (will not believe the feedback from his or her boss or colleagues) and seeks an evaluation of himself or herself.

The same beginning may be followed by the client (who disagrees with the assessment received from his or her boss or colleagues) saying "Let's skip this issue". He or she may not even be willing to complete a test addressing that field. However, after a few sessions, it may occur that the coachee opens up to the coach and that owing to the confidence established between them, they return to the issue later and the coachee ultimately completes a self-assessment test.

Coaching is very personal in nature. Many individuals opt for e-coaching (mostly in the US), which involves the use of e-mail, Skype or the telephone. In Europe however, many coaches prefer undeniably personal meetings because of the opportunity to observe gestures and every movement. For the same reason, they normally do not send tests by e-mail in advance and ask clients to return them when completed nor do they have a preference for emailing the appraisal for they consider such a medium to be too impersonal.

Ideally, a test takes an entire coaching session. It proceeds as follows: Both the coachee and the coach sit back in their comfortable armchairs. Coach asks a question. If the coachee provides a definite answer, then the coach writes it down, but generally, this is not the case. The coaching work begins when the coachee asks for clarification or replies "it depends." Completing a questionnaire and submitting the results based on a template is not rocket science. Any college student filling in basic market research questionnaires on the street can accomplish the aforementioned. However, the point is that we discuss the ideas on the agenda prior to furnishing an answer. In such an event, the client usually explains many cases. We might not even complete the test because sometimes when we raise question no. 3, the coachee shares an actual case from the past and exclaims: "Oh my God, I really must be aggressive if I did that... What am I going to do now? I didn't even realize I was so aggressive at work! Could you help me?"

Coaching would be much less effective if the coachee only responded with a "yes" or "no." With the approach in question, the client encounters many 'A-ha' moments and is able to build something from many small pieces.

It has its advantages if a coach has a few tests at hand. There are a vast number of resources where you can find tests, which also means that you should carefully check for quality. There are test books available in every language, and many websites offer downloadable tests for a small amount. I also have dozens of tests in my toolkit (including confidence, stress, time management, charisma, delegation, conflict-handling, etc. tests, i.e. nearly every issue that my clients face). Many times I prefer to create a tailor-made test for the specific case from several resources. This allows us to identify with every single question on the test. There are very sophisticated tests focusing not only on a specific issue (e.g. stress) but covering a wider scope, e.g. those able to map the entire personality profile, such as MBTI or GPOP, its business version.

36. MBTI – Myers–Briggs Type Indicator[32]

Based on the typological theories advanced by Carl Gustav Jung, the MBTI assessment was created as a result of fifty years of research and development. Pursuant to Jung's preference theory, everyone has inherent preferences in the same manner as being left- or right-handed. These preferences appear in four fields of the personality profile. The MBTI describes the individual features of one's behavior using four pairs of preference:
- On what do you focus your attention? Where do you get your energy from? (extroverted – introverted)
- How do you perceive things? How do you obtain information? (sensing – intuition)
- How do you make decisions? How do you view your environment and the world? (thinking – feeling)
- How do you approach the outside world? How do you resolve your problems? (judging – perceiving)

Based on these pairs of preferences, the system defines sixteen distinguishable types of equal rank. The contours for the types typical for an individual are not rigid. In accordance with Jung's idea, knowing the type and the system can further self-development appropriate for one's age.

This tool enables you to learn as well as understand yourself and others better. It also promotes a non-judgmental stance towards others who are different than you. The MBTI system treats difference as a value and does not assess IQ or EQ.

There is a list of recommended jobs/occupations for each of the 16 enumerated types based on the test. Some types are more suited for academic research and others are born to be actors. Clearly, this does not mean that you should not apply for a certain job unless you have the same letter combination, but simply that complying with the given role will involve less effort if you fit that type. These codes change during one's life. Many people whose parameters changed even in two dimensions over the course of five or ten years. This is another reason why you should not regard your type as fixed when choosing a career. Nevertheless, it is interesting to note (because clients are often leaders) that there are four types out of the 16 that are defined as natural leaders. (Again, I would like to emphasize that anyone from another type out of the 12 others can also become a leader, but it involves less effort for a natural leader.)

- ESTJ – traditional leader,
- ENFP – catalyzing leader,
- ESTP – troubleshooting leader,
- ENTJ – visionary leader.

Besides career coaching, the MBTI can be applied in many other fields in business and corporate coaching:
- *Motivation:* Each person is inspired by a different kind of motivation. To learn how a leader can motivate his or her staff, it is useful to know the latter's MBTI code.
- *In case of suspected burn-out* or if the leader fails to perform well in the given role, then it can be reasoned that he or she was a type other than one of the four natural leaders. In that case, it involves too much effort for him or her to comply with that role.
- *Stress management:* Each of the 16 types regards different things as stress; they experience stress in a different manner. Also, stress resolution techniques must be applied in a different way with each type.
- *Team-building:* It is valuable for the leader to know the types of their team members. A good team does not necessarily consist of the same types. However, you have to be careful if, for instance, all

team members are judging types and the leader is a perceiving type. This will result in either the team members feeling frustrated because they prefer exact deadlines for their tasks and need quick decisions as well as controlled processes and the leader being the polar opposite, or conversely the leader having to exercise self-control to comply with these expectations and not delay their team.

• *Conflict management:* If you are aware of the fact that some conflicts originate from different personality profiles then you can still decide to proceed with that relationship and accept differences, or, adopt the Mercedes Symbol, which recommends exiting the given situation in either your private or professional life.

CASE STUDY (EXCERPT)

A lady consulted her coach about a problem in her family. She was raised with the notion that a family should be together on weekends. They would attend picnics and go hiking, do a lot of cooking and baking, and go to the movies together. Hence, this served as a model for her. Yet, she realized that if she kept forcing her family to stay together all weekend, then everyone would get frustrated by Sunday evening although she could not explain why.

They were discussing which programs the family members were keen on. It turned out that the father and the son preferred going to the library, staying home and reading, whereas the daughter and the mother disliked the idea of staying home because they found it boring and always wanted to go out and do something, such as visit friends or engage in any other activity.

This was the coachee's point but she explained that because her husband was a very rational man, it would be advisable to have a tangible tool to enable him to understand the problem and resolve it. While she was explaining their situation, the coach deduced that, in this family, girls are extroverted and boys are introverted, and so she came up with MBTI. All four of them completed the test, and the observation was confirmed. Given this knowledge, the rational father and mother decided to separate for one day of the weekend and spend the following day together.

At the next coaching session, the coachee reported on their first weekend spent apart and later together with a smile on her face. She explained how she and her daughter had a great time shopping, spending time with friends and going to the movies, while the boys went to the library and read in silence next to each other for hours. She could not understand why the boys would enjoy spending a whole day together without uttering a word, but said that she simply had to accept it, rather than understand it...

37. GPOP – Golden Personality Profile

As CPP, the owner of the original version of MBTI decided not to allow the distribution of the questionnaire either for commercial or research purposes, there is currently no legal MBTI questionnaire available in many countries. Instead, it is recommended to utilize the GPOP questionnaire.

Developed by Isabel Briggs-Myers and John Golden, this questionnaire also defines 16 distinct personality types of equal rank that work differently. This system also describes how the individual completing the test copes with stress. It is an ideal tool for talent management, leadership development and an enhancement in communication and cooperation. The profile also specifies your personal stress factor and level of optimism or pessimism.

These preferences form specific personality types. Your personality is manifested in the manner that you approach people and your environment, as well as in the way that you act and communicate and the traits that you find pleasing or displeasing in others. By familiarizing yourself with these factors, you will realize important elements of the foundations and root causes of your successes and failures and get closer to finding the way to and the direction of the desired change.

By becoming acquainted with your personality type and recognizing the features of other types, your consciousness about yourself and your environment will increase. Furthermore, this knowledge will facilitate self-development, a more constructive cooperation with individuals of other types, a more effective communication, networking and more successful leadership.

Knowing how you react to stress, how you can tackle it and what you can learn from it when it is at an unmanageable level serves a useful purpose.

Personality profile as a tool is mainly applied in coaching where the purpose is to improve self-awareness, better acquaint oneself with others and increase cooperation. Therefore, it can be used in any situation necessitating the application of cooperative skills or knowledge of how others normally react to environmental factors. By becoming intimately acquainted with your type, you can better understand the origins of family conflicts, which means that this tool can also prove to be beneficial in life coaching.

38. Diary

This is one of the most frequently used coaching tasks that is performed by the coachee as homework between coaching sessions, rather than during the latter.

The duration of the observation can be one day (if it is sufficient since you need to record things that you can observe in a day and it is better to avoid observation for several days because it might adversely impact your work). However, records are typically kept throughout the period between two coaching sessions, i.e. for one, two or three weeks.

No complex technology is needed. Some prefer to keep records on a graph paper but most do so on an excel worksheet and deliver it either as a printout or as a file on their laptops.

Records can encompass a wide array of themes, as in coaching itself. Therefore, it can be applied in the Situation stage as well as in the Key Obstacles, Leverage, and Evaluation stage when outcomes are evaluated.

Consider a coachee who hires a coach because he or she wants to say "no" more often. At the first coaching session, he or she submits records evidencing the response "no" given twice a week, and that by the eighth week, records attest to the fact that he said "no" 15 times per week. This demonstrates a positive tendency.

It is good to have a quantifiable figure for the diagnosis and to set a target figure because then you will be able to numerically gauge the coaching. For example, up to now it has been three but I am aiming for ten. Sometimes, the coachee plans to raise the number. In other cases, the coachee may want to achieve a smaller target number – e.g. some individuals would like to reduce the number of conflicts they face and others who avoid conflicts may want to raise that very figure.

It is plain to see that records can cover events of a relatively high frequency, e.g.
• conflicts faced;
• saying "no";
• times of interrupting others, which points to the degree of impatience;

Alternatively, they can be very unique as the following case study illustrates.

CASE STUDY (EXCERPT)

A coachee was assigned the following as homework: For the period of one week, he had to record each time he uttered a specific curse word. After three days, he called me and confessed that he was feeling painfully embarrassed. He had suddenly become aware of his own behavior: he said it 27 times on Monday and could not resist uttering it on Tuesday, saying the word 6 times...

39. Happiness and Success Curve

The client has to mark his or her successes in the following coordinate system:
X coordinate: duration from date of birth to the present; then narrowing the time frame: the past 10 years, past year, past month, then for a week, one element of happiness in hourly increments;
Y coordinate: level of happiness and success from 0 to 100%.

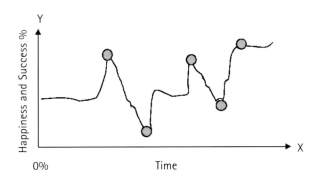

The coach can ask the following questions:

- Where were you at a specific point? Why?
- What is the goal?
- What is the source of your happiness/success?
- What do these points have in common?
- What is the secret of your own happiness/success?

Success and happiness have a different meaning for everyone. There might be clients who can better describe the ten most significant moments of the past year.

This tool can serve as an aid for confronting work-life balance issues (because they only record moments from their work). Once a client demonstrated signs of burn-out but he did not want to face them. He drew this curve down and recognized that he only marks success/happy points that can be bought: his first car, his first house, his first yacht, but did not mention the birth of his kids or any other family event. It was a useful exercise for him to become aware that something is not OK.

It can also help clients who lack self-confidence to become cognizant/to become aware of their successes. For example, they might observe that in the first coaching session it took twenty minutes to cite ten successes from the past year. In the second session, they might recall ten successes during one month and within the same time frame, and in the third session they might record in twenty minutes ten memorable moments from one week.

There may be a number of indicators linked to the happiness and success curves, which are entirely dependent on the individual. There was one coachee whose success curve correlated entirely with the number of cigarettes he smoked, while that of another coachee corresponded to fluctuations in her weight. She noticed that whenever she was working on an exciting challenge, she was down to her "competition weight" but whenever she felt distressed and had to perform too much operative work, she ate significantly more to achieve her desired level of happiness.

Case Study (excerpt)

Nearly all coaches who specialize in cross-cultural coaching spent several years abroad, which means that they have first-hand experience with the struggles of collaborating with people of different nationalities.

One classic coaching case involved the Hungarian Chief Executive Officer at the local subsidiary of a large international company. It was the American owner who requested the coaching since he felt that the Hungarian executive had a rather negative general attitude. He stated the coaching should continue until the Hungarian CEO's automatic reply to his boss's first question on their weekly phone calls: "How are you?", becomes "Very good!".

The coach knew that this would be quite a challenge due to the fact that when the American boss dubs someone a pessimist; the latter may very well view himself as a realist, since the many of Hungarians tend to be more pessimistic than individuals of other nationalities.

The first tool that the coach employed was the happiness curve.

She asked the coachee to plot his approximate level of happiness from the day he was born to the present day and then to mark the high points when he was very happy and explain why.

The points he marked on the curve included his graduation, the purchase of his first car and of his home, all professional successes and assets that are of a material nature, but conspicuously missing were things such as his wedding, the day when his daughter was born, and their vacations in exotic places.

The coach then asked him to narrow down the time frame. Initially, she wanted him to consider the past year, but when she saw that there was no high point marked on the curve for the past four years, she eventually asked the coachee to begin there. Next, they narrowed down the time frame again to the last month, at which point the coachee almost lost his composure, grumbling about the purported objective of the exercise in question and the whole notion of coaching. (In retrospect he found this exercise to be the most beneficial and in fact claimed that the best thing that happened to him in (or the highlight of) the past four years was being granted an opportunity in the form of an eye-opener, the coach.) He had a difficult time recalling and listing some positive experiences he had in the past month. We concluded up the first coaching session with this exercise.

Meanwhile, the coach was intrigued by the absence of time constraints since the American boss had stated that he would be willing to pay for the coaching indefinitely. Still, she knew that she would bill the client for one session only, since the latter will not be willing to return for a second one. She decided to assume the risk that her coachee would be reluctant to consult her again, but she would not back down. Moreover, since the end justifies the means, thought the coach, she would assign the following homework.

For the next two weeks, the coachee was required to list in a table containing an hourly breakdown all the positive things that happened to him. While it can be any frivolous occurrence, two conditions must be satisfied: No cell may be left blank in the table consisting of 14 days x 14 waking hours, and everything can only be entered once.

When the coachee learned of this, he was already making grimaces his displeasure non-verbally so that even the coach had to exercise self-control. In the next few days, she often reflected on that moment. Interestingly, many individuals who, judged by an outside observer, seem to be extremely content (they have a good job, big house, beautiful wife, intelligent children), are in fact pessimists and consumed by negative feelings. Although harboring the fear that the coaching assignment would be drawing to a close, she was aware of the necessity to test her coachee with this homework. A refusal on his part to do so will demonstrate a reluctance to change.

On the 8th day, the coach received a phone call from the coachee:
"I just wanted to let you know that I am working on the table and did not leave a single cell blank... Oh, and my American boss just called me this morning and asked me how I was, and before I knew it I replied 'I'm feeling fine, just fine.' I also accompanied the children to kindergarten this morning, and my four-year-old daughter kissed me goodbye, even though it is not customary for her to do so. Therefore, I was over the moon as I was coming in to the office and bought a box of chocolate for my secretary, who shed tears of joy because she had never received anything from me since the day I became her boss. I was in such high spirits for being on the right track that when the cleaning lady entered a few minutes ago to take out the trash, I gave her all the coupons and collectible stickers that I picked up at the stores and that I would have otherwise discarded. I then proceeded to offer my employees the newspapers and magazines that come in the mail and that I never have time to read but that I tend to leave unopened and to discard. But wait a second, does it mean that the coaching is now over? Then maybe I should have confessed to my American boss instead that I feel miserable?"

Indeed, he had completed his homework and realized the many little pleasures in his life that had previously went unnoticed. There were many small items on his list that he read at the second coaching session (because there was a second session, of course). It included observations such as his happiness upon taking a peek in the children's bedroom at 10:00 p.m. and seeing his two children sleeping in the same bed, rather than in separate beds, and all cuddled up. It also included how, when it was announced on the radio that an all-time heat record had been broken, he realized how lucky he was to be in his air-conditioned car and not sweating outdoors all day like the road construction workers. Additionally, he mentioned the good joke he received via email from an old, long-lost friend.

The first homework was a success, and both the coach and the coachee were pleased, and so they continued to work together/collaborate enthusiastically.

He also replaced his screen saver with the following maxim: *"I complained that I had no shoes until I met a man who had no feet" (Persian proverb).*

He even set up a reminder on his cellular phone, which sent him the message three times a day: "Don't sweat the small stuff!"

He read the books recommended by his coach, including *The Happiness Equation* by Manfred Kets de Vries.[33]

He also recruited a "helpmate" within the company, whom he asked to kick him under the table whenever he utters negative, pessimistic sentences at meetings.

At the third coaching session, he was asked to write down twenty of his own positive traits, which made him sweat his guts out. When he had completed the assignment, his coach told him, "Okay, let's have a coffee now, and then we are not going home until you add ten more traits to the list." His homework at the end of the day was to ask five friends or family members to send him five qualities each in writing.

He also had to create lists of the following:

• What joys do you envy from others? (This is aimed at making you aware of the simple pleasures we are wishing for and how easy it would be to obtain them, and that therefore, we should pursue them.)

• What activities do you enjoy participating in and make you feel good? Sports? Culture? (It can be anything, and answers will vary from one person to the next. You should make sure you engage in one of them on a weekly basis.)

• What are your favorite dishes? (Take your wife out to a restaurant.)

• What is some of your favorite music? (Find it online on the same day and listen to it with your wife

or download it and keep it in your car. Listening to music can be a source of pleasure and may bring back joyous memories or even help you unwind.)
- What are your favorite clothes? (Do not save them for special days but wear them today.)
- When was the last time you saw your favorite movie? (On your way home, stop by the video store and rent that film for an evening.)

On the fourth session, he had to list 10 individuals from his environment and write next to their names why each would have reason to envy him. There was one who had wanted a child for years, whereas the coachee had two. Another had been unemployed for years. There were many others among his friends who were divorced, whereas my client has just returned from a romantic getaway with his wife. The real punch line, however, was that the last person who he added to the list was his American boss. The coach was surprised and asked him why, to whom he replied: "Because he does not have such a wonderful coach as I do."

They have been good friends ever since.

40. Activity Records[34]

This tool is a sort of hybrid combining the tools of Keeping records and Happiness and success curve. Derived from cognitive therapy, is an ideal tool for describing a client's daily activities whereby days are listed along the horizontal axis and hours along the vertical axis. I utilize this tool in coaching.

Activity records may also be used for addressing time management problems. However, it is useful if, in addition to activities, the client records the level of happiness generated by the specific activity as well as the level of activity. The curve will reflect the times when the client has the highest levels of activity and helps identify the times when he or she can schedule important actions.

Besides time management problems, this tool can be employed effectively prior to a career change since it helps identify the types of tasks that generate happiness for the client and the direction in which he or she should proceed. Thus, this tool can be used in the Situation and Positioning stages.

Furthermore, you can add another parameter to this tool. In addition to asking what the coachee is engaged in and how he or she is feeling in the given time frame (fifteen or thirty minutes), the coachee can also add what he or she would like to do then. It is advisable to review records at the end of each day:

Did the coachee engage in variable or repeating activities? (Which ones did he or she repeat frequently?)

Did the coachee have variable or repeating thoughts? (e.g. if the same desired activity is mentioned numerous times)

What is the proportion of actual and desired activities? (Did they coincide many times or were there only a few overlaps?)

41. Old House – New House

This is an extremely useful tool for coachees who prefer visual techniques. The coach instructs the coachee to draw two two-story houses, one illustrating the current state of affairs and the other displaying a desirable situation. The first floor represents personal life and the second symbolizes work. You can draw information from the size and the location of each room.

It is often utilized to resolve work-life balance issues. I recall a case when it was used for a strictly business issue: The client drew the hierarchy of the board of directors (e.g. the power of the HR area) in one house and the ideal structure he sought to achieve in another house.

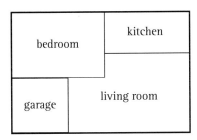 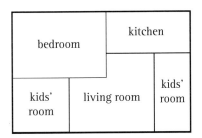

Case Study (excerpt)

The department head of an international company hired me as his coach. He was uncertain about what he hoped to accomplish through coaching, but since his boss offered him this opportunity, he decided to seize it.

Notwithstanding this, coaching is a future- and objective-oriented process, so that a purpose is definitely needed. In light of the fact that during the first five minutes of his introduction, he mentioned how busy he had been lately, as he was recently appointed to this new position and was in the process of building a new house, I immediately thought of using the "old house – new house" coaching tool.

Coach: So, did you see many floor plans recently?
Coachee: Tons of them! You know, our house is being built on a hillside, and so we had to figure out how to ensure sufficient room while at the same time not having to climb the stairs all the time.
Coach: I see. Would you be interested in using floor plans to identify your coaching objective?
Coachee: My boss didn't mention that you were also offering architectural services. If I had known, I would have asked for a quotation," he said with laughter. "But sure, let's give it a try.
Coach: So imagine that you have a two-story house where the first floor is your personal life and the second floor, your professional life.
Coachee: Wait, that's not good!
Coach: Why?
Coachee: Because a house would not be statically strong with twenty square feet downstairs and a second floor that is a thousand square feet."
Coach: Are you suggesting that there is an imbalance between your work and your personal life?
Coachee: We haven't even started drawing, and you have already identified the objective? That was rather quick since we haven't even been talking for seven minutes.
Coach: It must have been just a coincidence, a stroke of luck. But let's examine this in greater detail. If you can already think along these lines, then tell me presently how large is the children's room, the bedroom where you sleep with your wife, and the living room where you entertain friends and family?
Coachee: OK, so this was not simply a lucky coincidence, but it is really a good tool. Funny you should ask, because we do have a bedroom in our apartment, which is approximately 12 square meters, but in reality it's zero. One of the reasons why we embarked on this construction project is that our three

children currently share a 20-square-meter room and in the new house each will have a 15-square-meter room. However, I presently devote enough time to them; in other words their share would not have to be modified as they demand and obtain what they need, but that is not the case with my wife. Would it be possible to really think out of the box here?

Coach: Absolutely, if we were to do it somewhere, it would certainly be it!

Coachee: Can I draw a balcony?

Coach: Of course, if that's what you would like...

Coachee: Very much so! And I will immediately remove my mother-in-law from our living room!

Coach: Could I summarize the past two minutes?

Coachee: (nods)

Coach: If I understand correctly, you have a problem balancing your professional and personal lives. However, this is not the classic scenario where your children hardly know you. Rather, it is you and your wife who do not have enough time for each other. Your other problem is that your mother-in-law is accorded too large a role in the family.

Coachee: Yes! I would never have thought that a coach, being an outsider, would be able to see things so clearly.

Coach: With respect to the two issues, the latter (the one concerning your mother-in-law) is clearly a life coaching issue, whereas with the former, although it is also related to your lifestyle, it has its origins in your work. As you know, I am an executive coach, and your company is paying me to help you become a more successful leader, and therefore, if you also agree, we should primarily focus on this issue.

Coachee: I agree. I will solve the problem with my mother-in-law on my own.

Coach: This floor plan is a coaching tool which helps us define the objectives, but not find the solution. Therefore, let me ask you now, taking into account all of this, to make a drawing of your current home and the home of your dreams.

Coachee: (busy drawing)

Coach: OK, so as I can see in your current 'living space,' nearly 80% is devoted to work and 20% to your personal life, out of which 18% belongs to your children, 2% to sports, and 0% each to your friends and your wife. Then, in the new house you would like to devote 50% to work, 18% to your children (meaning no change), also 18% to your wife, and 7% each to sports and friends. If this house was to be achieved at the end of the coaching process, would you consider it a success?

Coachee: Yes.

Coach: So, let's get down to business, shall we?

Coachee: Sure. Just a second. As I understand, this tool was used for defining the objective of the coaching, so can we stay with it a little longer?

Coach: OK. What would like to do?

Coachee: I think we could make progress if I could break down the 80% devoted to work in the same way I did with my personal life. That way, I would not only see that I would like to go from 80% to 50%, but also what the 30% to be cut would be comprised of. We could then take another step and determine how it could be reduced. Could we do that?

Coach: Of course! Coaching is all about helping you.

Coachee: If I divide up my work on the basis of time devoted to various tasks, I would say that out of the 80% approximately,

40% is spent attending pointless meetings,

5% in productive meetings,
5% on strategic tasks that cannot be delegated,
20% on paperwork,
10% on listening to and helping my employees speak their minds...
Coach: I see. And what would it look like in an ideal world?
Coachee: Yes, I can see the solution already! If I could cut back the time spent at pointless meetings to 10%, then it would leave me with exactly the needed 30% to solve my problems.
Coach: In which percentage of the cases do you realize this in the first five minutes, and how often is it that you only conclude that a meeting is pointless only afterwards?
Coachee: In the majority of the cases, when I look at the list of participants and the agenda, I know already that there is no real point in being there, but I usually go nevertheless. I always find out by the end of the fifth minute at the latest; I never realize this afterwards.
Coach: Alright. So, what are your options?
Coachee: I could avoid attending the meetings, or I could stand up and leave.
Coach: Which one is more difficult for you?
Coachee: Well, I guess it's harder to stand up and leave once you are already there.
Coach: Try the following: Next week, choose one meeting that you will not attend. Then the week after, choose three, and on week three, either cancel all meetings that you consider to be pointless for attendance purposes or send someone else in your place.
Coachee: This homework will be a significant challenge, but I'd like to try it and see whether the company would collapse...

42. Coat-of-Arms

This is another favorite tool of coaches who prefer visual techniques. The coach instructs the coachee to draw a fictitious coat-of-arms that reflects his or her current situation. Upon completion, he or she will draw another coat-of-arms that illustrates the scenario he or she wants to achieve in five years.

An ideal tool for work-life balance issues or in career coaching, this technique can be used both in the Situation and the Positioning stage.

If the term 'Coat-of-Arms' sounds a bit outdated for the coachee, then you may use the word 'logo' instead. It's not about how talented you are in drawing but the meaning of your picture. To illustrate the above take a look at these 2 Coat-of-Arms below. The first represents the current situation whereas the second the desired outcome. The blue color on a client's drawing shows a cold, unwanted love whereas the red color on the 2nd picture stands for true love. The yellow-white work-life balance would turn into a well-balanced green color symbol with music involved that the client has been missing from his life. He wishes to keep the yellow sun that, for him, means optimism.

This is a tool that can be applied not only in individual coaching but also in team coaching. We once had a client who was so enthusiastic about the outcome that he ordered mugs with the designed logo (coat-of-arms) for the entire team for Christmas, and they went to the traditional Christmas market in their city to drink mulled wine together.

Case Study (excerpt)

Once, I instructed a group of 18 prospective coaches to draw individually a fictitious coat-of-arms which best reflected their current situation as well as one that illustrated a desired goal for the future. Clearly, each coat-of-arms included coaching in some form or another.

Prior to assigning this task, I had concerns about how they would view coaching. I was hoping that there would only be a few out of 18 students who would draw a dollar sign or a moneybag. I was very pleased to see that coaching was portrayed in every coat-of-arms and was not depicted as a source of wealth. Instead, most symbols included paths and the support of others as avenues towards success.

43. Reverse Job Advertisement

At the outset of the coaching process, you can evaluate the situation in many ways. While most techniques may be implemented in all categories listed in the book, "reverse job advertisement" is a tool that is generally intended for career coaching. It is ideal for issues involving career change, self-confidence or assertiveness although it can be used in many other cases as well.

While a job posting, written by an employer, outlines the type of an employee that is being sought for a particular position, a reverse job advertisement is prepared by an employee and includes his or her strengths, skills, abilities, interests, accomplishments and how he or she will serve as an asset to the company. It is not a cover letter because it is not intended for a specific position. Rather, it offers a profile of the individual as if he or she posted a job advertisement that reads 'Hello, this is who I am. Please tell me if you need me/if I can further your company's interests and if so, in which capacity'. When the client is ready and has drafted a paper of approximately half a page, then, following a short break, he or she should read it back and state what he or she would recommend to an individual posting such an advertisement, i.e. what job he or she should hold, whether he or she is an asset etc., depending on the focus of the coaching.

Many people are uncertain about their professional goals. They simply drift with the tide from one job to another. This is where career coaching can help, by guiding coachees towards their purpose in life and a career that is not solely an avenue for making money but also offers an opportunity for self-realization. Here, the client can set his or her thoughts free since it is only the assessment with the remaining stages to follow.

44. Analogue Environment

This is a tool that places the evaluation of the situation at hand into the context of an activity or hobby that is familiar to the coachee (and the coach), thus making the situation analogue to that. This process can be continued in the Positioning stage. The point is to discuss the to do's, the situation, the professional state of affairs etc. using terms that are more familiar to the coachee, instead of relying on general terms, technical or business jargon.

As an analogy, you can discuss, for instance, motorcycling, hiking, cooking, fishing, police investigation, medicine, art, teaching, gardening, journalism or anything that enables one to view the given situation through different lenses.

Case Studies (excerpt)

A top-level executive of a large oil company shared with me both this tool and case. As he put it, 'he was over trained', so the coach had to invent a new and unconventional tool for the Situation stage. His hobby was motorcycling, and it was used as an analogue environment for his work environment:
- Who plans the route if you go motorcycling?
- Do you prefer riding alone or in a large group?
- What role do you normally play in the team?
- How do prepare yourself for the trip?
- What do you pay attention to en route?
- How important is it for you to arrive on time?

After the first, Hungarian edition of this book many clients of mine asked me to use this tool. One leader's hobby was military history. He used the following phrases during the Situation phase:
- Feels like somebody is holding a gun against my head
- The air has gunpowder,,
- I don't want to be in a "ready to be deployed" position all the time, it is rather tiring...

45. Free Association

A colleague of mine who is an executive coach specializes in empowering female executives who often struggle to find a balance between pursuing a career and raising a family. She often uses free association as a tool. She asks the coachee to jot down any thought that comes to mind upon hearing the term "female executive." They then sort out the thoughts, feelings, opinions that are not owned by the coachee (i.e. stereotypes, external expectations, etc. which are others' thoughts or feelings). These are the ones that she has to eliminate first to be able to identify her own needs and thereby specify the areas necessitating improvement so that she may find her own balance.

The most commonly-encountered issues are:
- Remorse work-life imbalance,
- overexertion,
- bad mother, bad wife,
- conflicting roles,
- compliance,
- success,
- conflict.

Clearly, you can use any keyword for this task to assist the client in identifying the various dimensions and inherences of a complex problem.

46. Fantasy Ladder[35]

It is a visual tool used to map and manage self-limiting beliefs. The goal is to help the client achieve the point of objectivity, by progressing from clouded subjectivity.

CASE STUDY (EXCERPT)

I liked Mick Cope's story about a person lacking confidence who was making a presentation. His thoughts were: The man in the third row is not paying attention. This must be because my presentation is boring. The attendees are not interested either and are just feigning interest for the sake of politeness… I'll never make another presentation.

He was pushing himself into a spiral. He was thinking in ever more general terms and found the situation increasingly negative although his starting point was wrong. The man in the third row was not paying attention, but the reason was not that he found the presentation boring. On the contrary, he was really enthused about it and was searching for a sheet of paper in his bag so that he could take notes.

Climbing the ladder:
- Attenuation: we pay selective attention to certain aspects.
- Alteration: two people watching the same movie have different ideas.
- Amplification: we draw global conclusions.

Fantasy – Presently, it has little relation to the original fact and has turned into a myth or story.
Fiction – The story is rooted in fact, but critical details have been altered.
Fraction – One person has put a spin on it, and while in essence, it is still accurate; it now has a personalized edge.
Fact – All persons involved in the experience would agree on about the details

Fantasy
Fiction
Fraction
Fact

The client has to climb down from the fantasy ladder. The coach can only help reverse the three processes:
- Turn it down: try to strip away the generalization – "this always happens".
- Clean the distortion: What makes you think that? Why is that so?
- Add missing data: What else happened? How might others view this?
- Face the facts.

Based on this description, these four steps might seem simple, but in fact, it is very difficult for a coachee to climb down the ladder on his or her own.

47. Fantasy Domains[56]

As earlier mentioned at least a few times, helping the coachee draw the most objective picture possible of himself or herself is one of the coach's key tasks. Embedded fantasies may cause the coachee to either overrate or underrate himself or herself. Both reactions might be problematic. These fantasies may come from the person's socialization, comments that parents, friends or teachers made when the coachee was a child, etc.

The four fantasy domains can be described by two parameters. Negative/positive indicates the direction in which the fantasy deviates from reality, and high/low strength points out the degree of the deviation. Mike Cope[36] offers a very lucid example for the four cases.

	Negative	Positive
Low strength	Doubt	Delusion
High strength	Demon	Demi-god

- *Doubt:* the client does not dare to apply for admission to a music academy because of one or two vocal slips in one of his or her karaoke recordings (it can be resolved by listening to the recording again so that he or she realizes that it was only one or two vocal slips and that the DJ was shouting in the background).
- *Demon:* the same girl today is a 35-year-old married woman who, for twenty years, was conditioned to think that she has a bad voice.
- *Delusion:* the client quits his job because his girlfriend compliments him for being a talented guitarist (an objective opinion from a music teacher will be enough).
- *Demi-god:* this boy receives the most cutting-edge guitar from his parents – It is his hot guitar, rather than his talent that makes bands want to play with him (it is difficult but he has to look in the mirror to see that he is surrounded by opportunists).

When there is only a slight deviation from reality, the coach can succeed quickly in most cases. In cases involving either overrating or underrating, an objective assessment can help the client be cognizant the actual situation. However, if there is a wide gap between fantasy and reality, then change can take a long time. This tool may be of utility in the Situation stage when discussing the current situation and what the coach and the client can expect.

48. Wisdom Cards

While working as a project manager at Accenture, I had the good fortune of having an internal coach and of then being asked to serve as an internal coach. Later on, I had an external coach, and currently it is my profession.

A few years ago while searching for an external coach for myself, I encountered many professionals. The very first time I even became uncertain. After introducing ourselves, the coach took out a pack of cards but not playing cards but the kind with images on them. I had to pick a card and explain what it reminded me of, what feelings it evoked in me, how it related to my present circumstances, and what it tells me. I felt awkward in this situation.

On the way home, I began thinking and found that I had a completely different notion of what business coaching is. For me, this case was similar to a gypsy woman or a fortune teller reading the cards. Since, many years have passed. Today, I find the tool to be useful; it was simply poor timing when it was introduced to me as a coachee. It might have worked well after a few sessions, but prior to establishing trust, it had the opposite effect of discouraging me. This indicates the importance of knowing the appropriate timing, situation, and person, among other things when utilizing a specific tool.

Quotes have served as a source of inspiration for most people since a long time because they encapsulate essential thoughts in a few words. They can shed light on your opinion regarding a particular situation or life in general and enable you to discover your own knowledge or wisdom as well as bring you to a better understanding of yourself. This was the basic idea of the so-called wisdom cards. They inspire clients to add their personal experiences and memories to the given themes.

Any group of images can serve as a base for such free association. Alternatively, you can collect wise sayings and thoughts and create cards out of them to integrate some creativity into the activity – as if fortune-telling was also a part of the coachee's current objective. Interestingly, it matches your current life situation...

A few wise sayings that match many common life situations include the following:[37]

"There is no duty we so much underrate as the duty of being happy." *(R. L. Stevenson)*

"You only have to start dancing and the music will come somehow." *(Zorba the Greek)*

"...the only simplicity to be trusted is the simplicity to be found on the far side of complexity." *(A. N. Whitehead)*

"A stumble may prevent a fall." *(T. Fuller)*

"People are just as happy as they make up their minds to be." *(A. Lincoln)*

"Man cannot discover new oceans unless he has the courage to lose sight of the shore." *(A. Gide)*

"It's useless trying to help those who don't want to help themselves. You can't push anyone up the ladder unless they want to climb up." *(D. Carnegie)*

"The tragedy of life doesn't lie in not reaching your goal. The tragedy lies in having no goal to reach." *(Benjamin E. Mays)*

"If one does not know to which port one is sailing, no wind is favorable." *(Seneca)*

The coach may ask the following questions:
- How could you take advantage of on this wisdom?
- Can you apply this thought to your life?
- What does this wise saying tell you?
- How does this thought inspire you?

Alternatively, the coach can present the coachee with a list or collection of wise proverbs and quotes to choose from, such as:
- one that is suited to him or her
- one that he or she can identify with,
- one that is atypical or unclear to him or her,
- one that he or she could forward to his or her colleagues,
- one that could serve as a guide,
- one that previously matched his or her life but that is no longer applicable to his or her current situation.

A quote creates an opportunity to discuss its content and the reason why the coachee selected it, highlighting values and ideas and recalling the examples of wise "masters".

Case Study (excerpt)

This is unquestionably a versatile tool may be used in many ways. Sometimes it is not the coach but the client who discovers another method of utilizing a technique.

There was a coachee who worked as CEO in one of the European countries of a German multinational company. Corporate policies regulated every aspect of work there, and the coachee displayed initial signs of burn-out. In coaching, the CEO was allowed to indulge his creativity without breaching any of the rules while still spicing up his monotonous life. They made a lot of small accomplishments, including eliminating the mailing of the standard corporate Christmas cards to the client's direct subordinates. Instead, the CEO decided to write them personalized cards. He used wisdom cards to select the most appropriate quote for each of his executives because he wanted to personalize the bland Christmas cards used by multinational corporations.

By the simple act of reading through each of the hundred cards, the CEO was able to view many things in a new light. On the other hand, he managed to find quotes that were the perfect fit for his subordinates. Between Christmas and New Year, he could strike up conversations with each of the six executives which elevated their relationship and collaboration to a higher level. They could start the New Year with this achievement.

49. Task Lists

The type of list that the client should create depends on the challenge to be addressed by coaching. A coachee struggling with the issue of low self-esteem can start by gathering the following information:

• Which individuals around him trust him or her, appreciate him or her, value him or her? They you may add their reasons for doing so.
• When, where and why have you been especially pleased with yourself in your life? What achievements are you proud of?
• What are your strengths?
• What good qualities did you have when you were a child? Which ones remained and which others have you improved on since? Are you missing any of those attributes? How could you bring them to the surface?

With respect to issues relating to goal-setting:

• What are your wishes for the future? Save them and read them again in a month. Determine what has changed and if there is any progress towards the realization of your wishes.
• What are your obsessions?
• What excuses do you have for not doing the things you should do?
• What are the things you really like and dislike doing?
• What are the things that you keep postponing?
• What are your weaknesses? In what aspect do you want to change?
• What things always arise regardless of who you are talking to? What are your major themes?

Creative Writing – Introduction[38]

Creative writing is not simply a coaching tool but a set of coaching tools, which explains why I devote a separate introduction to this topic.

Creative writing is a guided writing exercise utilized both in team and individual coaching. Rather than addressing a topic in general terms and attempting to create a work of fiction, participants tackle the issue of self-awareness, as well as personal problems or other areas to be explored during writing. It's a Guided Writing Exercise.

GUIDED – This includes the purpose-oriented nature of this exercise. Writing is not solely a hobby; it also serves a purpose.

WRITING – The human brain functions differently when we speak or write. Writing facilitates reveal one's hidden thoughts and enables one to immerse himself or herself in the given topic. When writing, you think over what you wish to convey in a different manner. In the writing process, there is a different timeframe and a unique relationship between your thoughts and the manner in which you communicate them. Sometimes you write things that you would never have imagined. Your education and socially and morally-embedded habits may limit or influence you putting your thoughts down on paper. People tend to write what they think they are expected to or what they expect from themselves. This writing exercise is aimed at capturing "first thoughts." You must transcend a level of awareness in order to avoid writing down what you want – this is usually your second, third, or subsequent thought – and instead write what spontaneously comes to your mind. This facilitates the attainment of a deeper level of self-awareness.

EXERCISE – A tool for discussing issues and problems. It is applied writing.

Creative writing – How it is applied in practice

1. Defining the topic and the timeframe.
2. The coachee writes.
3. Processing the text from a particular aspect and analyzing the process of writing, i.e. how it affected the coachee's emotions.

Creative writing can be applied to any issue or problem. However, there are fields that are especially suitable for using this tool, e.g.:
- decision-making;
- organizing things, e.g. ideas;
- introducing a new project;
- self-awareness;
- stress resolution;
- revealing a problem;
- conflict management;
- improving creative skills;
- in team coaching, identifying and resolving issues that affect the team and that are difficult to recognize as well as to manage conflicts.

Creative writing can be utilized at most stages of the SPARKLE Model i.e. in the Situation, Positioning, Alternatives and Route stage, depending on the specific instruction.

A few practical tips

• *Write by hand,* without being concerned about of paper and pen to be used. Establish a convenient setting for writing. The most important consideration is being able to write quickly with the pen you have in your hand. Nowadays clients sometimes find it strange and ask to do it on their laptop or tablet but it is essential to write by hand.
• *Timeframe:* always set a timeframe for the coachee.
• Always have a *topic* defined by you or the coachee. Alternatively, if there is no topic, then you should identify a purpose and the coachee can write about anything.
• *You can make it as a daily exercise (as a homework):* it is recommended that one write for 10 to 15 minutes every morning. Allow yourself a month for reading back what you wrote.
• *Keep writing...* without interruption. You need not use flowery language or write well. There are no spelling requirements. You must let yourself go and not think about what you want to write. It does not have to make sense; instead, you can jot down on paper thoughts that are only meaningful to you. You are not required to be logical; you can be absurd, awkward, humorous, unconventional, and the like.
• *Never plan* in advance what you are going to write.
• *You are not required to show* or read what you wrote. It can remain private. The purpose of the exercise is finding out what it inspired you to do and how you can put it to use.
• Actually, you can write about anything.
• For the first few times, it is a common occurrence for the coachee to have *nothing to write about.* How can you find a topic? Draw inspiration from your environment, e.g. start by describing the room in which you are sitting. There are topics that can be usually discussed by everyone, e.g. childhood, your daily routine, etc.
• If you experience writer's block, then simply write what is on your mind, i.e. "now I can't think of anything."

If you want to use this technique as a coaching tool, then you should try it in advance. You will then gain experience in analyzing your own writing. Furthermore, you will have experienced how it feels to be confused or fearful vis-à-vis the subject of your writing. It is recommended to write for at least one month, ideally, on a daily basis. You need not wait for a grand inspiration or brilliant thoughts to emerge. The aim is not to produce a masterpiece. By the same token, you may write on the topic of your choice and may also write a text that is meaningless and serves no purpose.

Creative writing is recommended for use as a complementary tool. You can engage in it when seeking to introduce or close something or when experiencing difficulty in reviewing a process. You can also use it when the coachee is unaware of his or her feelings or his or her own approach to certain issues capable of resolution or when you wish to address self-awareness in a different manner than in a test. The writer will draw on his or her own experiences. Writing brings out your intuitive, hidden, emotional side as opposed to your organizational side functioning through logical thinking.

There are many coaching tools based on creative writing. In this book, we only present a few, but we encourage you to use these in a creative manner and to inform the author if you explore new paths so that he or she can be included in the extended edition.

General topics

• A sentence that you heard in a bus or a restaurant.
• A memory from your childhood. What is your first memory? Write about it.

- What are your dreams?
- Write about life without mentioning the word 'life'. The same can be applied to 'work', 'career', 'me', etc.
- Write anything about yourself. Then revise what you formulated as questions and made as statements.
- Write about yourself, then analyze the usage of words: Which nouns, verbs and adjectives did you use and how often?
- Write about your favorite activities when you were a child.
- What is your greatest fear?
- Write about your family in a childlike style.
- Begin sentences with: "I remember..."; "I don't remember..."; "What I want is..."; "What I don't want is..."; "I know that...", etc.
- Start your composition with the following sentence: "At this moment I don't know what I should write about, maybe about..."; "What I really want to say is..."; "If I die, I'll miss..."; "What I know is that..."
- Provide an explanation – it can be about something ordinary or simple, e.g. how was your morning. Then write how it really was.
- What kind of an animal or plant would you like to be?
- Write about what abstract concepts mean (for example, freedom, life, lie...).

Example:
The process of assigning a written task to the coachee:
After clarifying the type of writing you expect, provide him or her with the following instructions:
I. Imagine that a year has passed. This period has been ideal in every aspect, with everything having been accomplished and all that you had wished for having come true. Also, you had a stroke of luck (it must be realistic, i.e. avoid mentioning winning the lottery). Describe what happened. Then, set a time frame ranging from ten and thirty minutes.
II. If completed, assign the next task without discussing the prior one: Consider how you achieved the point that you wrote about in one/five years. What efforts did you make to achieve it? What steps did you take? Then set a timeframe that should not be shorter than in the previous task.
III. Processing the text. Raise questions and set points of reference:
1. How did you deal with this topic? If it was difficult – why? How did you find the period of one year/five years – was it too close, too far out, too long? How do you normally carry out the planning? Do you plan at all? If the coachee disliked the topic, then you should discuss the reasons.
2. Did the coachee accomplish anything by writing? Are there new things on his or her mind, or is it rather a summary of what he or she wrote?
Thus far, questions explored the writing process and the coachee's content, which is an account of his or her experiences. The next questions will analyze the writing itself.
3. Did you make any decisions? Are there consecutive steps that you take to achieve a point? Are there any thoughts in particular on your mind? Is there anything you failed to address? If yes, why?

Although the discussion generally takes approximately 20 minutes, there are coachees who need to devote an entire session to this tool because of the emergence of numerous situations.

If the writing exercise is successfully completed, then you can begin preparing, for instance, an action plan. Note that you should continue analyzing even after the account of the coachee's experiences and should not forget to draw conclusions.

50. Creative Writing: Fairy Tale[39]

Not every coachee welcomes creative writing; it is a specific tool that I would primarily recommend for use in life coaching. Nevertheless, coaches who have become aware of when and with whom it is advisable to apply this tool have reported a high level of success. It is a self-awareness game in a symbolic language.

Draw yourself as if you were a character in a fairy tale. Write a tale using this character. Upon completion, analyze the tale using the following questions:
- Which character would you be in this fairy tale? Good/bad/outsider?
- What actions do you take in the fairy tale?
- What kind of relationship do you have with other characters in the tale?
- What is the mood of the tale? How could you categorize its genre? Is it romantic/horror/ adventure, etc.?
- How did you feel when you were writing it?
- What are the lessons learnt?

51. Creative Writing: Map[40]

This is another self-awareness game in a symbolic language for clients who prefer visual techniques. The coachee has to draw a map of himself or herself or describe what is on the map. The objective is not to create a beautiful picture. Upon completion, he or she will write a poem about it. At first, this might cause apprehension, but there is a rationale behind having a drawing followed by a task requiring the channeling of your emotions into words: The former task is rather intuitive and the latter one makes one think. They both activate different parts of the brain. This game can improve your ability to set aside what you are doing when attempting to resolve a problem and view it as an outsider.

Vogelauer[41] uses map as a tool in yet another effective way. He asks the coachee to gather all the concepts, keywords, persons that are significant in the given situation and draw a map using them. As with a map, dimensions and distances have importance. Clients may approach mapping as a task in various ways. They may come to a solution in the form of a social atom, but the task may result even in a relief including cross sections.

52. Creative Writing: Funeral Eulogy[42]

While it may sound a bit morbid, this is a very effective tool particularly in raising self-awareness and self-confidence. However, you must exercise caution as it is not intended for all clients.

The coach asks the client to draft a funeral eulogy – one that others would write for his or her funeral:
- What do the questions touch on? What do the statements cover?
- Analysis of word usage: What nouns, verbs and adjectives did he or she use and how often?

53. Mind Mapping[43]

Mind mapping involves jotting down ideas, problems, questions, issues and thoughts in an unrestricted manner, not bound by the requirement of a listing or sequence and displaying the former visually. Since there is no sequence, you can map inherences and due to their visual representation, they may be analyzed much more easily than in creative writing.

Case Study (excerpt)

I opted to employ this tool with a client who had a difficulty articulating his dilemma. He drew a picture to better observe the predicament involving his company and him during an economic crisis. He was pleased to know that he did not have to define a hierarchical relationship between family/personal life and work/company. They were all represented as branches of the same thickness. He could be proud to conclude that, "It is a tree from above, and as I can see, the branch of profit growth needs little support to prevent it from breaking because of its seemingly heavy weight."

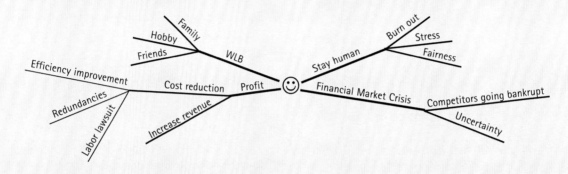

Notes

1 http://thinkexist.com/
2 Peter Drucker: *Innovation and Entrepreneurship*. HarperCollins, 1985
3 Paulo Coelho: *The Pilgrimage*
4 Mick Cope: *The Seven Cs of Coaching*. Pearson Education Ltd., 2004
5 Ibid.
6 http://paulenglish.com/trust.html
7 Werner Vogelauer: *The ABC of Coaching Methodology*. Trans. Zita Delevic, Luchterhand (Hermann), 2011
8 Ibid.
9 http://en.wikipedia.org/wiki/Johari_window
10 Mick Cope: *The Seven Cs of Coaching*. Pearson Education Ltd., 2004
11 Thomas Gordon: *Leader Effectiveness Training – L.E.T.* Perigee Trade, 2001
12 Ibid.
13 Myles Downey: *Effective coaching*. Texere Publishing, 2003.
14 http://hbr.org/product/swot-analysis-i-looking-outside-for-threats-and-op/an/5528BC-PDF-ENG
15 Werner Vogelauer: *The ABC of Coaching Methodology*. Trans. Zita Delevic. Luchterhand (Hermann), 2011
16 Ibid.
17 P. Tonagh – F. Barber – J. Duck: www.bcg.com
18 Nix Savage – Blair Whitehead: *Strategies for Assessing and Managing Organaizational Stakeholders*. Academy of Management Executive, 1991
19 http://www.leeiacocca.com
20 Jonathan Fox (ed.): *The Essential Morena, Writings on Psichodrama, Group Method, and Spontaneity by Moreno*. Springer Publishing, 1987

21 Mick Cope: *The Seven Cs of Coaching*. Pearson Education Ltd., 2004
22 John Whitmore: *Coaching for Performance*. N. Brealey, 1996
23 Graham Lee: *Leadership coaching*. Chartered Institute of Personnel and Development, 2003
24 Mick Cope: *The Seven Cs of Coaching*. Pearson Education Ltd., 2004
25 Martin Seligman: *Learned Optimism*. New York, NY, Pocket Books, 1998
26 Ibid.
27 Ibid.
28 Thomas Gordon: *Leader Effectiveness Training – L.E.T.* Perigee Trade, 2001
29 Ibid.
30 Ibid.
31 Martin Seligman: *Learned Optimism*. New York, NY, Pocket Books, 1998
32 https://www.mbticomplete.com/en/index.aspx
33 Manfred Kets de Vries: *The Happiness Equation*. Vermilion, 2002
34 Martin Seligman: *Learned Optimism*. New York, NY, Pocket Books, 1998
35 Mick Cope: *The Seven Cs of Coaching*. Pearson Education Ltd., 2004
36 Ibid.
37 http://www.goodreads.com/quotes/
38 Julia Cameron: *The Artist's Way*. Tarcher, 2002
39 Ibid.
40 Ibid.
41 Werner Vogelauer: *The ABC of Coaching Methodology*. Luchterhand (Hermann), 2011
42 Julia Cameron: *The Artist's Way*. Tarcher, 2002
43 Buzan, Tony: *The Mind Map Book*. Penguin Books, 1996

II. TOOLS OF THE POSITIONING STAGE

> *"People are not lazy, they simply have impotent goals...
> that is...goals that do not inspire them."*
> Anthony Robbins[1]

> *"The tragedy of life doesn't lie in not reaching your goal.
> The tragedy lies in having no goal to reach."*
> Benjamin E. Mays[2]

> *"If one does not know to which port one is sailing, no wind is favorable."*
> Seneca[3]

I am often asked what my role as coach entails. Although I have answered this question in numerous ways, depending on who asked it and when, the following keywords are, for the most part, always included in my response: I help executives set and achieve their goals. While this trite, often-cited story ultimately proved to be an urban legend, I decided to include it in this book:

"In 1953, a team of researchers interviewed Yale's graduating seniors. Twenty years later, the researchers tracked down the same group of alumni and found that the 3% among them who had set specific goals at the inception had accumulated more personal wealth than the remaining 97% of their classmates combined."*

The moral of the story is that theoretically, setting goals is a very simple task, yet there are very few individuals who do so. Although it might seem self-evident to fix an objective, a coach can facilitate the task and identify the path to accomplish the aim.

To view goals in a more realistic manner, they may be divided into two categories- that of final goals and performance goals.

A *final goal* is one which you set often even though you have hardly any influence on it. For example, you may set your sights on becoming a market leader or winning a championship. Although attainment of that goal partly hinges on your efforts, it also depends on the competition. Therefore, delivering your best performance might not guarantee a victory due to your rivals' superiority. This does not mean that you should only fix an objective if its attainment depends entirely on you, but that you should exercise caution to avoid disenchantment in the event of failure.

There is greater utility in setting a *performance goal* that might well facilitate the realization of your final goal and yet focuses solely on factors that you can influence. Refrain from setting your sights on becoming an Olympic champion. Rather, plan on improving your past performance by 5% annually. You have a greater chance to achieve the latter and with fewer excuses and pretexts and as a result to commit yourself more easily to that objective in question. A coach should make the client aware of this fact and strive to set a performance goal, rather than a final aim, as the outcome of the coaching process.

54. SMART Goal[4]

Goal-setting is of key importance, and the type of the aim you set is pivotal. You should strive to set a SMART goal.

- S – Specific – It should be specific for you- one that is important for you, not a third person. You should avoid stereotypical statements such 'I would like to be happy'. Rather, specify what would make you content and set it as a goal.
- M – Measurable – This can refer to a variety of parameters. You can set an aim in terms of square feet (the size of your ideal house), dollars (your desired salary), pounds (you want to lose). In addition to facilitating the assessment, this step helps you better identify the point at which you have achieved your goal and progress from your points of measurement onward. Although there are undeniably goals that are difficult to quantify, the possibility to do so always exists. For example, a life coachee first defined her goal as 'I would like my marriage to improve', an objective which she could quantify. She stated that that her marriage would be restored if her husband bought her flowers more than ten times a year without any special occasion, as he had a habit of doing in their earlier years. She also considered that her marriage would be saved if they went out to the movies/theater also ten times annually and talked for at least ten minutes each night prior to going to sleep instead of turning their backs to each other in bed and falling asleep. She even set for herself measurable tasks because she knew that flower or movie tickets would not be forthcoming in the absence of a contribution on her part. Therefore, she offered a massage to her husband for one hour each week (he had been urging her to do this and was surprised by her sudden willingness to do so) and baked one of his favorite cakes once a week. Lo and behold, it did not even take ten weeks for the first bouquet of flowers to arrive.
- A – Attractive – The goal should pose a challenge. You should invest efforts instead of setting your sights on a goal that you have already achieved or that can be realized with ease. For a straight A student to get into a good college may not be attractive enough but it can be if it is Harvard or MIT.
- R – Realistic – The goal that you set should be within reach. You should not aspire to become a ballet dancer at the age of sixty or an astronaut at a time of his or her life exceeding the age limit set by NASA. It is advisable to set only goals on which you exercise at least a minimum of influence. If you have no means to impact it, then search for another goal. It is unrealistic to aspire for the fourth Olympic gold medal of the Hungarian national water polo team unless, for instance, you are their coach.. If your profession is not related to the goal in question, then you should consider setting a goal over which you can exercise an influence.
- T – Tangible – Set a timeframe for your goal. If you want to accomplish it by winter, then picture a snowfall. If you wish to achieve it by your retirement years, then visualize the underlying emotions because a deadline serves as a source of motivation. (It should be a realistic deadline, that is, one that generates encouragement rather than panic.) My experience shows that if the client announces at the first session he already has a well-defined goal and we can skip the Situation and Positioning phase for not to waste time and money, I just ask him to take a minute and check whether it complies with all the SMART parameters. The 'Measurable' and 'Tangible' part is missing in 99% of the cases.

55. Integrity Coaching[5]

Thomas J. Leonard (1955 - 2003) is considered to be a major contributor to the development of personal coaching. In 1992 he founded Coach University and in 1994 the International Coach Federation. He wrote 6 coaching-related books and founded CoachU, the oldest professional coach training organization. He has developed plenty of coaching models and tools, you can find 31 unique and powerful ways to coach different types of clients in the following presentation: http://www.surpassy ourdreams.com/CoachingModels.pdf.

Let us see one of them that is most related to the Positioning stage. Clients often come to coaching with the following: "I have already gone through some of the stages such as the Situation, Positioning, Alternatives or even the Route stage but nothing has changed, I have not reached my goal. In a situation like that (even if the clients says it is just bad luck) we can start the coaching process right from the beginning. If the client insists he or she does not want to waste time and money with the Situation stage, the coach can raise the question whether the client is willing to rethink the goal setting (Positioning). If so, this tool can be a useful one.

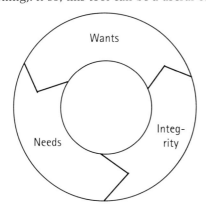

First step: look at the 'Wants'. If the client can not get what they want, it is probably because key needs are not being met. Unmet needs often mean many wants.

Second step: look at the 'Needs'. If needs can not seem to be satisfied, it is probably because integrity is weak in a key area of the client's life.

Third step: look at 'Integrity'. Once integrity is solid, one wants less, naturally, and needs are more easily satisfied.

Be aware that it should be used only if the client goals are consistently not being met and he or she is feeling stymied. So it does not mean that the coachee can not define challenging goals to accomplish during the coaching process, it is more about whether it is realistic or not (like in the SMART tool's 'R' that stands for 'Realistic').

56. PURE Goal

PURE is another acronym. A PURE goal meets the following requirements:
P – Positively stated. U – Understood. R – Relevant. E – Ethical.

P – Positively stated.
Always state a positive goal. Never formulate a negative statement as an aim since it can direct your attention to what you should avoid, rather than on what you should do. Consequently, you will be expending energy escaping, as opposed to pursuing your goal. For example, the statement 'My company should be a market leader' is assertive, direct and unequivocally ambitious, whereas

'My company should avoid being a runner-up' connotes accomplishment of the goal in question even if ranked third.

U – Understood.

A goal should be understood and accepted by all stakeholders. Do not complicate it too much.

R – Relevant.

In this context, "Relevant" is a hybrid of the 'Realistic' and 'Attractive' features of the SMART framework. A goal should be relevant, i.e. achievable, but at the same time, it should involve a challenge.

E – Ethical.

Upon seeing this requirement, I questioned its inclusion because it was self-evident. However, I acknowledged my naiveté as it is not understood by everyone that an ethical coach can only support a coachee who has set an ethical goal. This explains the importance of meeting the criterion in question.

57. CLEAR Goals

The acronym CLEAR also helps in evaluating whether the established goal meets the following requirements.

C – Challenging – You cannot consider it a goal unless efforts are invested.

L – Legal – It is as important as the 'Ethical' criterion of a PURE goal.

E – Environmentally sound – This principle also applies to individuals. It exhorts you to refrain from harming your environment and this includes human beings.

A – Appropriate – It should be adequate and tailored to your situation.

R – Recorded – You have to put it in writing. 'Words fly away, writings remain' is also applicable to this issue. Both the coach and the coachee share a common interest in recording the original intentions.

58. MbO–KPI[6]

MbO signifies 'Managing by Objectives', and KPI is the acronym for 'Key Performance Indicator'.

Peter Drucker was the first to address Management by Objectives in his book *The Practice of Management* in 1954. This concept became the most popular management practice in the '60s and '70s – first in the United States and then spread throughout the world.

MbO combines assessment techniques based on agreed-upon objectives. It is a management approach that focuses on the accomplishment of objectives jointly decided and recorded with the employee. The manager assists the subordinate in breaking down the company's strategic objectives to an operative level, i.e. actions, and in accomplishing them. Performance reviews are an important component of this approach in that they enable the parties to define personal objectives and gauge continuously their accomplishment of the latter. Together, managers and employees establish the objectives to be accomplished by the employees.

Most companies have a performance appraisal system in place. Some hold quarterly reviews, whereas others perform either semi-annual or annual appraisals. The key point is that they review performance and utilize MbO, which can serve as an ideal base for coaching.

Coaching that centers on the accomplishment of such a well-defined KPI also offers another benefit: When closing the coaching process, it is easier to calculate the ROI (Return on Investment). This is an advantage for both the coachee and the principal because it demonstrates that the coaching was a worthwhile investment. Furthermore, it facilitates the assessment of the coach's performance.

CASE STUDY (EXCERPT)

The trade director of a large manufacturing company contacted me the other day. He had prepared an MbO for that year, and he would commence with three of the four goals. Although he knew the means to reach them, he sought a coach's assistance to achieve the fourth goal. The first three goals were strictly professional and consisted of a) increasing revenue, b) increasing margins, and c) decreasing costs. The fourth objective, on the other hand, was not so evident. Although the latter was also stated in figures, the trade director felt there was too much risk because while he could track the daily increase in revenue on his monitor, this factor could only be measured once, that is, at the end of the year. The fourth factor was as follows: If 70 percent of the approximately 500 individuals he managed would state that he was a good leader, he would receive 100 percent of his salary as bonus. If 60 % of them concluded the same he would earn 50 %, and where only less than 50 % thought so, he would receive no compensation in that area. Although this last objective included percentages, it was less measurable than increasing the revenues by X %.

Because a quarter of his annual bonus depended on the fourth factor, there was a great deal at stake because he was rewarded by tens of thousands of dollars that year in bonus. Therefore, the coach's fee, which only constituted a small portion of the bonus, it was a worthy investment.

Hence, this time the objectives were set in an expeditious manner and we were able to base the SPARKLE model on it, which generated a considerable amount of funds for the leader's bank account.

59. Balanced Scorecard[7]

In 1992, Robert S. Kaplan and David P. Norton introduced the balanced Scorecard concept, several elements of which are based upon the practice of MbO. The Balanced Scorecard is an achievement-management technique that links the strategic goals to the operational objectives and activities. This concept evaluates a company's or business' productivity according to four pivotal aspects, taking into account the cause-effect connections because tracking the financial figures alone does not guarantee effective intervention into the process. The four aspects are:
1. Finance
2. Customers
3. Internal Business Processes
4. Learning, Innovation, and Growth

The BSC is searching for answers to the following questions:
- What strategic goals have we achieved?
- What is our position in the market?
- What processes should we develop? Why? How?

- To what extent is a product or a service profitable to each client?
- How do our customers value our performance?

Example:

How do each of the indicators in question relate to the strategic goals? Highly-motivated and independent employees (Learning, Innovation, and Growth) are able to fulfill the requirements for shipping deadlines (Internal Business processes). This in turn leads to greater customer satisfaction, thus generating more clientele and leading to increased turnover (Financial),

Success factors for the operation of BSC:
- selecting appropriate index numbers;
- project management behind certain elements of BSC;
- collecting data;
- selecting appropriate benchmarks.

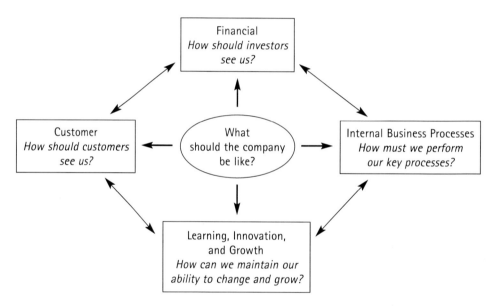

The main areas for the implementation of BSC are the following:
- supporting the deployment of the strategy
- rendering the strategy comprehensible; identifying the operational goals
- harmonizing the strategy and the financial planning
- harmonizing the strategy and the organization
- incorporating short-term strategic reviews and experiences into the strategy

We can also apply the BSC concept during the coaching in view of the fact that BSC involves breaking down a larger goal in a logical manner and transforming it into smaller, clearer, and more concrete goals. It can serve as a valuable tool to motivate employees because if we can clearly deduce what we expect from them, they are more likely to devote themselves to their tasks with greater ease and accomplish them successfully.

60. Benchmark

Around year 2000, during my international management consulting work, my clients have often asked me to create a benchmark for them. They wanted to know the size of the average outstanding account in their industry, the deadline for paying within competitors' companies, and the extent of staff turnover etc. The benchmark allowed them to compare and contrast. More specifically, they could see more clearly how much they are behind, to what extent they are ahead of their rivals.

Leading international management consulting companies used to treasure these benchmarks because they were invaluable. Furthermore, if a leading consultant examined one parameter of hundreds of his clients in nearly 100 countries, the latter would have a greater advantage in the competition. The world has changed a lot since, with a lot of such data being accessible on the Internet free of charge and with little research. Benchmarks can be used not only very successfully in leading consultancy but also in coaching. Most leaders feel reassured when they know they are not alone in certain burdensome situations. There are ample resources which can simplify a coach's life, which is why they need to keep their eyes and ears open. These days, much is expected of coaches, who must be able to see the whole picture and help to effectuate fresh changes. This is precisely why they need to be constantly developing innovative ideas. In the absence of such data, we can rely on feedback provided by our clients' experience to further contribute to our coaching. This means that if you have coached numerous managers, you can discuss the overall average encounters and competence with your coachees.

These benchmarks can be extremely useful in goal-setting in order to help the client identify whether or not his or her objectives or goals are in fact SMART i.e. realistic. If the industry average staff turnover is 40%, then setting a goal of 5 % might be inappropriate or unrealistic.

CASE STUDY (EXCERPT)

Benchmarks or 'comparing data' are not only useful to verify whether the target we set is realistic or not but also to realize –either during the Situation or the Evaluation stage that our predicament is not extraordinary, and that we should not strive for 100 % perfection.

A colleague of mine cited data according to which leaders dislike providing negative feedback to their colleagues to such an extent that 35 % of them would rather do a parachute jump, 27% shave their heads for charity and nearly 8 % eat insects for a week. I could not help but smile. However, while coaching a financial manager whose strengths did not include providing negative feedback, I shared with him the recently-acquired information. He called me the following day:

"Laura, guess, what happened? You know I have that team leader who did a bad job recently. We lost tens of thousands of dollars and I did not dare to tell him that it was his fault and that he should do things differently in the future. But I finally did it today!"

"Great, congratulations! Will you describe to me how it happened?"

"I told him that I had just heard some statistics according to which one-third of the leaders would rather resign than communicate to their employees their source of dissatisfaction. I stated that I also belonged to this 35 % and therefore brought a parachute with me and was planning to pull the cord. However, I also indicated that he had really botched that issue last time!"

Thus, he did not use a benchmark in the Positioning stage but gave a substantial boost to the Key Obstacles and Leverage stages. The essence is that he reached his target.

61. Specification

As earlier mentioned at SMART, it is critical that our client have a specific target. When I ask a client at the first meeting what he or she would like to accomplish through coaching and what his or her aim is, I often get the answer: "I would like to become a better leader". It is very difficult to commence with it because it would be quite hard to measure whether we reached the intended target. This explains why it is worth investing some time and energy into narrowing the target. One of the follow-up questions is:" Alright, but what is your definite goal?" This question is repeated over and over until either the client or the coach grows weary, which sometimes happens early on. For purposes of defining a specific objective, I would rather suggest another tool that of a self-evaluation test or a form that helps to narrow the field with greater precision. The client is asked 60 questions relating to the different sub-sections. In this manner, after having examined the results, a client can conclude that it is unnecessary to develop his or her presentational technique in general, but that it may be sufficient to focus on one of the six areas, e.g. increase in efficiency.

CASE STUDY (EXCERPT)

Our client, who was a CIO with a very well-structured thinking never encountered any difficulties with the visual aids and was also very thorough. He had always been well-prepared before his audience and this ensured that he would avoid mistakes in setting his goals and preparing his lecture. We illustrate this with the following graph:

Of course, this can be broken down even further since the 'Increasing efficiency' category can also be divided into several additional sub-categories, the majority of which the coachee performed well in. Therefore, it sufficed to concentrate on only a few categories:
• Striking introduction with surprising statistics or a colorful example. • Varying the tone and the volume during the presentation. • Using simple, energetic sentences. • Including the audience in the presentation with a few questions • Eye-contact with the audience. • Pause to ensure maximum attention between the major topics. • Memorable conclusion including either a joke or surprising statistics as an engaging illustration.

The process and coaching tools became so different that I grew dissatisfied with the usual target, namely that the leader wanted to make better presentations. We did not spend much time on the elements at which he excelled. Thus, we simply had to focus on the introduction and the conclusion. That is to say, he should always have a captivating introduction and ending for which we gathered a lot of ideas in the Alternatives stage. He then selected those ideas that best matched his personality and still made the presentation noteworthy.

62. Let Us Complete the Sentence

You may have experienced this tool at a Dale Carnegie training course but it is equally applicable in, it not better suited to coaching. It is often employed in a leadership or business coaching situation whereby clients are asked to complete the sentences below with their own words but without thinking at length. They should first write down their spontaneous thoughts:

- My mother taught me that a good leader ....
- My father thought that a good leader ....
- When I was a teenager, I saw that a good leader ....
- When I was a student, I learned that an good leader ....
- Through my previous managers, I observed that a good leader ....
- Through my role as manager, I have discovered that a good leader ....
- For me, the biggest challenge in becoming a good leader is ....

This game-formed tool, which can be introduced for a few minutes usually, yields very surprising results and creative thoughts on the part of managers that they may elaborate on for hours or days. Many coaches have a great appreciation and consider it to be a really useful tool.

Naturally, depending on the target of the coaching, the sentences cannot only begin with: 'The good leader.....' but can be replaced with an alternate phrase. For example for life coaching topic the sentences could start with:' The good mother...', or as a career coaching tool: 'The best job...'.

CASE STUDY (EXCERPT)

A middle-aged male coachee solicited my help, explaining that he was feeling unwell. He felt that he could not please everyone, even if he was bending backwards; he could not be a good man.

The term "good man" caught my attention. I asked him to help define what "being a good man" meant – both for himself and me – using the tool 'Complete the sentence'. First he indicated whose opinion mattered to him and then stated what they would tell him.

- According to my wife, a good man is a caring husband who often takes his wife out.
- According to my daughter, a good man is a good father who plays a lot with his child and refrains from constantly using his cell phone.
- According to my mother, a good man is a good son who cares for his elderly parents and spends at least one evening with them each week.
- According to my boss, a good man never makes a mistake in his job and stays longer at the office every night than his boss.

He went on and on, listing the vast number of people whose expectations he wanted to satisfy.

"And what makes a good man according to you?" – I asked him. – "A good man does his best to come up to the above expectations, but is intelligent enough to realize that a good man is not a superman, and therefore he turns to a coach and surrenders to the latter his need to comply with everyone's expectations..."

63. Mercedes Symbol

This symbol has significance when a client finds himself or herself at a crossroads. The situation becomes too unbearable for him or her. "It's terrible this way, but how will I go on?"

The solution can only be three variations, namely, the three elements of Mercedes Symbol:

1. Adaptation

First, we ask our client to list the advantages and disadvantages of the current situation. We then instruct him or her to prioritize both lists. Depending on the client's personality, these lists are more transparent on 'post-its' for those who are visual types.

When performing an assessment, we can identify different aspects depending on the particular problem:
- We can prepare a priority list.
- We can calculate in dollars any significant differences between salary-income/profit.
- Time can also be an issue for clients with time-management problems.

CASE STUDY (EXCERPT)

For a woman with a large family, looking after the latter was the most important task. She had been working at the same workplace for six months and was dissatisfied with a lot of things there. Resigning was on the forefront of her mind. Having prepared the list, she realized that as the children were the most important for her, and that her workplace was a short distance from home and the kindergarten, the job was advantageous to her. Hence, she decided to stay and adapt to her working environment. Later, she viewed the company and its hardships in a different light and before long, adapting to the workplace became second nature.

2. Change

When listing the pros and cons as well as prioritizing, it usually turns out that none of them poses a real problem. Therefore, throwing in the towel would not be wise because one stands to lose too much.

This time, the coach and the coachee review together the issues that may be modified and determine what may be realistically expected.

Case Study (excerpt)

When we began coaching one of our clients, she was "fed up with everything" and wanted to resign the following day. She asked for a coach to help her find a solution. When we were engaged in analysis, it was quickly deduced that she perceived trendy, open-plan, large offices as extremely hostile. She felt that she could not even make a telephone call, and that everyone was disturbing her. In the following weeks, our client was, with a coach's assistance, able to set up a cubicle and was even able to separate it with pieces of others' furniture. Thus, our client's predominant concern was resolved to everyone's satisfaction, and much to her boss' delight, she did not resign.

3. Resignation

When the disadvantages exceed the advantages both in size and in priority, resignation becomes evident. In such cases, the coach's tasks are change, the search for a new workplace and new goals.

There are three obstacles when making the decision to step out of the comfort-zone:
1. The imaginary committee: There are values that we take over from others (parents, bosses, etc.) and that we later adopt. Furthermore, we act as if there is an imaginary committee in charge. When we decide to effectuate change, we need a considerable amount of inner strength so that the end result matches our values rather than those of others.
2. Walls: We often feel that our commitments and borders build a wall around us, and that the more we do something, the higher this wall becomes. Understandably, it is very hard to tear down these walls. This can be illustrated by the following scenario: An individual who has been employed at the same workplace for a long period of time, perhaps decades, and he or she cannot or is not willing to make a change and is unable to change because of the high wall that the latter has built over the years.
3. Fear of change: Many people would rather live with a problem than resolve it. They fear that change would result in failure. Therefore, they refrain from trying as they feel others would not consider them as being very successful. Should they become successful, they fear that others would dislike or even envy their success.

Case Study (excerpt)

One of my colleagues often uses the Mercedes Symbol as a coaching tool. He shared this case with me.

His client was the branch manager of a medium-sized company. The firm had an owner/ managing director and two branch-managers who were engaged in such a fierce competition that they spent most of their energy wielding their superiority over one other rather than being productive.

With the owner intending to gradually cease working full-time over the years, the two branch-managers were delegated increased authority, which led to a bitter rivalry. The two managers were of the same age but different backgrounds. One of them had been working for the company since he graduated from college, whereas his colleague had transferred from a 'multinational' corporation a few years before. Each one thought that his experience was more valuable than that of his rival.

My colleague was contacted by his client, who informed the former that he was considering to resign because he was weary of the infighting. However, because he was appreciated at the company and had been granted a great deal of authority powers, he was reluctant to resign. Upon drawing and explaining the Mercedes Symbol, my colleague then he expressed surprise at the result because he thought it would help to appease his client and lead to a sound decision.

The very rational young man started listing the pros and cons under the three options, and 'change' won. To briefly sum up the two hours of hard/intense work: His situation at the company was too difficult to adapt to, but too good to resign from.

After the decision was made, the coach's task was simplified in that he only had to assist his client in fleshing out step by step what he planned to do in order to change the situation (e.g. he had a discussion with the owner/managing director and the other branch-manager to highlight the different competences). His coach guided him in making these steps.

This coaching has become a success story, attested to by the fact that the two managers have lunch together every week, an event which had never occurred in the previous five years. They also found solutions to problems that did not impact exclusively the branch of one of two managers but the entire company (e.g. bonus system to decrease staff turnover). Consequently, the cost of coaching was quickly generated a significant return on investment, not simply because a competent leader remained at the company but also because their cooperation was given great momentum.

✸ 64. Miracle Mountain Metaphor – 5P[8]

While you can read about this tool in greater detail in Mick Cope's book, here is a short synopsis:

There are a numerous coaching cases where the client has a problem, finds a seemingly suitable solution, and accomplishes his aim, but the issue is yet to be resolved. In such a case, it is worth tracking the progress: Why did he or she want to achieve that goal? What final goals of his or hers are situated on top of the 'Miracle Mountain'?

CASE STUDY (EXCERPT)

The owner/managing director of a company with 100 employees was seeking a coach for his time-management problems as he had been late for all the meetings. The coach first introduced generalized solutions and asked her client to purchase a diary. (This tool became his 'property' according to the methodology.) However, it is not enough to buy it and keep it on the shelf; he also had to record his appointments (this became the 'process'); and when the secretary called him to tell him where to go, he put it down in his diary. It turned out that the young man lacked the proficiency to manage his time efficiently. The coach could have taught him time management but instead the company saved money sending him to a two-day time-management training (so called: 'proficiency'). So, they made the first three steps starting from the bottom of the Miracle Mountain. However, there was no change because they did not clarify the long-term goals on the mountaintop. It was apparently useful to make the first three steps but until he found out why he had wanted to arrive to these meetings on time, the diary and training were both useless. On the third occasion, when they had covered 'property', 'process', and 'proficiency', the coach, who was unsettled by all of this, asked her client with a little irritability: 'Why do you want to get to these meetings on time? What is the real goal of the coaching?' Her client, who was pondering about this subject, realized that being late did not pose a real problem for him because he was not interested in getting anywhere on time. He would be content if there were no meetings for him to attend in the future, and if his employees and his branch managers unburdened him so that he could address strictly the strategic elements of his work, e.g. the countries to which they should be expanding. He would be pleased if the branch managers managed to negotiate about all the issues in connection with such an operation.

It took some time to uncover that his ultimate goal was not arriving to meetings on time but having an independently-working team. They continued coaching along these lines.

Owner/managing director's time management

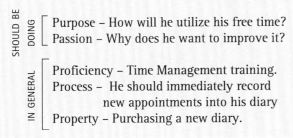
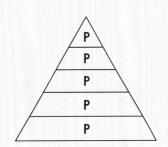

SHOULD BE DOING
- Purpose – How will he utilize his free time?
- Passion – Why does he want to improve it?

IN GENERAL
- Proficiency – Time Management training.
- Process – He should immediately record new appointments into his diary
- Property – Purchasing a new diary.

65. ABCDEF Method[9]

The chart below is also taken from Mick Cope's books, and it speaks for itself.

	Intention	Long-term results	Present situation
A	Action	Abort	Intemperate zeal, but the coachee lacks resources.
B	Better	Bluff	Sometimes things improve at first, then worsen.
C	Cure	Chaos	Sometimes the cure is worse than the problem – depression/drugs: addiction.
D	Deliver	Delay	False solution, postponing the real problem.
E	Easy	Embarrass	It is easier for the coach to apply a widely-used tool but it might not be applicable/in the situation at hand.
F	Faster	False	The coach would follow steps 1 2 3 and the coachee steps 1.

While one may not appreciate the proverb" Even the road to hell is paved with good intentions", those words, alas often ring true. I am familiar with more cases where a coach helped his or her coachee to reach the goal that the latter had set for himself or herself with clear intentions. However, the coach could have been of even greater assistance if he or she had inquired about the reason for wanting to achieve that goal.

CASE STUDY (EXCERPT)

The following chart contains data relating to the scenario involving the purchase of new clothes by a woman to attract men. If she does not achieve the desired result, the next possible step is plastic surgery. My plastic surgeon friends report that, in most cases, women- go under the knife much far more willingly following their first operation and then their life becomes a tread wheel. They are constantly saving money to be able to pay for the next operation because they not only view their nose as ugly but next their knee and so forth and so on. It needs to be considered whether the operation is an appropriate solution to their problem if they also do not feel well after the third or fourth operation. Otherwise, they should consider other solutions.

Target	Tools	Failure
Time management	New diary	Looks great on the shelf but she does not use it.
Attracting the opposite sex	New clothes	Her next problem: nose too big.
Weight	Anti-hunger pills	After losing six pounds, she takes up junk food again.
Drink	Change to Cola	'I only make exception on my birthday'.
Mastering skills	'Increased smile' training	She is tired of smiling on the second day of the training.
Problematic partnership	Holiday	Shouting already at airport.

66. Positive Visualization

We must determine the Positioning stage by considering the following questions: 'What is good?' 'What is the likely goal?' 'How would the client be satisfied at the end of the coaching?' It is imperative to identify the goals so that the client knows when he or she achieves them and does not overlook them.

The coach must assist the coachee in viewing the target very precisely. Prior to setting the goals, the coach must train the coachee to consider things from a different vantage point.

Clients should verbally describe the goals they set and with as much detail as possible. They should draw each goal and imagine what they will feel, hear, and see upon achieving it. NLP (Neuro

Linguistic Programming) literally means programming by language. This means that when speaking about something, we recall the feeling and its effect will change. The acronym VAKOG is described as follows:

V – *Visual* – I imagine the captivating blue sea, the movement of the waves...
A – *Audio* – I recall the squawk of the seagulls, the soft sounds of the waves...
K – *Kinesthetic* – I feel the sun is shining caressing my skin and the gravels pressing on my back...
O – *Olfactory* – I smell the scent of algae...
G – *Gustatory* – I can taste the salty gush in my mouth...

Positive visualization, tell us psychologists, is the act of practicing mentally instead of physically and training ourselves for victory. As Olympics champions say, "success is in the head". Thus, that is why they have a trainer for their body and a coach who galvanizes them for success.

In Ohio, a research team was performing a study on three basketball teams with similar abilities. One team was practicing free throws; the second one did not even need to look at the course as it was also training mentally. The third team was on vacation and so was training neither mentally nor physically. The values were measured again one month later. The third team's score decreased, but the two other teams' successful throws increased by 27%.

A boy named Conrad used to work as a bellboy at a five-star hotel in the United States. He posted a photo of himself on the inside part of his metal locker in the basement. On the photo, he was standing with his shoulders squared back in front of the hotel. The caption beneath the photo read: 'My hotel'. The other bellboys were mocking him, saying: 'If he wants to ingratiate himself with the bosses, why does he post it inside the locker instead of outside?' But Conrad was not doing it for his supervisors but for himself. Conrad Hilton proved the success of positive visualization, and in fact, the hotel became his property a few years later. Currently, nearly 500 hotels in 124 countries around the world belong to his hotel chain. In these hotels, nearly 150 000 rooms are at the disposal of guests, whose satisfactory index exceeds 70 %.

Some of our clients keep pictures of the goals they wish to achieve, such as a desired car; others have this picture on their monitor or as a screensaver.

Case Study (excerpt)

The director of a large bank had been seeking to become a member of the Board of Directors. When one of the BODs transferred to another bank, he was temporarily appointed as Deputy Director. He was aware that the bank was recruiting for this position. Therefore, as he intended to keep his position, he engaged in positive visualization. He identified with this role to such an extent that he behaved as if he were the director. He imagined what he would feel, do, hear and see. He started to behave in real life as in his vision. He started to wear tie and jacket and share his opinions at every board meeting, not being afraid of the risk. After finally being named Director, he sought another challenge a few years later. He is currently an executive coach who, with great pleasure recommends this tool to his own clients.

67. Post-it

When my five-year old daughter pulled 'post-it' in the 'Activity' board game, she described it as follows: "the sticky tag, usually square and yellow, that we have in every room. Mom uses it as a coaching tool, and Grandma writes the shopping list on it.' Hence, this is the official definition of a 'post-it'.

I recommend this tool to visual types who might not find the 'creative writing' technique very useful. Moreover, this technique has also shown utility in cases when the clients have great expectations. They have too many ideas about the aim of the target. Ideas are simply flowing out of them. One part of these ideas is contradictory, while the other part originates out of the other, indicating that there is a cause-effect connection between them. Here, it is useful to apply this tool and ask the clients to jot down only keywords on the Post-its (that way, they can condense their ideas), ask them to disregard or even eliminate of the unnecessary ones (not real, cause-effect, independent from them...), and then continue the work with the rest. Post-its are also beneficial because they are easier to prioritize when the issues are narrowed down, i.e. they can be arranged in order on the table.

CASE STUDY (EXCERPT)

I was coaching the branch manager of a company. As he was the one who was financially responsible for the coaching and not his company, he wanted to be dually-effective. After introducing himself at our introductory session, he immediately got straight to the point: "I don't wish to waste too much time in the introduction because I don't want to become friends with you but would like to focus on reaching my next goal". This time the water flowed, and everything poured out. After 20 minutes, he took a breath, and I seized the opportunity by placing a package of Post-its in front of him. I asked him if he knew what it was, and he replied "yes of course, a pack of Post-its". I informed him that he was right and that however, it was not only Post-its but also a coaching tool that may be employed in the Positioning stage.

I instructed him on what to do, and he set 74 Post-its on the two tables joined together at the café. It was hard work, but finally he managed to discard 73 Post-its in the waste basket. He constantly stood up, walked 20 yards to the waste basket and returned because the latter was fitted on the wall and could not be pulled closer. That way, he was able to think more efficiently while walking. The only remaining Post-it had simply three letters: WLB, that is Work-Life Balance, and so, the balance between work and private life became the starting point, because all the rest of the post-its were either less important for him or related to this.

68. Role Models

Who have been the client's role models from childhood until now? These individuals should be included on the list even if they were appealing to him or her because of only one characteristic. Why do they appreciate these individuals and what can be learned from them? The client should list the attractive features on the basis of the aforementioned and indicate on a scale from 1 to 10 where he or she is now, where the role model is, where the others are, and to where he or she would like to arrive.

Case Study (excerpt)

The Role Models scale is a commonly-used tool. What follows is a memorable anecdote, but first a few cliché ones:
-My boss is very good at validating her own interests. She's 10 on the scale, I'm 2, but I would like to score an 8.
-The other director excels at time management and always meets deadlines. He is 10, I'm 2. I would like to be an 8.

However, one project manager did not mention such trivial ones, and that is why I am highlighting this one:
-Now I'm working Mediterranean style, I call it: 'Manana'. On the other end of the spectrum is the Nike logo with the motto 'Just do it'. This is one scale. On the other scale presently, I compare myself to a noisy little character and in reality would like to envision myself as 'The Godfather'.

This is also a tool that we used in our coach trainings. Once we developed together with the trainees a tool out of the former and dubbed it the anti-role model. It may also occur that the client cannot name any individuals that he or she views as a role model but conversely can cite 'anti-role models'. This can also serve as a good starting point.
There was once a client who indicated that she did not want to be an autocrat like her ex-boss who always unilateral decisions and managed his subordinates with an iron fist – although he did not always possess the philosopher's stone and should have consulted others. At the same time, the client was also reluctant to be as democratic as another manager at her company who assumed the role of a democratic leader because she was unable to make decisions and always proceeded to ask her subordinates' opinion. Those two extremes were a great help to my client since she could gauge her progress on a weekly basis to ascertain how she moved on the scale and towards which anti-role model.

69. Attribute Card

This coaching tool is not very complicated. It consists of 100 cards of positive attributes and 100 cards of negative attributes. If a coach lacks such a deck of cards, he or she can create one. Compiling a list of 100 of each attributes is relatively simple. It can be used at various stages and for different goals. It can be applied in such a manner that the coachee cherry-picks those positive and negative attributes that:
• characterize him or her the most; this is done individually – Situation stage;
• characterize him or her according to his or her boss (or other important relationship, e.g. spouse) – also Situation stage;
• he or she would like to develop – Positioning stage.

This tool also helps in cases where the coachee cannot verbalize his or her situation or goal due to an insufficient vocabulary. In such a scenario, the cards may aid in generating a precise definition.
We can also apply the attribute card when supporting a career change: what qualities the client currently possesses, what qualities are necessary for his or her current job or desired occupation/position and to what extent they harmonize.

The attribute cards may be used not only in a bipolar way, i.e. whether we are good at something or not but also taking into consideration the grades. Specifically, we are evaluating the particular attributes for our situation on a scale from 1 to 5.

70. Choosing an Object or Animal

This coaching tool consists of choosing an object/animal that embodies a group of adjectives and functionalities and then discussing the choice and qualities.

The coach takes some objects (i.e. utensil, cutlery, office tool, toy, photo, souvenir) with him or her and lets the clients touch them and make a selection. After choosing an object, the client tells the coach how he or she is similar to the chosen tool, what common features they have with it and how they differ. Thus, the clients describe themselves from a different point of view.

This exercise can also be performed when choosing a specific animal instead of an object: which qualities of the animal the client possesses, how they differ and what characteristics resemble to those of the animal would he or she would like to have. Therefore, this tool may be utilized both in the Situation and the Positioning stage.

71. Positive Feedback

A prestigious newspaper interviewed me in spring 2008, and the journalist (who has been working as a coach ever since) assigned the following title to the article: "The person conversing with you gives you courage, not brain".

This title comes to mind all the time because although at that time this journalist had not even enrolled in the coaching training course at our school, she could wittily see an. Indeed, in most cases, our clients are a bit insecure even if they make a sound decision (especially when it is a really important question and it serves them well to obtain an objective feedback from an outsider.

The medium-sized IT company cited in the article had finally made a decision, namely to assume the risk of launching overseas, and today it is has a presence in eight other countries.

72. Rubber Band[10]

Mick Cope's book also includes the 'rubber band', as a coaching tool. The coachee also must be aware of the necessity of stepping out of his or her comfort zone during coaching if he or she seeks to develop traits or change their attributes. For visual types, a Rubber Band is a useful tool in deciding whether the coaching is worth pursuing and revealing the challenges the coachee may face.

The client has to draw an angle and answer the following questions:

- What is his or her current direction?
- What new direction does he or she intent to take?
- How different is the new direction from the current one (degree of variation)? The range should be from 0 to 180. Clearly, there are coaching topics that set radical changes as goals, for example a bad habit (i.e. drugs), and there are others with a smaller circle of change. Among the latter there might be goals that the client can fulfill gradually and also those that the client can achieve in one step, for

instance, cutting the Rubber Band. As the proverb says: " It is impossible to cross the canyon in one leap." Either we make one big jump and sink (cut the rubber band) or we keep our heads above water and make some progress, in which case the rubber band will pull us back.
- How strong will the reversion Rubber Band be?
- How strong are the forces pulling someone in the new direction?

The coach's task is twofold:
- to aid in cutting the old Rubber Band,
- to anchor a sturdy, new Rubber Band; otherwise it will pull the client back into his or her comfort zone.

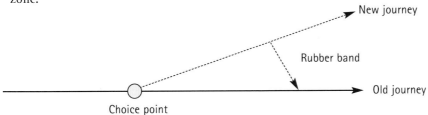

I usually apply this tool in two cases.

On the one hand, I use it when I sense that the coaching partner is unaware of the concept of biting off more than he or she can chew. In such circumstances, I endeavor to clarify the process by utilizing this visual tool to make them conscious about the task they intend to take on, and whether they are committed enough.

The other case is where the client would like to set additional goals since the tool assists in prioritizing.

The coach can also aid in stretching out, knotting, and strengthening the new Rubber Band, for instance, by practicing the new form of behavior in a sheltered environment. With the help of the aforementioned, the client gains positive experiences, and the new rubber band becomes stronger.

CASE STUDY (EXCERPT)

A manager contacted a coach because he wanted to become more democratic. The coach did not find him to be convincing enough because he was describing the disadvantages of democracy in long sentences and its application in the decision-making process. The latter, he stated, would be delayed or potentially lead to a poor decision, but nevertheless, the leader should assume responsibility, and so on.

To strengthen the new Rubber Band, as part of his homework assignment, he sought to engage in decision-making regarding a holiday in a democratic way. However, he reported at the next coaching session that he did not succeed in making a decision concerning this current family issue. As he observed: "Again, I pressured my family to visit natural parks -because I am paying for the holiday- in lieu of Disneyland, which is my two small children's preferred destination. " There were some other attempts, but after a few similar coaching sessions, the client himself indicated that he would abdicate since in his case, cutting the Rubber Band would be the optimal solution. This meant that if the company were sold and the new owner believed in 'empowerment' as a miracle weapon, he would be able to choose between leaving and changing. However, until this strong pressure is felt, efforts to coach him are pointless.

73. Wheel of Life[11]

When *Co-Active Coaching* was first released in 1998 by Laura Whitworth, Henry Kimsey-House and Phil Sandahl, this pioneering work set the stage for what has become a cultural and business phenomenon and helped launch the profession of coaching. One of the most commonly used tools in co-active coaching is the Wheel of Life. This is primarily employed in life coaching but it is easy to modify so the coach can utilize it in many scenarios (e.g. identifying priorities, evaluating management competencies, etc.).

„The eight sections represent different aspects of one's life. This exercise measures one's level of satisfaction in these areas on the day that the client works through this exercise. With the center of the wheel marked 0 and the outer edges numbered 10, the coachee can mark his or her level of satisfaction with each life area by drawing a straight or curved line to create a new outer edge. The new perimeter represents the wheel of the coachee's life." The coach and the coachee then can review together if this were a real wheel, how bumpy would the ride be? Where does the coachee want to improve his or her level of satisfaction? What specifically can he or she do to accomplish that?

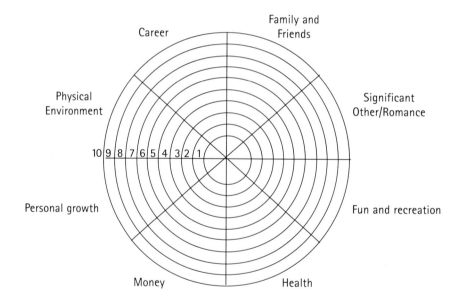

The coach can also use this wheel by starting out with a blank one, suggesting aspects and ideas to evaluate, and even modifying it. To be able to live a well-rounded life, it is important that it revolve not exclusively around work. Although what constitutes 'completeness' is a subjective consideration that varies from one individual to the next, some factors appear more frequently than others. In the Wheel of Life, family, friends, health are often present, but some individuals also have adventure or religion as well. In cases where the Wheel of Life is too bumpy, the wheel might not be able to carry the burden, and either the work overload results in burdensome costs or leads to failed marriages, neglected children or a decline in the client's health. This is a simple tool for helping clients examine how they are functioning in their life. The clients are not in need of an outsider to confront them with their problems and opportunities.

As mentioned above, this tool can be easily modified for example in a business coaching situation. As with the Wheel of Life, the clients set parameters in the "Wheel of Business". What are the important things in their work?

Case Study (excerpt)

A concrete example is apparent on a drawing in which a manager sought to make change in four areas but considered that three of them could be combined successfully. He set the goal of enhancing his assertiveness and applying his professionalism so that he could create a more successful team. He proved to be right, for as a result of applying himself in those areas, he also earned a higher income, (the fourth area to develop).

74. Drawing a Tree

Coaches with a psychology background often use this tool with remarkable results. The coachee is asked to draw a tree. When ready, he or she is asked to draw another one and a third one. He or she is then asked to look at the three trees and say everything that comes to his or her mind when observing them. At this point, the coach displays the key. The first tree symbolizes how we present ourselves to the outside world, the second represents how we live inside ourselves, and the third how we would like to be.

This tool has already produced very unique results. There was a client who did not draw apples or pears on the tree but little hearts. Another one drew a conventional design of a bench under the tree with himself and the coach, because the coaching was so important part of his life.

This tool can be applied very well in topics involving self-knowledge. Because each client is unique, we must coach him or her at the stage where he or she is in his or her personal development and in the areas that are in fact the most pressing for them at the moment. Some clients arrive at the introductory coaching session with the purpose of not simply being able to attain a definite, measurable business target but also to develop their general self-knowledge so that they will become increasingly efficient and successful in their occupation. When a client is uncertain about which areas he or she is experiencing problems or facing obstacles, this tool sheds light on the differences, possible contradictions between our self-image, roles, and desires.

An experienced coach has enhanced this tool so that when the coachee draws the tree, she makes six photocopies of the drawing. She then hands out three copies to the client, who distributes the drawings to three individuals who are important for him or her (it can be anyone: spouse, boss, colleague), and the coach keeps three copies with her. The coach jots down her own thoughts and feelings on one of them and asks a coaching colleague to do the same on the other copy. Finally, she sends the third one to a psychologist who specializes in analyzing children's drawings.

According to the experiences, interpretation of the drawings from additional viewpoints renders this tool even more effective, particularly with clients who have self-confidence issues.

Case Study (excerpt)

One of my colleagues shared the following case with me.

One of her clients is a young, hopeful team-leader of a multinational company. Spirituality not being foreign to her, she set, at the introductory coaching session, the goal of becoming a more effective leader. Towards this end, she sought to improve her inner-self. She believed that finding inner harmony was the key to successful leadership. During the discussion, it seemed evident that the client was very well-prepared and self-aware. She had attended different training courses and read numerous books, i.e. she knew the general answers to the questions. Therefore, her task was to confront the reasons for her own struggles.

After analyzing some concrete situations, my colleague introduced the tree-drawing method in order to uncover personal obstacles or the common reasons lurking behind the conflicts. By looking at her three drawings, the client perfectly conceived her unresolved problems- those which might cause difficulties in her human relations (and also leadership issues). Finally, they reached the root of her problems and hence were able to continue searching for solutions.

75. Training Courses

Unfortunately, many individuals do not work in jobs that match their personality. Rather, they only work to earn a living.

This coaching tool can be applied very well in career coaching, and it can also be used in a multitude of ways. When applying this tool, clients list those training courses that they would like to enroll in now or in the future, either because the topic of the course is their forte and they would like to hone their skills in that area or because it constitutes their field of interest. They may even want to attend a course to develop some suitable skills. Clients can provide their input without inhibition and even list training courses that are unknown or humorous. (One of our clients was laughing about attending a poker course in order to be able to make decisions with a poker face in the business world. It turned out that there was such a poker course, and the bank, as principal, paid for his attendance!)

They should also list the aspirations they had at the age of 14 because it might unveil to light a repressed or hidden desire.

By the time we become adults, our world can limit itself to work and obligations. What did we strive to contribute to the world? What can be realized amongst these ideas? It is worth considering all of these not only before a career change but also to prevent burnout so that we do not persist in the same patterns. While every upper-level manager need not play golf, it is desirable if everybody spends their free time engaged in personally meaningful activities.

76. Creative Writing: Ideal Day[12]

Creative writing is a useful tool in both the Situation and Positioning stage. The client should imagine that beginning today (and it has been an ideal year) in one (or five years) great things will happen to him or her, all the while remaining in reality. The client should describe in detail that day. What do they do? Who are they with? What clothes are they wearing? What country do they live in? How is the climate? What scents are they smelling? What sounds can they hear?

Then, they should write about the path that they took to arrive at that destination.

77. Creative Writing: Letter[13]

This is a writing role-play for leaders. Clients should assume the role of someone who would willingly offer them advice or feedback. The coachees should then write a letter on behalf of that person: "How does he or she view them as a leader, and what attributes would the coachees need to change?" Subsequently, the client should write a letter to this imaginary person describing what he or she plans to do to effectuate this change.

Notes

1 http://www.goodreads.com
2 http://thinkexist.com/quotes
3 Jay Rifenbary: *No Excuse!* Possibility Press, 2007
4 Peter Drucker: *The Effective Executive.* Butterworth-Heinemann, 2007
5 http://www.surpassyourdreams.com/CoachingModels.pdf
6 Peter Drucker: *The Effective Executive.* Butterworth-Heinemann, 2007
7 Robert S. Kaplan – David P. Norton: *Balanced Scorecard – Measures that Drive Performance.* Harvard Business Review, 2005. Vol. 83.
8 Mick Cope: *The Seven Cs of Coaching.* Pearson, 2004
9 Ibid.
10 Ibid.
11 K. Kimsey-House – H. Kimsey-House – P. Sandahl: *Co-Active Coaching: Changing Business, Tranforming lives.* Nicholas Brealey Publishing, 3rd Edition 2011.
12 Julia Cameron: *The Artist's Way.* Tarcher, 2002
13 Ibid.

III. TOOLS OF THE ALTERNATIVES STAGE

„*Impossible is just a big word thrown around by small men, who find it easier to live in the world they've been given than to explore the power they have to change it. Impossible is not a fact. It's an opinion. Impossible is not a declaration. It's a dare. Impossible is potential. Impossible is temporary. Impossible is nothing.*"
Muhammad Ali[1]

„*The reason so many people never get anywhere in life is because when opportunity knocks, they are out in the backyard looking for four-leaf clovers.*"
Walter Chrysler[2]

„*Our greatest weakness lies in giving up. The most certain way to succeed is always to try just one more time.*"
Thomas Alva Edison[3]

In this stage, we are concentrating on finding and displaying options and possibilities: how to follow and achieve the agreed-upon direction and target. This stage is also pivotal so that the client would not make an appropriate decision. He or she could have the opportunity to make a sound decision in the next stage after having studied more options. At this time, the quantity of alternatives is even more important than their quality, i.e. we should not discard ideas that we deem unrealistic either from the standpoint of time, ability, or cost. Let us welcome and jot them down because they may lead to a brilliant outcome when combined with another idea.

One of the coach's main tasks in this stage is acting as the catalyst for the generation of ideas and encouraging the client not to engage in self-censorship.

If it helps, the coach could also create notes so that no ideas are overlooked. He or she should write down all ideas, even if they seem silly because a basic thought may be developed in the presence of other ideas.

In the words of the management consultants: The outcome of the Situation stage is the 'AS IS'. The result of the Positioning stage is 'TO BE', i.e. the state of the goal. This time, we create the GAP analysis which consists of examining the differences between 'AS IS' and 'TO BE'. Although this is not always a conscious step, we should be aware, even subconsciously, that this is the purpose for which we are gathering the alternatives.

"In math class, we add numbers and obtain the right answer. It is no use wasting more time on adding for once we have the correct answer, we cannot get any further. Many individuals operate this way throughout their lives. They are satisfied with their first answer. However, real life is very much different from exercises at school. Generally-speaking, there is more than one right answer, and some answers are superior to others because, for example they cost less, are more reliable, or are easier to achieve. We have no reason to assume that the first answer is the best" –says Edward de Bono, before providing the following explanation: „Only three alternatives exist. Either we maintain the price on the same level, decrease it, or increase it. We cannot do anything else."

It is true that any of our decisions relating to price may only fall under one of these three categories. On the other hand, there are also numerous other alternatives. We can decrease the price later. (How much later?) We can decrease the price of some individual products. We can change the product and choose an alternative that is less costly. We can also change the promotion of the product in order to justify the higher price. We can lower the price for some time and then raise it later. We could also leave the price as is and make special offers. We can lower the price and ask for additional charges for the extra items. After having weighed all the alternatives (we did not list all of them here), we will be able to place them in one of the above-mentioned three categories. At the same time, listing the three basic categories does not in itself generate all the cited alternatives. The typical error of those who think in an inflexible manner is to list the alternatives and then continue.

„People easily acknowledge that creativity is a matter of talent, and that if they do not possess it, they should leave that domain to others. There are better and not so good ones, but most of them are able to reach quite a good level."[4]

78. CREATE Model[5]

We can read about this tool in Mick Cope's book and in greater detail. What follows is a brief summary.

It is very important to use this tool in writing so that nothing essential is excluded.

C - *Challenge*. What should be considered a favorable result? In accordance with which criteria should we evaluate it? What is prohibited? What is the cost-limit?
R - *Randomize*.
E - *Explore*. What would happen if ...?
A - *Appraise*. Surveying possibilities pro and con: the coach should determine whether the possibilities are not achievable or the client harbors any fear.
T - *Test*. Control on the basis of fixed criteria.
E - *Evaluate*. Ranking (the coachee has to reason through them).

As is shown in the following drawing: in the first three steps, we are expanding and broadening the possibility, then in the following three steps, we are narrowing it.

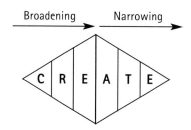

79. Paper Clip

This tool is useful at the beginning of collecting alternative ideas and as an icebreaker exercise in order to make the client think without restrictions.

A paper clip is one of the simplest devices produced in the largest quantities in the world. Its basic function is keeping sheets of paper together. It also has several other means of application. Everything depends upon creativity and the freedom of thinking.

Upon announcing the task, the coach should give the coachee ten minutes brainstorm and jot down ideas. They should then review original individual ideas (without criticism), and the coachee should be accorded ten more minutes to generate other ideas. (There may be hundreds of new ideas, so only time can place a limit on them.)

Experience helps broaden thinking and identify the possibilities that have not been presented thus far. It also enables us to be cognizant of our own limitation and to discuss them when cherry-picking certain ideas. (How did these ideas come to mind? Why are they important? Does he or she feel that there are any similarities with other ideas? How many ideas does he or she think that his or her boss would have written? etc.)

80. Illogical Ideas[6]

The coach may also present deliberately some irrational ideas but must make it clear to the client that the aim is generating ideas and not actually choosing any. If the coach presents an extremely illogical idea, he or she might trigger laughter in his or her client or break the ice so that the latter will generate a great deal of good ideas. By the same token, if the client observes the coach also making audacious statements, he or she will also display bravery by expressing some unusual or imaginary ideas. It may also happen that the coachee's idea is not completely unrealistic, but that he or she is simply insecure to communicate it. In such a scenario, a preposterous idea propounded by a coach may help deliver a flash of genius which was initially concealed.

CASE STUDY (EXCERPT)

In a brainstorming session, the participants proposed that the factories polluting the environment should pollute their own factories. Although some of them broke out in laughter, this thought led to the promulgation of the law requiring factories being built along the river to satisfy their demand for water from the lower part of the river where they poured their wasted water.

81. Film and Book Recommendations

Although this tool cannot be used with every coachee, it is applicable in numerous instances:
• communicating their knowledge: the coach is neither a trainer nor an advisor, i.e. when it turns out that the client lacks sufficient knowledge, the coach can choose between transmitting his or her savoir-faire (if this can be accomplished during one session, it may be the most affordable and

effective solution), or he or she may suggest a training course (e.g. presentation technique) or a book.

• 'enlightenment': when the coach does not want to inform the client that he or she is on the wrong path because it is preferable if the client realizes it himself or herself and quickly becomes aware of it.

The situation is facilitated if the coach has a copy of the proposed book and lends it to the client or provides the latter with a photocopied version of the relevant pages. The books suggested depend on the coach, the topic, and of course the client. Below is a list of often recommended books.[7]

Leadership Development
1. The Leadership Challenge, Kouzes & Posner, 4th Edition
2. Leadership and Self-Deception, The Arbinger Institute
3. What Got You Here Won't Get You There, Marshall Goldsmith

Career Management
1. The Likability Factor, Tim Sanders
2. The First 90 Days, Michael Watkins
3. Encouraging the Heart, Kouzes & Posner

Work-Life Balance
1. The Seven Habits of Highly Effective People, Stephen R. Covey
2. 132 Seize the Days, Amelia Thomas
3. The Sixty Minute Family, Rob Parson

Strategy and Vision
1. Thinkertoys, Michael Michalko
2. Competitive Strategy, Michael Porter

Onboarding Success
1. The First 90 Days, Michael Watkins
2. What Got You Here Won't Get You There, Marshall Goldsmith
3. The Next Level: What Insiders Know About Executive Success, Scott Eblin

Executive and Leader Presence
1. Leadership Presence, Halpern & Lubar
2. Executive Charisma, D.A. Benton
3. The 8th Habit, Stephen Covey

Healthy High Performing Teams
1. The Five Dysfunctions of a Team, Patrick Lencioni
2. The Wisdom of Teams, Katzenbach & Smith

Corporate Culture Dynamics
1. Crucial Conversations, Patterson, Grenny, McMillan, Switzer
2. First, Break All the Rules, Buckingham & Coffman
3. Fit In! The Unofficial Guide to Corporate Culture, Mark A. Williams

Emotional Intelligence
1. Leadership Presence, Halpern & Lubar
2. Anything by Goleman!! The father of emotional intelligence

Diversity Management
1. A Whole New Mind, Dan Pink
2. Go Put Your Strengths To Work, Marcus Buckingham

Happiness
1. The Happiness Equation, Manfred Kets de Vries
2. Sex, Money, Happiness, Manfred Kets de Vries

Out of the Box Ideas/Creativity
1. Blue Ocean, W. Chan Kim
2. Six Thinking Hats, Edward de Bono
3. Good to Great, Jim Collins

Empowerment vs. Autocracy
1. The Secret: What Great Leaders Know and Do, Blanchard & Miller
2. An Autobiography, Lee Iacocca
3. Leadership and Self-Deception, The Arbinger Institute:

Ethics
1. Winners Never Cheat, Jon Huntsman
2. Musashi, Book 1 : The Way of the Samurai, Eiji Yoshikawa

If the client has read the book (even years preceding the coaching) or has seen the film, we can highlight characters, features, and scenes from them.

Nowadays, due to the financial crisis, many of my clients who have reached very high positions are now questioning 'where now?'. Some of them have already watched the movie 'Bucket list' with Jack Nicholson and Morgan Freeman from such a perspective. In the 'Bucket List' we rank all those things that we want to do and experience in our life before we 'kick the bucket'. Many people's bucket list is slowly turning into the sad list - a collection of missed opportunities.

The billionaire, played by Jack Nicholson, has always been busy with 'money-making' and building his own empire. Therefore, he never really thought about what he needed beyond closing his next big business transaction until one day, Fate sends him an unexpected and urgent warning. The other character, played by Morgan Freeman could have advanced in life but for family reasons could only become a mechanic. Together, they decide to fulfill their dreams, as a burning desire awakes in them the desire to do what they had really wanted to do for the rest of their lives. Thus, the 'bucket list' does not simply train the brain from that time onward but becomes an appointment calendar. The two men, who are different only on the surface, leave the hospital, setting aside their doctors' instructions and relying on their common sense. They go on a world adventure. They travel everywhere from the Taj Mahal to the Serengeti National Park, from the five-star restaurants to the most appalling tattoo-saloons, and from the driver's cabin of old racing cars to the open door of an airplane. All they need is a sheet of paper and their passionate instinct to move them on their way. This film has led many people to reflect on life.

Case studies (excerpts)

On one occasion, a successful businessman invited me to have coffee for the introductory session at an upscale coffee shop by a river. Although there was a 'No Parking' sign in front of the café, he parked his big $200,000 car right up to the window so that he could keep an eye on the whole time (and prevent it from being stolen). As he was parking directly in front of me, I could not see the river but noticed a 'handicapped sign' on his windscreen to avoid parking fees. Needless to say, my first impression was not too positive. At that time, I headed a team of eight coaches and therefore contemplated rejecting him and recommending him another coach. Finally I acknowledged that it was a significant challenge for me. While having coffee, it turned out that he had a dilemma, namely that as he had become wealthy enough, he sought to be charitable and perform a good deed. When I asked him: "Why, what is his true intention?', he replied that he had so many sleepless nights and had been suffering from pangs of conscience. While my intent was not to interrogate him; I felt it necessary to ask him if he really meant that charity would solve his problems and put an end to his sleepless nights. He replied that he was working in retail trade that is rather challenging and demanding. I was able to instill in him the importance of healing the wound instead of putting a Band-Aid on it. He had achieved the standard of living he had always sought, in fact, exceeded his own expectations. Thus, he could afford to be respectable. In the following weeks, his order to his shop manager employees that they issue a receipt to everyone stunned them. Doing so was worthwhile because already before the next coaching session, his employees informed him that they were able to work with greater ease since they no longer harbored the fear that the client was a tax collector and consequently were able to serve their clients in a professional manner.

I do not recall on which session I assigned this homework, but I recommended him to read John M. Huntsman's *Winners Never Cheat*.

One of his choices was bandaging the wound with thousands of dollars of charity, and the other option was treating it. He chose the latter, i.e. although he attended the first meeting having completed the Situation-, Positioning-, Alternatives-, and Route stages and insisted that I only help him with the details of the charity. We resumed the activity of brainstorming alternative ideas so that he could achieve his goals and sleep peacefully at last.

We held a coaching session with the owner of a 100-employee company. The owner and the managing director were one and the same; he had built the 5 million dollar-worth company from scratch in a few years. His strategy was to employ directors who were superior to him in a particular area. One of them had better sales skills, while another one excelled at development, and still another at operational tasks, etc. Our first meeting was in an upscale café, where he actually walked in haphazardly. He didn't come in, but he slipped in. He sat down and folded his arms, hiding his hands in the sleeves of his sweater but not for purposes of staying warm. He spoke about himself and his company and praised his employees and team while devaluing his own performance.

I also observed him delivering a presentation at a conference under the auspices of 'shadow coaching'. He was talking in the same manner: the remarkable team and company he has, the office they had opened abroad, and the celebrity clients throughout the world. But the message was not effective, coming from a leader who appeared less than confident in his own value. I also knew that if he were so run-of-the mill and average, as he portrayed himself to be, there would be many similar companies in the country. This client surely excels at something.

As he requested initially coaching in time-management, I tried not to be persistent, although I felt that he should boost his self-confidence and polish his personal image. Therefore, I introduced the following tool that we usually utilize for building such clients' personal image, where there is a disparity between the latter and that of the company. I asked him to list the names of corporate competitors and their leaders and rank their image from 1 to 10. In most cases, the leader's grade was higher than that of the company, but where it was lower, it was only by 1-2 points. At the same time, he assigned a grade of 9 to his company and 2 to himself.

The situation was evident; so he immediately asked if there was any possibility to change it. Naturally, he was skeptical.

Later, we watched a few scenes from different films:
- Benjamin Zander (the conductor of the Boston Philharmonic Orchestra) presented a lecture at the 2008 Conference in Davos.
- How did Steve Ballmer encourage the developers of Microsoft?
- "The Godfather".
- Since when was it obvious who won the Nixon-Kennedy election?

We also watched some interviews and excerpts of conferences about other top managers, who he considered to be his role models. Based on the films, he gathered the elements he wanted to work on. He became increasingly objective on his avenue of change- shaking hands in a different manner, entering a room in a new way, and communicating with the press, his employees, and their competitors in a novel way.

82. Parable

A parable is an inspirational, cautionary tale, which communicates a moral, social, or philosophical truth that would be difficult to understand in its abstract form. One of the main sources of parables is the Bible, where we can find several anecdotes (e.g. 'The parable of the prodigal son'). Among other well-known collections are Valerius Maximus' *Nine books of memorable deeds and sayings*; P. Alfonso's *Disciplina clericalis,* or the *Gesta Romanorum. The Nasreddin Hodja tales*, the *Esopus*, and *Andersen tales*. Numerous masterpieces of parable-compilations became the part of fiction in different works.

Sometimes the client cannot see the forest from the trees, and while he or she is analyzing the situation (usually for a long time), various tales and metaphors come into the coach's mind. In such cases, the aim is for the client to step back from the ordinary interpretation so that he or she could view the situation through different lenses, in the mirror of a parable.

I would also proceed cautiously here. During a coaching session, reading out a short parable could be very effective but certainly not on the first occasion. Prior to doing so, we must determine whether our client is open to it or not. In such cases, the coach may make the following introduction:
- As you were sharing with me this specific situation, a parable came to my mind. Would you like me to share it with you?

When the coach finishes telling the story, he or she could raise the following questions:
- Do you possibly see any links between your case and this story?
- What does this story teach you in this specific situation?

We can also find the tale of King Midas in Manfred Kets de Vries' book *Sex, Money, Happiness and Death*,[8] also a classical parable in our materialistic world. King Midas once received Dionysus, the god of wine, who in turn expressed his gratitude by offering the former to grant him any wish. The greedy king did not consider the consequences of his desires before wishing that everything he would touch would turn to gold. He confronted the first hardships when even the food and drinks as well as the scent of his roses turned into gold in his hands. The biggest sorrow struck him, when his warmly-beloved daughter also transformed into gold. It was then that he realized how greedy he had been.

83. 'What if...?' questions

When the client is brainstorming and compiling alternative implications, he or she often forms sentences with negative comments. The coach may add a „What if...?" tool to these sentences.
When the client says:
- This would be a great idea, but there will not be any funds for it.
The coach should respond as follows:
- And what would you do if money was not an issue because there was an unlimited budget?
That way, not only do we fulfill our goal that the client conveys to us his or her original thought but that he or she may also generate a new one. It is equally true for the following statements:
- My boss or the owner would not consent to it.
The coach's response:
- What might be the solution if you were the owner or CEO?
Another common remark that coachees make:
- This would be an extremely time-consuming solution; I am too busy to adopt it.
The coach may pose another question:
- And what would you do if you didn't lack time and were a time-millionaire?
This enables us to expose all the self-limiting factors, and even if it is impossible to achieve all the goals, according to my experiences, part-solutions including very useful alternative ideas, always surface.
Therefore, we the coaches know our clients best and how to serve them, and we take heed not to overlook such setbacks but challenge the self-limiting comments.

84. Stepping Out of One-on-One Coaching

In the case of personal sessions, only the coach and the coachee are present
When the coachee comes to a halt while thinking outside the box, i.e. he or she is unable to generate enough ideas, then the client can call on the intervention of outsiders who are impacted by the topic. The individuals who are sought depend on the issue at hand. It may be subordinates, other leaders, or anyone that the coachee thinks can contribute to the brainstorming. The coach may also participate in this meeting if the client invites him or her, but the client may also solicit an outsider between two coaching sessions and bring the result with him or her. Neither the coach nor the coachee should feel awkward about not producing enough ideas. This alternative could provide a solution. We call in others to uncover more ideas so that we could multiply resources. Those who are support us will participate with pleasure and will not consider it as a burden.

What is brainstorming?
Brainstorming is teamwork involving at least two individuals- the client and the coach- that focuses on idea-searching. It centers on finding new ideas devoid of criticism and offers the opportunity to

develop new ideas or an association of thoughts. The objective is to gather up as many ideas as possible with the understanding that quantity is more important than quality.

The ground rules:
- We must jot down all ideas (words are flying around).
- The ideas cannot be criticized, or judged.
- Others' suggestions may be developed.
- Participants should also express their seemingly less useful ideas because they may often serve as starting points of other, greater ideas.
- Let us encourage the participants to develop more and more ideas (with praise, candy...).

When a coach facilitates a brainstorming session well and effectively removes responsibility from the participants, then, they obtain much better results and may even have a FLOW experience.

85. The Coach's Ideas

In the Alternatives stage, the aim is that the coachee develops as many ideas as he or she can. The coach can assist him or her by asking questions or offering some ideas.

One of its advantages is that if the coach also conveys ideas, the client will muster more courage and share ideas that he or she had been reluctant to because he or she deemed them unintelligent.

The other main advantage is that the coach has already encountered similar situations in the past and knows the best solution. At this time, the coach must consider the following:
- At which stage does he or she communicate the ideas? If the coach informs the coachee in the Situation or Positioning stage that he or she had already encountered similar situations and knows the solutions, then we dub it counseling rather than coaching. Therefore, we should try avoiding this before the Alternatives stage.
- When in the Alternatives stage? Not at the beginning, when the client is thinking, because he or she would likely swoop down upon the idea and fail to produce any personal or self-generated ones. The coach should wait until all the client's ideas come to the surface and then introduce some other tools that intensify the brainstorming and the 'What if? questions'. After making a note of all of these, he or she can share his or her own ideas after permission.
- How to introduce brainstorming? Clearly, it is not worth saying: "Alright, thanks for your ideas, but the philosophers' stone is with me, and the right solution is the following:...". This is because the coach would then be assuming the role of counselor. It is worth asking the coachee if he or she has any more ideas, whether he or she is curious about the coach's ideas, and if so, now or later. At this time, the coachee must decide whether he or she wants to hear the ideas or proceed to brainstorming.
- What next? In the Alternatives stage, the coach and coachee review all the ideas that were generated and prioritize them from different aspects in the Route stage. At this juncture, the coach should ensure that the client does not place any ideas at the top of the list simply because the coach suggested it. Rather, those should be ranked with the same consideration as the client's own ideas.

86. 10+10 Minutes

The client should set aside the topic of brainstorming and write for ten consecutive minutes. Everything that comes to his or her mind. They should stand up, stop analyzing or thinking, walk for a while. They should then resume writing again for another ten minutes and write down everything that comes to mind. Many individuals are skeptical that if someone has been brainstorming for ten minutes, no more ideas will surface. However, according to our experiences, the second ten minutes have never proven to be unproductive. Moreover, a short break has often led the client to produce more ideas than in the first round.

87. Change in Emotions[9]

Most people, when thinking about options, limit themselves to a logical world. This tool helps us to move them out of it with questions such as these:

- What would be the most humorous solution? (Let us not solely consider serious, rational options!)
- What solution would astonish others?
- What would you do if you had no emotions and did not have to be mindful of others?
- What would you do if you had no fears?
- What would you do if you were not angry?

Hence, an endless line of questions may be developed, with the coach's creativity as the sole limit.

88. Consulting the Encyclopedia

This alternative-searching tool involves consulting the encyclopedia and linking the words there with a specific topic. It might seem trivial. At first glance, I too found it to be banal until I tried it. Now, I can attest to its effectiveness and suggest that you try it!

The case below is derived from Edward de Bono's book:[10] "We search for some ideas in connection with television sets. The randomly-selected word was 'cheese'. There are holes in cheese, and there may also be holes on the screen of television sets. What does it mean? It means that there could be 'windows' on the screen, which would signify the different programs on other channels."

CASE STUDY (EXCERPT)

A client working in sales had come to the coaching session with the dilemma of being burned out. The coach thought that she would not ask the usual time-management questions or apply the Mercedes Symbol. Instead, they were going to try 'Consulting Encyclopedia'.

The client welcomed the idea of not having to think of banal solutions. The coach, who did not have an encyclopedia with her at that moment, randomly jotted down some words such as sunshine, carpet, flower, hat, and bread- which were irrelevant to the topic at hand.

She wrote a number in front of all of them, and the client was asked to select from 1 to 20. He chose 4, which was 'hat'. They were both smiling and wondering how would it be linked to the topic, but as there was harmony between them, they were brainstorming diligently.

- Could it be that 'hat' is pertinent here in the sense that I should take off my hat, i.e. resign?
- Or does it refer to my wish that my boss tips her hat off to me and acknowledges my work?
- Or does the hat, which protects the head (from cold, pain), symbolize the need to protect myself, i.e.

after some preparations, making notes, should I solve the problems and reason through solutions with the management?
- Or does the hat protect me from everything, i.e. I do not need to address the problem, it will be resolved on its own?
- Even the notion of 'begging' is evoked with the word 'hat'. Could it be that I should request a pay raise?
- Is it the 'Magician's Hat'?
- Don Quixote, i.e. is it a senseless fight?
- Must I adapt? Is this my hat at my workplace?

As the reader can discern, this tool proved to be highly-effective, but both the coach and the coachee had to be open to the new solutions.

89. Reverse[11]

In other professional books, this tool is referred to as 'directional-change', but the essence is the same. The client is delegated the task to form ideas that oppose their goals. This tool is also applied in research and development and has led to the invention of the following products.

- Disposable razors: at this point, the long-lasting razor was the final goal, yet the disposable one became the company's most profitable venture.
- Post-it: its developer was almost terminated because he invented a sticker which sticks and can be removed at the same time.
- Wafer seller: He had been selling hot wafers, but with this method, he only had a large turnover in winter. He was thinking of ways to attract customers in the summer too. What if he sold them cold, not hot? Furthermore, he would even fill them with something colder. And so, the coned ice cream was born.

We can also apply this tool in coaching when the client is searching for ideas and questioning what he or she can do to decrease the revenues from sales (e.g. downsize the sales team) and then tailor the new ideas to the situation.

90. Combining[12]

Mendel combined mathematics with biology, which yielded genetics. Gutenberg combined grape-press with coin-press, which produced the pressing machine.

According to a legend, the hot dog was also born this way: A seller would serve his customers a plastic plate with the sausages to avoid burning the customers' hands. The plate cost more than the sausage. A more affordable solution presented itself when he learned that he could provide cotton gloves although this also cost more. Moreover, both solutions resulted in considerable waste. He later heard his neighbor complain the bakery isn't so profitable with so few crescent/bread rolls sold, and he is already considering product development, namely to fill the crescent rolls to increase sales.' They combined the two products and achieved two goals at the same time because both businessmen's sales increased and waste was decreased. Now it is called: Hot Dog.

Naturally, combinations cannot only be used in product development but also in coaching. It is worth examining whether goals or unveiled alternatives can be combined.

Case Study (excerpt)

Generally-speaking, I work with leaders in coaching; however, sometimes, I also work for non-profits pro bono. I feel especially compelled to reach out to mothers with little children facing dilemmas. I often hear about a mother's extreme discomfort at the thought of returning to her former workplace following a longer maternity-leave. Except for this hesitation, however, she does not take any further steps. I had a one-one hour conversation with two mothers the other day. They both told me that they were only qualified for their original occupation but they did not want to work in that field. We listed their hobbies, leisure activities, favorite books, etc. They both said that they appreciated the skills and abilities that they utilized in leisure activities. However, they acknowledged that no one would remunerate them for those.

One of them, an English-Hungarian translator at a multinational company, had completed a lactation counselor's training course during maternity leave. In her view, there was no such position where she could integrate both her existing knowledge (English) and her hobby. She is now cognizant of her error because, as a result of coaching, she is now visiting the wives of diplomats to offer them advice on breast-feeding. She is well-paid and loves what she is doing. This was her goal.

The other mother's hobby was shopping and gleaning fashion magazines. She too thought that it would be impossible to marry work and her hobby. Today, she works with me, helping those managers with image problems to dress more appropriately for their position. Presently, she is still gleaning fashion magazines and shopping, with the difference being that she is now remunerated for her hobby.

Combination was useful in both cases.

91. Grouping[13]

It may occur that in the Situation, Positioning, or even in the Alternatives stage that the client lists so many goals or alternatives (even dozens) that cannot be addressed with ease. In this case, a coach with structured thinking can greatly assist by grouping these ideas around 2-3-4 main ideas. After communicating to the client the latter, a new group of ideas may come to the coachee's mind. Alternatively, he or she may include some elements in another group or adds new ideas to his or her list. Either way, this tool is always valuable.

92. Adaptation[14]

There is nothing new under the sun, i.e. many solutions can be adapted to a particular situation but must be individually-tailored. The coach can help his or her client think with the following questions:
- Do you know someone with the same dilemma? Can his or her solution be adapted?
- Have you ever been in a similar (if not the same) a predicament before? What was useful then?
- How could this problem be resolved in another country or corporate culture? (E.g. a managing director of an American-owned company studies his dilemma in a Japanese environment. Or an autocratic

leader is receptive to the solution of a democratic manager; he or she does not adapt the solution entirely but is inspired by some of its ideas.)

93. Magnification[15]

Magnification consists of enlarging a certain parameter of an idea in an unrealistic manner. The beer known as 'Utopia' was born out of product-development with the help of this tool. The alcohol content of this beer was substantially increased, that is to say by 25 %.

Anything can be magnified, e.g. time limit (what would we do if we had no time constraints), the budget-limit, or any other parameters.

Case Study (excerpt)

A group of friends founded a small counseling company. At the time of its creation, all the members had another job so that employment was not on their minds. All of them accounted for their work once the projects were completed. However, they were not remunerated for performing the administrative and marketing tasks as they could not employ anyone for the job. A few years later, the company started growing, with the gratuitous contributions of friend who were not owners playing an important part.

In the beginning, they could not tell how far the company would grow and were not concerned that was only one owner because the company did not post a profit. When they closed the year with considerable profit, the colleagues-friends expressed their disapproval of providing pro work. The owner searched for a coach to solve this dilemma, and we applied the tool of magnification. The owner regarded this issue as something that cannot be resolved as the ten other colleagues sought a share in the ownership. However, he did not want to offer them a share, but at the same time did not want to lose them. We used the tool of magnification in the Alternatives stage by exaggerating the company's income and profit. We asked the owner what he would do if the revenue were half a million dollars instead of 100 thousand and the profit were 200 thousand dollars instead of 20 thousand. He answered that he would employ all the counselors and thus eliminate all grumbling stemming from performing unpaid work. We then examined how this idea could be adapted to the new situation and instantly came up with two ideas. On the one hand, the idea of employment had not been considered beforehand. The owner could now agree that it is not necessary to employ at once all ten individuals on a full-time basis, but that he could also simply hire one person full-time for administration and marketing. Alternatively, he could employ, on a part-time basis, two of the existing counselors, namely those who may be already dissatisfied with their current employer. The owner's repertoire was expanded with two new ideas, and so this tool also proved to be useful.

94. Reduction[16]

The antithesis of magnification, the tool of reduction may also be applied effectively.

"The problem has reached new heights. What would you do if it were half its current size, or one tenth of it?"

The other variation of this tool involves dividing the procedure into elements, i.e. the client is attempting to solve the problem piecemeal, instead all at once.

95. Ideal People

"What would your role model do in this case? What would your wife do? What would the Prime Minister do? And your father or your best friend?"

This tool helps the client to approach the problem from a different perspective and consequently offers him or her a new opportunity to generate even more ideas. If these solutions prove to be inappropriate for him or her, it does not matter as it is only the Alternatives stage.

96. Consultant

"What would you suggest if you met someone with the same problems? Step out of your role for a minute! It is much easier to offer advice to someone than to yourself."

We may even incorporate it in role-play, whereby the coach pretends to be at a loss and asks the client for help.

Case Study (excerpt)

One of my coaching colleague's client was a newly-appointed manager. In this new position, the coachee was expected to conduct sales activities, make cold calls, and set a good example to her staff. Additionally, there was a special clientele that only she was allowed to contact. These high expectations made her nervous.

During the coaching, they first drew a Mercedes Symbol with the client validating the following cases: adaptation to the new situation; resignation, and a change. It was seemed obvious that she wanted to remain working there but wanted to change.

Instead of opening the encyclopedia randomly, they verified the expression 'cold call' in a dictionary, but it produced no results.

The next tool was the 'Reverse', i.e. 'warm call' or where the respondent knows the caller. This was a fruitful approach because either the secretary made telephone calls or introduced herself first in an e-mail, or searched for the individual on Facebook to see if they had common friends so that the phone call would no longer be so impersonal.

Using the 'Magnification' tool, the coach asked her:
– What if you had to do it all day?
– I would resign - she said. Therefore, this tool proved to be ineffective.

As an alternative idea, the client proposed a 'cold meeting' (blind date) instead of 'cold call'.

Then she asked five people what helped them cope with the stress from cold calling.

They were also engaged in brainstorming and acknowledged the importance of the following points:
- To be conscious that the refusal is never personal but a business offer.
- To count her successes which boosts her confidence.
- To offer herself a reward when she completes a telephone call (chocolate, five minutes of private conversation, browsing on the Internet, etc.)
- To schedule the task of making calls when she is in a good mood.

- To recall a previous situation that she disliked – how she overcame it, how she felt while it was occurring, how she coped with it.
- To carve out time for devising her own method – the optimal time, place, and manner to make the calls.
- Positive visualization – she should link positive experiences to the task (e.g. sunshine, chirping of birds, seashore… – anything that is pleasant for her).
- To have a standard formula - for persuading the people she called – which also encompasses words of 'success' such as 'success-rate', 'system of relationships', etc. She should also explain that the high price ensures high quality, which enables the client to save his or her own time and energy.
- To set her own goals in connection with the 'cold calls' and when she achieves them she could delegate a portion of her tasks because she will know what to expect, or otherwise signal to her bosses that she would like cold calls to be a minor part of her work.
- To view this job as a learning process during which she may acquire new skills.
- To think of a worse professional situation, so that her job would seem pleasant in comparison.
- There will be elements in every life situation that she will find displeasing, and yet still they have to be dealt with – especially, if she is satisfied with the rest of her work.
- To seek out a colleague among her junior staff for whom this task is more suitable, and they could perform it together.
- To be conscious of the fact that she does not want to sell the particular product/service, but the opportunity of shared success.
- To collect information about the person she is going to call.
- To try tailoring the 'language and style' of her call to the potential client's requests.
- To ask her clients why the specific product/service is useful for them in terms of money and time.
- To ask her clients about other potential companies which might be interested in their products/services.
- To create an introduction of approximately 30-40 seconds, in which she describes herself, her job, and the reason for her call, as well as mentions references and their significant outcome.
- Magic words that are worth including in the introduction are: saving time/money, relationships, success, information, special product/service.
- If there is an answering machine, it is worth recording the introductory message. It is important to provide the prospective client her name and telephone number both at the beginning and the conclusion of the message. An email may follow the message, containing the main information and the time when she will call again.

They spent an entire coaching session searching for new ideas and then narrowed the circle to those that are realistic. For example, at this point, the idea of delegating the tasks to a subordinate was discarded because she would find it inappropriate. She would have considered it as giving up and she is just not that type…

Afterwards, they chose the client's favorite ones, and discussed how to time the probes, in what order, and for how long.

The client was satisfied because she left the session with an action-plan.

Moreover, her coach reviewed the benchmark according to which, depending on the caller's skills, only 15-30 % of the cold calls lead to an actual introductory appointment. This fact convinced the client to not panic if she is rejected after the first cold call.

Notes

1 http://www.goodreads.com/author/quotes/46261.Muhammad_Ali
2 http://www.todayinsci.com/C/Chrysler_Walter/ChryslerWalter-Quotations.htm
3 thinkexist.com/quotation/our_greatest...lies_in.../264484.html
4 Edward de Bono: *Six Thinking Hats*. Little, Brown & Company, 1985
5 Mick Cope: The Seven Cs of Coaching, Pearson, 2004
6 Michael Michalko: *Thinkertoys*. Ten Speed Press, 2006
7 www.pebblejam.com
8 Manfred Kets de Vries: *Sex, Money, Happiness and Death*. Palgrave, 2009
9 Michael Michalko: *Thinkertoys*. Ten Speed Press, 2006
10 Edward de Bono: *Six Thinking Hats*. Little, Brown & Company, 1985
11 Michael Michalko: *Thinkertoys*. Ten Speed Press, 2006
12 Ibid.
13 Ibid.
14 Ibid.
15 Ibid.
16 Ibid.

IV. TOOLS OF THE ROUTE STAGE

> „One doesn't discover new lands without consenting
> to lose sight of the shore for a very long time."
> Andre Gide[1]

> "Choosing a path means having a miss out on others-if you try
> to follow every possible path you will end up following none."
> Paulo Coelho[2]

In this stage, the coach is assisting his or her client to determine the method of selecting from among compiled list of alternative ideas. This stage is successful if the client leaves the session with an action plan, which instructs him or her on what and when to perform in order to reach the goal.

97. Pros and Cons Analysis

For the first reading, this tool also belongs to the others with which almost everyone is familiar. Why is it included then in this book if it is so evident?

Although this is one of the most obvious tools, sometimes the client overlooks it. Therefore, with a coach's assistance in writing and reaching into deeper dimensions, it can be extremely effective.

It is a simple tool since all the client has to do is list the alternative ideas previously presented, writing down the advantages and the disadvantages. Upon completion of the list, the client reviews the direction that the scales are moving. He or she can immediately make a note of it in his or her notebook in Word or if it is preferred, on a large flipchart and even including others in this activity.

CASE STUDY (EXCERPT)

The manager of one of the subsidiaries of a large multinational company was seeking a coach to help to solve her problems. The first meeting was a catharsis for both of us, but I knew that she had to interview two other coaches that day who also applied for this position.

The HR manager called me at noon to inform me that the manager wished to work with me. I was very pleased because I had the FLOW feeling (defined by Csíkszentmihályi) at our first meeting. I admit, that in such case, I would even accept a pro bono assignment.

The manager sought to develop her leadership skills but she felt she could not improve any further. Her most pressing demand was obtaining objective feedback about her work.

This company was comprised of several small, national businesses, but the '180/360 degree assessment', typically conducted at large multinational companies, had not been prepared yet. Therefore, we drafted one and worked together in 'shadow coaching' for a day. The aforementioned confirmed to me that, on the one hand, the manager was a competent leader who could become even greater with a little feedback about her performance. On the other hand, the only skill that she needed to develop was strategic decision-making.

These two factors were very much intertwined, as she was insecure about her critical decisions because she had not received any feedback as to whether or not she was an effective leader and performing well. Following this, she had more courage to undertake her next step. She had been racking her brains for months about the following: She thought that their multinational parent company was not effective enough having six separate subsidiaries with separate operational systems (Finance, HR, Top management). However, she did not dare to communicate her new idea of merging the subsidiaries because she was not certain if she was on the right track.

After having built her self-confidence vis-a-vis her leadership with 'shadow-coaching' and the '180/360 degree assessment', we spent the next session analyzing this strategic question with a pro-con analysis. The arguments in favor of the merger benefited the owner, i.e. the multinational company while the cons were advantageous to my client. i.e. if she conceived the idea, and it doesn't come to fruition, her self-confidence would diminish again and she would jeopardize her enhanced image inside the company. Moreover, her managerial position was also at stake due to the fact that if the six subsidiaries were merged, not so many leaders would be necessary. Her subsidiary was not the largest one of the six subsidiaries either with respect to income or number of employees. The other possibility was to keep the proposal to herself, notwithstanding the fact that she thought it would be highly effective. After having included this alternative on the flipchart, she immediately added the following note under it: 'I couldn't sleep well.' When she had only been thinking about this alternative idea or when she had just expressed it, she had different feelings about it than when she jotted it down. She instantly deleted this idea, arguing that it would not be a possibility.

The decision was made. It was a stronger argument than the risk of being fired.

From our very first meeting, I sensed that my partner was a fantastic leader and that she had the potential to become even greater. Prior to our next meeting, she undertook to schedule an appointment with the CEO of the multinational company to share with him her suggestion.

The result: She was appointed CEO of the holding company which was comprised of the six subsidiaries.

We applied an easy tool, but it was unmistakably evident that the only decision was one made by a conscientious, honorable, and loyal leader.

98. Pros and Cons Analysis with the Time Dimension

Vogelauer[3] supplemented the simple 'pros and cons' analysis with time as a dimension. He noticed that his clients sometimes overvalued certain alternatives, either because they were thinking short term or fell into the other extreme. Thus, he guided his clients with the following chart:

	Pros	Cons
Presently		
Momentarily, today		
Tomorrow, as a consequence, in the future		

99. Pros and Cons Analysis with Post-its

The 'Pros and Cons Analysis' can be combined very well with the Post-it tool.

CASE STUDY (EXCERPT)

With one of our clients, along with the SPARKLE Model, we had completed the Situation stage and the Positioning stage, and he had identified two alternative ideas, i.e. he could choose from two alternatives when we entered the Route stage. His dilemma was whether he should be an employee or launch his own business. He was assigned the task to compile a list of the advantages and the disadvantages of both alternatives. He brought a package of Post-its but was allowed to write only one item on one Post-it. When he had completed approximately 30 of them, he stuck them in groups on the large table and ranked them within the groups according to his own priority. He also numbered them in the corner of every Post-it to indicate their significance. Afterwards, he added the numbers on the pro-, and con Post-its and was also surprised by the results. However, he was able to reach a decision in accordance with them. Ever since, he has been a successful businessman because the coach not only supported him during the Route stage but also the Key Obstacles and Leverage stage.

100. Win-Win

We utilize this tool when the leader's dilemma has potentially multiple solutions, i.e. there are a lot of alternatives. Moreover, it is imperative for the leader that the decision is beneficial for the others involved.

CASE STUDY (EXCERPT)

We also applied this tool at the small consulting company which I discussed in the rubric on the 'Magnification' tool. The owner considered that the problem could not be resolved because when the ten other colleagues also demanded a share from the company, he refused. However, he feared losing them; therefore, he had to find a solution that was acceptable to both the ten colleagues and him. With help of the following chart, we realized that there is such a solution that is beneficial also for our client and the ten colleagues. Sharing is not the only positive outcome. There is no longer any grumbling, and as a result of the new motivation, the company has become even more successful in the market.

Advantageous solutions for owner	Disadvantageous solutions for owner
- Profit-sharing. - Employing part-time those who have worked pro bono or accounted - Employing a marketing specialist and administrator from outside.	- Assigning a share of ownership - Dissolution.
Advantageous solutions for colleagues	**Disadvantageous solutions for colleagues**
- Assigning a share of ownership - Profit-sharing.	- Employment status (because they were also engaged in a different activity that they did not wish to relinquish - Employing other individuals for the marketing and administrator position…(because they knew that profits would decline substantially; and although they were complaining, they were enjoying the volunteered tasks, as those were creative).

101. Adenauer Cross

This tool, which is very similar to the 'Pros and Cons Analysis' is referred to here as 'Adenauer cross', which is how salespersons know it.

The following concrete example of the tool was provided on bank's website: 'Try it before applying for a loan. List the advantages on the left side and the disadvantages on the right column and make a very democratic, sensible, majority decision!'

Advantages	Disadvantages
1. Currently low interest rate	1. Interest rate risk 2. Exchange rate risk 3. Margin

102. Musts and Nice to Haves

Before making a decision it is imperative to identify the problem and more specifically, the pertinent issue. As Peter Drucker says: *"The manager who comes up with the right solution to the wrong problem is more dangerous than the manager who comes with the wrong solution to the right problem.*"[4] This evokes the image of a bull in the arena. The bull identifies the problem in an inappropriate way because the problem for the bull is not the red rag but the bullfighter. After poorly identifying the problem, the bull makes an appropriate decision because it attacks the rag over and over, which leads to its ruin. This is why it is critical to answer the following questions prior to making a decision:

- What is the problem?
- What are the reasons for the problem?
- What are the possible solutions?
- Which is the best solution?

This tool is based on the Kepner-Tregoe decision-making matrix, which can help us achieve the ideal solution (decision). 'Musts' are those requirements that have to be fulfilled under all circumstances during the implementation of a solution: e.g. when there are only five months to fulfill a task, all other tasks necessitating more time are eliminated. The existence of a 'Must' is necessary, without it the decision will not be acceptable. For example, if we illustrate it in a chart, as in the following one, we can even remove those solutions, in which not every 'Must' is fulfilled, and cease evaluating them.

'Nice to haves' are such requirements that are advantageous if they exist. However, the decision is also acceptable even if they are not met. For instance, it may be a 'Nice to have' to employ a handicapped or a former unemployed individual in order to enhance the team's quality and size.

We evaluate these solutions according to the 'Nice to Haves' and assign to them a score from 1 to 3 depending on the complexity of the decision. The one that obtains the most scores seems to be the best solution.

	MUSTS			NICE TO HAVES			Summary
	A	B	C	A	B	C	
1st possible solution	✓	✓	✓	2	2	3	7
2nd possible solution	X	X	✓				
3rd possible solution	✓	X	X				
4th possible solution	✓	✓	✓	1	3	2	6
...							

There are cases where the number of potential solutions and the number of 'Musts' and 'Nice to haves' is small. Although in such circumstances, we can do this mentally, charts have, according to our former experiences, been of tremendous assistance where more complex decisions are concerned.

We can apply this tool very effectively both in life and business coaching.

103. Labeling[5]

When the client has generated several alternative ideas, we can also apply a very simple tool known as 'labeling'. The client should label the particular options according to the level of his or her certainty regarding an achievable success.
- It must be successful.
- It can be successful.
- It might be successful.
- It cannot be successful at all.

While this tool seems to be straightforward, it is worth experimenting with it.

104. PMI Map[6]

This is an enhanced alternative of the 'Pros and Cons Analysis'. With a PMI map, we not only rank the positive and the negative factors but also those items that seem to be neutral at first sight or that, though they do not fit in any category, should still be mentioned and recorded.

Plus	Minus	Interesting
Pros	Cons	What is not obvious

105. Walt Disney Model[7]

The client should list as many objections and difficulties as he or she can for every option. He or she should then summarize them and select the one with the least significant weak points.

106. Autonomy Triangle[8]

Utilized in transactional-analysis, this tool can be successfully applied in coaching to analyze the clients' decisions. It is done along the three apexes of the triangle. You observe the "Efficiency", i.e. those skills that played a role in the client's decisions and guided him or her to the particular solution. Then, at the next apex you turn your attention to the "Support", people and factors that influenced the client's decision. Last but not least, you assemble those arrangements and steps that are worth performing to arrive at a successful decision. We call these criteria the elements of "Protection".

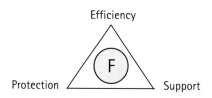

Case Study (excerpt)

A leader decided to collaborate with some of his rivals in order to tide over the crisis in an effective way. We analyzed this decision with respect to a future fellow by relying on the 'autonomy triangle' and obtained the following result:
• Efficiency - What appealed to him in this relationship: e.g. supporting stable clientele; broadening the visual range; expanding the sales potential of the products; more competitive offers; creativity; future assets.
• Support – What is encouraging him to have a good relationship: human aspect, e.g. sufficient sensitivity; resolving together many previous problems well; the ability of sacrificing some valuable opportunities for the sake of long-term goals.
• Protection – What arrangements must be done to enable that relationship to work: e.g. building communication; some offers in connection with certain products are not going to arrive so quickly; patients need to be treated individually for it is important to get to know them.

This tool can also be applied in an effective way when a client settles on a new position in career coaching.

107. Simulation

According to *Wikipedia*, simulation is the process whereby the expected or actual behavior of the system is analyzed on a physical or computer model of the latter.

There are several simulation options. The model may be an imitation that is only slightly different from the original phenomenon or process but otherwise identical to it, i.e. a smaller copy of it. A complex system is analyzed when simulating events and when a multitude of different events occur. Computer models are often used where these events are traced. If some unexpected effects manifest themselves in the system, they are replicated through the use of pseudorandom numbers.

During the implementation of the simulation model, a few statistics concerning the important events which are occurring and which relate to the operation of the system and the parameters comprising the system are developed. These statistics are the foundation of the evaluation.

Naturally, these all-encompassing computer simulations are not created for all events, the two reasons being time and cost. The likelihood is that the leader only has a few hours or a few days to make a decision, and by the time he or she would have explained it to the IT specialist, there would be no time left. This is why sometimes a 'living' model' is used.

I have also participated in a few business simulations where, on the basis of certain incoming parameters, various results along different scripts were produced at the end of the process. I assisted my partner in preparing these data so that he or she could make the best decision.

108. Black-White, Yes-No

Every so often, the client seeks a coach with the intention of skipping the first three stages of the SPARKLE Model and immediately starting at the Route stage. In this scenario, the coach tells the coachee in vain that first they should discuss the Situation, then move to the Positioning (yourself) stage, search for alternative ideas and only then to arrive at the Route stage where he or she can make a decision. It may be counterproductive for the coach to insist upon starting the process at the Situation stage because it could damage their budding relationship. It would probably be worth asking whether the client is 100% certain that there are only two alternatives and that he or she would like to begin the process there. If the answer is 'yes', then it may be a useful tool. Individuals tend to corroborate the decision they made with examples and often bring reality into the mix. However, if they glance at the scales on a daily basis, they may not get the same picture.

This tool can be applied both in business and life coaching. What follows is an illustration applicable to both contexts:

CASE STUDIES (EXCERPT)

A woman was soliciting a coach to help her decide whether she should divorce or not. First, the coach presented her the Mercedes Symbol so that she would understand that she was not limited to those two alternatives exist; but she was uncompromising. Nor did she want to elaborate on the situation, set the direction, or list alternatives. She explained that she was paying to make the decision, and that if she had wanted to analyze the past, she would have enlisted the guidance of a psychologist and not a coach. She undertook to complete the homework, which consisted of marking, for the following three weeks (until the next coaching session), a '+' or a '-' sign next to the date in her diary depending on whether her day with her husband went well or poorly. Every day, she would mark either '+', or '-' and write in the first sentence of her diary what she could have done to improve the day. 16 days out of the 21 were '-' yet, she decided neither to leave her husband nor to stay in the same situation but rather change because she could tell from this task that during the 21 days, she really could have done something to ameliorate it. Her next homework assignment consisted of completing one of the items on the list each day, which she did. Such items included: massaging her husband's back, taking their child to kindergarten one day so her husband could sleep longer, baking his favorite cake, among other small chores. A third session was unnecessary. While it was not financially lucrative for the coach, it offered her a great feeling of success because she was right in that there were more than two alternatives.

It is also a common occurrence in business coaching that the client can only discern two alternatives and sticks to his guns and insists on not paying for the first three stages of the SPARKLE Model. There was a coachee who sought help with a decision pending since four years, namely whether his company should expand in the future into the international market or simply continue operating in the national market. Another client was facing sleepless nights over whether she should terminate one of her employees. However, even more frequently, someone wonders whether or not he or she should resign from his or her position. The coach is not a counselor/therapist and can't tell the client what to do. Rather, the former can only help with coaching tools so that the coachee could reach his or her own conclusion. This tool also made it possible for the coachee to determine whether his place of employment was so unpleasant that there would be 21 '-' signs in his diary or if his perception stemmed from his negative mindset.

109. Decision-Making List

Listing is also an effective tool in the Route stage. Clients should list circumstances where they may ignore others' opinions and muster the courage to trust their own feelings.

We could also consider the flip-side of this tool where the client lists those situations where he or she failed to heed his or her feelings but listened to others' opinion, which ultimately led to an erroneous decision.

Upon completion of the two lists, even an entire session could be devoted to reviewing the listed items so that the client could make a confident decision. An additional session would likely be necessary in the Route stage, but the coachee could even spare four-five sessions in the Key Obstacles stage.

110. CHOICE Model[9]

This tool is utilized to evaluate the costs and the durability of the potential solutions. Six factors contribute to the long-term success of the decision. However, according to Mick Cope, fulfillment of those criteria of the former does not in itself guarantee success.

C – *Control:* Does the client have the required authority for satisfying them?
H – *Hunger:* Does the client truly desire the achievement, or do other goals more important?
O – *Options:* Has the client considered all options?
I – *Internalization:* Does the client take responsibility for the decision?
C – *Consequences:* Has the client considered all the consequences of the decision?
E – *End game:* Does the decision in question serve the long-term goal or distance itself from it?

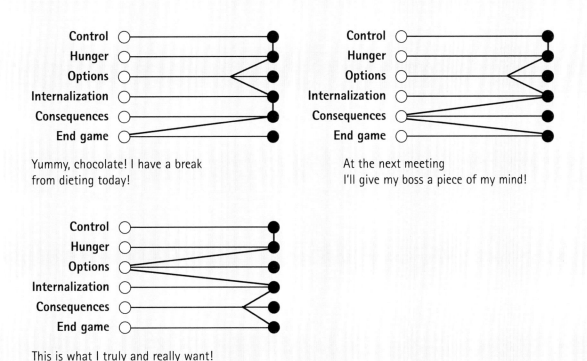

Yummy, chocolate! I have a break from dieting today!

At the next meeting I'll give my boss a piece of my mind!

This is what I truly and really want!

The questions of the CHOICE model as a tool:
C: Can you be influenced by your decision? Can anyone interfere with it?
H: To what extent and why is this decision important? What sacrifices would you make for it? What would you do if someone remarked that it certainly did not succeed?
O: How many options did you want and how many did you consider? How could you generate more ideas?
I: Would you like to carry it out yourself or someone else?
C: What costs, joys, and/or sorrows can this decision spell?
E: Does this decision draw you closer to the final, perfect picture? How do you know if you are working along the right lines?

111. Fishbone Diagram[10]

The Fishbone Diagram has a host of different names in professional books, such as 'Ishikawa' and 'cause-and-effect' diagram. This is also one of the tools that is widely taught at business schools and can be easily applied in coaching

Kaoro Ishikawa created this tool in the 1960s; it is one of the seven basic tools of quality control (the six other tools being the histogram, the Pareto chart, the check sheet, the control chart, the scatter diagram, and stratification). The Fishbone Diagram is a tool which presents our knowledge in connection with a problem by way of a drawing, together with the coherences. As a result, the diagram makes the problem more transparent and manageable.

The Fishbone Diagram, which acquired its name from its shape, is in fact a 'cause-and-effect' diagram. The head of the fish is the problem, the ribs are the causes, and the bones are the root causes. This method consists of searching for the causes triggering the evolution of a phenomenon, effect, or problem in groups of categories determined in advance with the help of team brainstorming. Typically, these categories are as follows: People, Material, Methods, Machines, Environment. They can be determined on a case-by-case basis depending on the problem (business policy, processes, systems, etc.).

Creating a Fishbone Diagram:
1. Gathering ideas: What is causing the problem?
2. Grouping the ideas.
3. New questions in each group of causes: What is causing the problem? More precise questions: Where, how many, how?

Advantages of a Fishbone Diagrams:
- Not only do they reveal the causes of the effect, but also the causes of the cause and place them into a logical system.
- They focus on the causes and not the history of the problem's evolution.
- They zero in on the causes and not the symptoms.
- They analyze the real causes and not the absence of something.
- Intervention can be planned according to the analysis of the causes.
- They display the connections between causes.
- Causes that were not previously analyzed are also revealed

Case Study (excerpt)

We were discussing with one of my clients who works for a less hierarchical organization the reason for the disproportion in workload of her company's staff. During an entire session, we endeavored to identify the possible causes. Upon compiling them, it was obvious that they could be rationally divided into logical groups. This is important because we have to approach those problems derived from the system one way and those which have a kind of leadership style associated with them another way. We set up action plans for the problems in each cause-group. In one of these action plans, we proposed to the manager a program of vision-composition, strategy creation, and team-building. The manager welcomed this idea, and the composition of vision and strategy were followed by a few workshops of organizational development where the team clarified the responsibility and competence issues and discussed the latent disputes within the organization. These programs not only contributed to a smoother division of labor but also significantly boosted the staff's motivation.

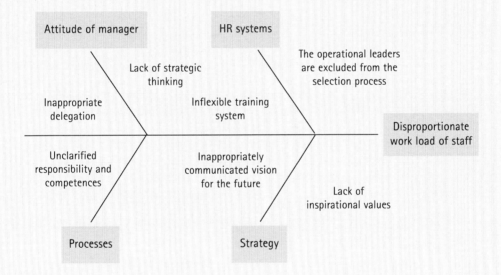

112. Action Plan

After the client has defined how he or she wants to reach the goal, either with the 'Pros and Cons Analysis' or the CHOICE model and then has taken it apart with a particular method, he or she is on the right path towards closure of the Route stage. However the client must not stop there. It is not sufficient to know the next step; one must also set a deadline.

During the coaching process, the next step following decision making (Route) is implementation (Key Obstacles and Leverage). The more elaborately the client works out the action plan, the greater the likelihood of success. We can encourage our client to prepare an action plan or flowchart.

Action plans are usually created in a chart which includes the steps, tasks, and deadlines. The sample below is the most simple variation; it can be liberally expanded with additional columns.

Steps	Description of tasks	Deadlines
1.		
2.		
3.		

Assuming knowledge of the answer may bring the devil out in the coach, i.e. the counselor in the Alternatives stage. He or she must remain low-key in such a situation. The realization of the action-plan does not fall within the province of the coach's duties. Therefore, it is the client, not the coach who sets the deadlines. We have to be particularly careful to not qualify the coachee's commitment, either pro, or contra. It can also make him or her feel insecure if we make statements such as:

– Why are you requesting so much time to complete this task? Why can you not perform it tomorrow?

Also, if we fall into the other extremity:

– Are you planning to take this step tomorrow? Do you not think it might be a bit premature? Are you sure about it?

The coach's main task, at this juncture is to encourage the client, and even if the latter is capable of taking the next step, the coach has to adjust to the client. If the coach fails to do so, there may not be a subsequent session, or they will spend the next session with the client's explanation that this step was not accomplished because he or she knew that the deadline was unrealistic but that the coach was insisting upon it.

To be able to devise a good action-plan, it is worth asking the client the following:

WHAT?
– What have you decided to do?
– It's time to decide. Which path have you chosen?

We should not ask conditional questions, such as 'What do you think you should do?' because presently, he or she must himself or herself commit.

WHEN?
– When are you going to do it?

Let us aim for the most precise answer possible, i.e. we should not accept the standard 'later'. It is worth writing down even the day or the hour; the client can write it in his or her diary.

WHY?
– Does this step further your long-term goals?

It is worth reviewing the Positioning stage to ascertain whether this step is helping it, or if the focus has shifted a bit. The established goals are usually modified by this stage in 70 to 80 % of coaching. Therefore, we should raise the client's awareness about this change to help him or her understand the process and ensure that he or she sees the value in it.

HOW?
– What objections can you anticipate will complicate achievement of the goal?

– How can you respond to these objections? How could I support you most in this stage? On a scale from 1 to 10, where would you rank the certainty of your capacity to do it? If it is not a 10, what could you do to make it a 10?

Some clients already have backing by sharing their action plan (i.e. with a spouse), motivating them further to realize the goals they established. Moreover, they do not want to fail and others to see it.

113. Flowchart

As a tool, the flowchart is ideal for displaying the completion of a task, or activity. We can mark the steps of the task with different plane figures to simplify them and to make their relationships easier to interpret. We should illustrate each step with a closed geometrical shape. The steps follow consecutively in a logical manner, and appropriate symbols render them easier to interpret. The classical flowchart elements are rectangles that signal individual steps, rhombuses which contain a decision point, i.e. a question, and narrows which point out the direction of the steps. Besides these, we utilize several existing elements at BPR- Business Process Reengineering, (e.g. process starters, triggers, finishers). However, for coaching, the easiest variation is sufficient, and we need not make it overcomplicated.

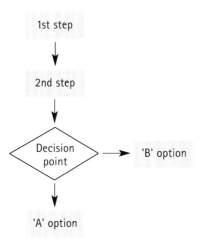

The advantage of the flowchart, compared to the action plan, is that it also includes decision points from where junctions may start, i.e. it is less static.

The developed alternative of the flowchart is 'swim lane', where we add a new aspect to the specific steps of the process such as 'Who creates that particular step?'.

It may be that there will be such steps in our flowchart where someone else's actions (i.e. our boss's approval) will be necessary. Therefore, it is important to clarify this already at this stage to avoid any caveats in either the Key Obstacles or later in the Leverage phase.

114. Gradual Task-Growing[11]

When the goal has been set and the decision has been reached by whatever means the client prefers, it may be tremendously helpful to search for alternative ideas about ways to achieve the goal. We can then divide the bigger steps into smaller ones that are not so intimidating, but instead attractive enough to start making them immediately.

We then proceed to rank these steps, adding a date beside them and even recording them in the diary: 'Which day, which part- task?'. We can also indicate milestones next to the tasks. It is ideal if the milestones coincide with the coaching sessions because then we may analyze and celebrate the tasks that have been set and fulfilled thus far. Therefore, if one or two tasks are dropped, there will not be a large quantity that is impossible to fulfill. If some tasks were not completed, it is possible to discuss with the coach both the reason and the manner in which they could be fulfilled in the following period. What is the coachee going to do? What is he or she going to try in a different way?

This cognitive therapeutic tool shows the client the way from the small steps towards the accomplishment of pivotal tasks. It is highly-effective in the Key Obstacles and Leverage stage because the path that the client follows to attain the desired goal can be viewed graphically. On the first stair-step, we indicate the task that may trigger only a slight discomfort to the client. At first, the coachee has to take this initial step. In the subsequent steps, we lump together the harder, and harder tasks. When can we say that the client has taken the step in question? When he or she has already put into practice that task, his or her distress concerning the latter has significantly diminished or has even become moot.

CASE STUDY (EXCERPT)

Splitting it into parts may be either when the goal is consists of sequential steps, or it may mean grades. An example for the latter is the following: A client contacted me the other day with the issue of the high staff turnover at a company, where he was the owner/managing director. It turned out that, at the 'exit interviews', everyone was complaining that they had been working there enthusiastically for years, but had never been given a 'thank you', 'congratulations' or any praise. The director was always protective about two things:
– 'If there had been any trouble, I would have told you.'
– 'Did they not see my satisfaction in their pay raise or bonus?'

Thus, he wanted to develop his ability to provide positive feedback. He took it for granted if the employees fulfilled a task well without an acknowledgment on his part. However on the other hand, if something was not timely or done erroneously, he immediately provided feedback. He failed to offer praise and appreciation; therefore, the employees began losing their motivation and did not dare to experiment in such an atmosphere.

We considered those situations where the owner did not offer positive feedback. It was clear that this was a characteristic that he displayed in each area of his life- namely, taking good things such as his wife and children for granted.

He conceded that it wasn't enough and that he had to change if he did not want to lose good people. In his case, gradual change was occurring in the following way:

1. At the coaching session, he tried providing positive feedback to me as a coach. Part-task completed.
2. As homework, he praised his three-year old daughter for having learned to swing, as he no longer had to push her. Part-task completed.
3. He should have praised his wife as homework but arrived at the next session without having completed this task. He felt frustrated as he had not done it for three weeks, and we did not leave until he thought of three practical things to praise his wife for that day.
4. As homework, on the one hand, he chose the employee who deserved to be praised the most, while conversely, he praised the one that he most feared losing. There was one more aspect: praising the one who would not be astonished at being congratulated because the director dreaded being mocked for ten years. 'What is this crazy thing he is learning to praise others?'

Staff turnover - partly due to his newfound knowledge of giving positive feedback - decreased from 20% to 7 %.

We also drew the steps because the client was a visual type:

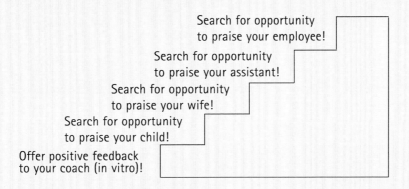

It was very instructive for the client to be able to visualize the upcoming tasks, particularly on a chart; and he experienced the climb to the higher stair as a success.

Incremental change works so well, that with this in mind, I would also like to share a few more cases.

The CEO of a 300-member company contacted a coach with the aim of improving his conflict management skills. He cited me several examples of measuring the success of coaching in an objective way. While most of those measurable goals were business-oriented, there was a personal one as well.

He had a bad relationship with his wife and lacked the courage to offer her feedback about what was not working well for him. Therefore, he chose to escape and found himself a paramour. He did not want to take on any conflicts and was postponing divorce. One of his personal goals in the coaching sessions was to be able to ask his wife for a divorce.

In business, his intended goal was taking on conflicts with his managers because, for example, he did not dare to inform the HR-manager of his coaching contract with me.

The cafeteria, where we were working, was a very discreet place, i.e. we were not disturbed while in session. When he had shared this information with me, we both sat back to think, and the waiter brought our drinks at that point. The CEO ordered green tea and some hot milk in a separate jug. The waiter brought the green tea, but with cold milk. My client commented on it to me, but not to the waiter. I asked him what he would do if we were at the end of the coaching process, and he was handling conflicts very well. He said he would immediately call the waiter and ask him to change the milk. Upon completing his sentence, there was silence for a few seconds. Silence is an important tool for the coach. Inexperienced coaches who lack sufficient confidence have an aversion to silence. They fear that their clients' dissatisfaction because they do not want to pay for silence. Yes, they do! Most new coaches start asking questions at this time. However, I saw it on my client's face; that it was unnecessary to ask how he would perform the next step. And, he succeeded: He asked the waiter to change the milk and said the following:

-"If the only benefit I reap from coaching is to dare sending the milk back, it was worth it. But, alright, I can see that we have started the work. For instance, when you were informed me about clients who you helped gradually towards the goal of being able to praise, it was the first step for me as well. Then came the conflict with my HR manager, and finally, I hope to garner the strength to take on 'the big talk' with my wife.

For gradual change, the following case also comes to mind, in addition to praising and taking on conflicts:

A top manager at a large, multinational company was invited to a global discussion where he should have delivered a one-hour lecture. He later canceled it but called me saying that he would like it if this was the last one he had backtracked. Such an event is organized once a year and he wanted me to prepare him to deliver his speech in English the following year overseas in front of an audience of 120 specialists.

He achieved his final goal by completing the following steps:
1. He delivered a lecture in Hungarian to 20 undergraduate students at his old university.
2. He gave a lecture in English to 20 MBA students at his university.
3. He gave a lecture in Hungarian at a Hungarian conference for 120 people.
4. He flew to attend an English-speaking meeting.
5. He participated in an English-speaking workshop with 20 people.
6. He gave a lecture at CEU (Central European University) in English.
7. And finally, he made a highly-successful presentation in English in front of 120 specialists, far from our small country. Even a video recording was made which we could watch together.

I worked with another a client whose process consisted of only three steps:
1. He presented it to me in his office.
2. He presented it to me in the large lecture room.
3. And finally he presented it successfully at a conference with 120 attendees.

If these tools which further the agreement (the Pros and Cons Analysis, the Adenauer Cross, and the others) are not helpful, the coach should still not postpone the decision but should make a selection, experiment with the option and perhaps even another other one if the first one does not work. This is why it is worth choosing the option which does not render the second one impossible once the first one has been completed.

The classical example is when a manager wants to discharge someone, he or she should give them a chance first because it is impossible to try it out the other way round. As André Louf wrote in his book: "If you choose the first one, you decide well if you choose the second one, you also decide well. God's will in connection with you at this very moment is only to choose something."[8]

Notes

1 http://www.quotationspage.com/quote/1937.html
2 http://paulocoelhoquotes.com
3 Werner Vogelauer: *Methoden-ABC im Coaching*. Luchterhand Verlag GmbH, 2011
4 Peter Drucker: *Innovation and Entrepreneurship*. HarperCollins, 1985
5 Michael Michalko: *Thinkertoys*. Ten Speed Press, 2006
6 Mick Cope: *The Seven Cs of Coaching*. Pearson, 2004
7 Ibid.
8 Ibid.
9 K. Mórotz – D. Perczel Forintos: *Cognitive Behavior Therapy*. Trans. Zita Delevic. Medicina, 2005
10 Ibid.
11 Andre Louf: *Grace Can Do More: Spiritual Accompaniment & Spiritual Growth*. Cistercian Publications, 2002

V. TOOLS OF THE KEY OBSTACLES STAGE

"Nature and education are somewhat similar. The latter transforms man, and in so doing creates a second nature."
Democritus[1]

„There is only one thing that makes a dream impossible to achieve: the fear of failure."
Paulo Coelho[2]

„All battles in life serve to teach us something, even the battles we lose."
Paulo Coelho[3]

In this stage, the coach is guiding the client along the chosen path to reach his or her goal not to throw in the towel at the first objection. Up to this point, the client is usually enjoying the coaching sessions because neither the Situation, the Positioning, the detailed description of the Alternatives, nor the Route stage is burdensome. However, in this stage, the coachee has to step out of his or her comfort zone. It is also possible that the client begins canceling his or her regular sessions. At this time, the coach should not take it personally, as it is a natural reaction, and the coachee should be made aware of it.

115. Measuring Trust and Faith

This tool is very much similar to the Rubber Band, i.e. it can also offer substantial assistance in establishing the goals, prioritizing, and progressing along the chosen path. However, while I would rather apply the Rubber Band theory with clients who prefer visual methods, this one is favored by leaders who work with numbers, such as controllers and IT managers.

At every coaching session, the coachee should indicate on a scale from 1 and 10 how much he or she believes in his or her own capacity to reach the desired goal. Then, the client should always discuss what triggered the change, for instance that either he or she had placed the goal higher or lower in comparison to the previous session. However, not only is the change worth measuring, but also the value of certain situations. For instance, if the score is very low, it is worth asking 'Why?' And also determine if they can filter out such a goal at the beginning, namely one which the client is not certain he or she can reach. Therefore, this tool can spare both the coach and the coachee a significant amount of frustration.

We can use the previous graphical description and indicate in the target how we are proceeding towards our objective:

This tool - although a bit differently - is also used in the Solution-focused Brief coaching methodology as well, called: scaling.[4]

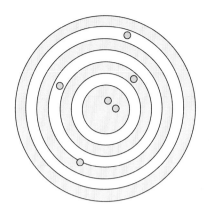

116. Creative Writing: Saboteur

As mentioned in the Situation stage, the creative writing technique has a lot of variations, some of them more appropriate for one stage than another. The 'Saboteur tool' is best suited for the Key Obstacles stage because the client is asked to identify his or her own saboteur.

Upon completion of the Situation, the Alternative, and the Route stages, the coachee must write about his or her self-created excuses and should make a step. He or she should try to recognize these excuses, assign a name to them, and list them. How can we utilize our own objections? What external objections do we have? Which ones are real and which are imaginary? And what can be done about them?

117. Learning from Our Own Mistakes

The CEO of a big oil company told me ten years ago that when he was recruiting managers for his team, he asked candidates about the mistakes in leadership they had made in the previous year. Interestingly enough, he was not asking about qualifications, success, or references.

On the one hand, he was testing their honesty and their way of assuming responsibility in the following manner: whether they would have the courage to own up to and act on their mistakes at such an unconventional job interview. On the other hand, his long-term goal was that the company would become a dynamic, quick response team instead of a sticky, slow oil spot. This explains why he was not seeking managers who were hesitant about their decisions and took one decision during the same length of time, but rather for leaders who made ten decisions and assumed the risk of failure in the case of one or two of the latter due to time limitation. There is a saying that clever individuals learn from others' mistakes. Of course, this is also a concept. However, if clients make a mistake and undergo the experience themselves they will make less mistakes in the future.

CASE STUDY (EXCERPT)

One of my clients who had always been enthusiastic and optimistic once arrived at the coaching session in a bitter mood. I asked him about his discontent. He explained that the large, multinational company where he was working had received three free tickets for an event in Cannes, France. As their department was the most successful one that year, the CEO offered my client to nominate three colleagues who would be awarded those tickets.

My manager-client, who was a highly-motivating leader, did not even think about keeping one of the tickets for himself, although he would have seized the opportunity to travel to the French Riviera with pleasure.

He discussed this issue with his three top employees who were very content. One of them had never received any company bonus before, the second one already purchased an airline ticket for his wife so that she could accompany him. The third one was the employee of the year. At that time, the foreign parent company had introduced a cost-increasing program, so they could get only two tickets rather than three.

The manager became exasperated and discussed the matter with one of his colleagues who he thought that the situation would impact the least. It was a poor judgment call on his part, for his colleague informed him that he had wanted to travel so much that if he could not do so, he would resign. The manager panicked and asked the second candidate whether it would be a great sacrifice to pass up the trip. He replied that he had already paid for his wife's ticket, although he would gladly cancel the trip so that his colleague, who he liked, would take his place. Moreover, he had already been to Cannes before. While the third colleague did not resign, he was deeply hurt.

My client asked me not to comment on this situation. He did not want me to solve the problem. He wanted to find the solution and expected me to support him only with my questions. He also added that he would like to use coaching that he had always used it for: he asked me to strengthen him in those areas that needed reinforcement and challenge him in areas where he was over-confident, which is precisely what I did. He then resolved his problem, and as he had learned from his own mistakes, he would no longer call me to solve a situation in the future with a similar issue because he now holds the 'philosopher's stone'. This is one of the greatest distinctions between consultancy and coaching.

118. Helpmate

The mentor and the coach are not the same. Neither one is superior to or less than the other because one of them is an apple and the other one is a pear. Often, everything is proceeding as planned very well in the first stages of coaching, with the client establishing his or her goals and making a decision, but there are roadblocks in the Key Obstacles stage. The coach cannot spend weeks monitoring the client, but if the latter really needs support in the form of someone observing him or her in everyday life and providing prompt feedback, and this could not be solved with 'Shadow Coaching', the client should look for an internal 'Helpmate'. This is a very useful method for those seeking to overcome their lack of self-confidence and who would like to use less negative expressions in the Key Obstacles stage although they fail to realize when they utter them.

One of the directors of a large company was the only female board member. She asked an empathetic board member to kick her on the ankle when she was explaining something redundantly or when she was half-hearted or pessimistic. She asked another member to touch her shoulder when she was thumping on the table with her fingers or rolling her pen. The coach did not have to be present, and the change occurred. Another client entered a board full of women. There were a lot of fights and intrigue, so she asked the eldest board member to be her mentor and help her to grow by not getting involved in every dispute with other women but instead to be broad-minded.

In this stage, two of us were assisting my client: a business coach and a mentor, which seemed to be a very good combination.

This tool is not to be confused with "Peer Coaching"[5] (developed by Andrew Thorn, Marilyn McLeod, Marshall Goldsmith), where each participant acts as both the coach and the client. In the case of "Peer coaching" both individuals have the role of a thinking and accountability partner, and of an objective supporter. "Peer coaching" is a two-way street whereas the 'Helpmate' is a one way street in a sense that the supporting person is the client's assistant or friend.

This tool can be utilized between two coaching sessions to practice new habits or after the engagement ends, in order to keep the client accountable with gentle reminders.

119. Magic Shop[6]

Considering that this is a playful coaching tool, we must exercise caution as to whom, when, and with whom we utilize it because it is not intended for everyone.

Moreno used to include this game in 1943; therefore, it is a well-known tool in psychodrama although in a simplified form and is equally effective in individual and team coaching.

If the client knows the target and what he or she would like to achieve, then it is worth discovering to what extent this aim is important for the client and what he or she would be willing to sacrifice for it. It makes the client conscious that everything has a price and has to be earned; it does not just happen.

The coach takes the role of the shopkeeper, the coachee that of the customer. The customer tells the shopkeeper what he or she wants to purchase, e.g. two hours of free time weekly and states what is in exchange for it- what sacrifices he or she would make (e.g. he would even risk a conflict with his wife because he knows that his wife will complain if he wants two hours of leisure time per week for himself but it will be beneficial to him).

The shopkeeper can now decide whether to give the customer the desired product in exchange, in this case, for the two hours of free time.

It is worth "provoking" the coachee a bit more so that the list of things the client is willing to sacrifice for his or her goal is expanded, and you reach the point where he or she points out: 'If I did so many things, and I still didn't obtain it, I wouldn't like to have it!' By this time, the list is usually so long that it could be spread out over the following weeks for purposes of experimentation. The coachee, having already explored some of the options can attend the next coaching session equipped with the ability to provide feedback to the coach about which solution works best for him or her or whether he or she still has to search for it.

When we use this tool in individual development, announcing the rules would likely be sufficient, and the game can start. For many clients, it is also helpful if they accord weight to the game and sit, for instance, at another table, as if it were a shop. Alternatively, they may choose some sort of symbol (ex. the client brings a plastic bag or the store owner is wiping the table with a napkin) and indicate that the game is over by setting aside these resources aside.

In the case of team coaching, this tool has shown more benefits. On the one hand, team members can obtain ideas from the others about the things they buy and give in exchange (more participants might want to buy the same thing in the magic shop, but there is only one such item; therefore, they will be further inspired to offer more for it and to bid). On the other hand, commitment to the objective and the support for accomplishing it are bolstered if the team members maintain daily contact with each other because this is a kind of competition for them.

This game is also useful if the client has multiple goals and cannot prioritize them. With the help of this tool, the client may examine which target is the most valuable the one in the magic shop for which he or she would give the most and is most worth its price.

120. Profit-Loss

When the client has identified his or her goal, it is worth examining to what extent he or she wants it. The answer 'very much' is inadequate. The client must convince the coach that the coaching will be successful because he or she really wants it. It could be a useful tool to create a list about the following:
– What is the client's profit if he or she attains the stated goal?
– What is the client's loss if he or she does not reach it?

Hopefully, both lists will be very long. There is an example in the Passmore book[7] that a client managed to collect 32 profit items about what he would lose if he did not quit smoking, and this facilitated their cooperation in the future.

121. Victory List

The client should list all those cases where he or she was consciously struggling to accomplish something, and the efforts proved to be fruitful. What were those recognitions, behaviors, features that drove to success?

122. Role-Play

The coachee can assume not only the role of himself or herself but also that of a third person. Role-playing can be applied, for example after shadow coaching when the coach can observe how the client behaved and the latter could then take his or her part, polarizing a bit. This way, it is not the coach who tells him or her if he or she poorly communicates with an employee (they can experiment with expressing volume or the expression he or she used, but rather the client who can see himself or herself as an outsider. In such cases, this tool has a confrontational aspect in that it holds a mirror up to the client.

However, we can also apply this tool in the Key Obstacles stage when the coachee has already decided what to do but wants to role-play it with his or her coach in a protected environment. They can role-play an important conversation, as with the coachee demanding a pay-raise from his or her boss. Oftentimes, however, the client has difficulty in providing positive feedback to the staff. In such cases the coach can assume the role of the negotiating partner, and they may explore different options, i.e. what the conversation would sound like if the partner (boss or employee) had a good day, and how it would be if he or she woke up on the wrong side (or if the coachee did not know his or her negotiating partner in advance, he or she might wonder whether the former was an extrovert or introvert).

It may also help the client a lot if they exchange roles, and the coach becomes the coachee so that he or she could see what another person would do in his or her place. They might as well role-play a situation that is important for the client and frequently for the sake of practice. The coachee could take notes of some concrete, sentences that he or she liked so that they could be incorporated into critical conversations.

Case Study (excerpt)

It is not only difficult to resolve but also to discuss a conflict. In individual coaching, only one of the participants is part of the conflict, i.e. our client is sitting across from us so we can only hear his or her side of the story. Consequently, the coach has to make a substantial effort to extract the most useful data from the client's statements relating to the conflicts: the client's attitude and most significantly the assumptions, prejudices and bad habits he or she holds in the course of understanding and solving his or her situation.

One of our clients had been trying to clarify a conflict with a colleague for months but found himself at a stalemate although he was trying really hard to rectify the thorny situation. He had approached this colleague numerous times to discuss how to solve the predicament but never made any progress. What is more, the situation deteriorated as his colleague always saw him in a nervous mood and not displaying any intention of cooperation.

To find out why the coachee had such a negative reception, we also had to examine more closely his intention in this case because we were already aware of his colleague's behavior in his eyes. The client's task was to describe in writing how he approached his colleague, what he told her when he approached her, what words he used, what he thought of his colleague, and what impressions he had of her.

According to the client's version, his colleague should address a practical issue so that then, the conflict would be resolved. It was in vain that he was attempting to convey this to her.

This 'conveying to her' really caught my attention, and we tried analyzing how it felt when the client 'wants to tell someone' what to do. They discussed the means of offering assistance when a problem needed to be resolved and how it seriously interfered the way of communication. They were honing the client's communication style while being an active participant of a problematic situation.

As I can always see and hear only my client and never the other party, we created a very simple situation where we could observe my client solving a problem. The situation was as follows: One of the participants is unable to call a plumber to fix a defective faucet and therefore, a friend comes along to lend a hand.

I took the role of the colleague refusing every idea and raising only objections because none of the tips suited her. My client was trying to solve the problematic situation in his role, which was not so complex in practice. However, we did not manage to get any further because of the following:

1. He did not ask questions but only made suggestions, and that is why he felt rejected.
2. After having offered me an increasing number of tips about where I could find a plumber, and I did not accept any of them, he grew increasingly cynical with me. He started his sentences with a negative evaluation about me and implying that I was not receptive to any propositions.
3. Then there was a turning point in the story...

Suddenly he asked me a question, leading me towards the resolution of the problem. He did not make any suggestions but was simply inquiring, which in turn led me to search for solutions.

Following the role-play we reached a conclusion. On the one hand, I confronted him with the feelings and thoughts that his cynical attitude evoked in me, and he made negative comments about my inability to solve the issue. On the other hand, my client also began feeling better when I began approaching the problem in a cooperative manner, and this was dependent on his discovering what his friend in need would like to do.

By walking into someone else's shoes for a few minutes, we are able to obtain a broader view of past events, understand our behaviors, and as it also proved to be helpful in our case, prepare ourselves for future occasions by realizing what we should do differently.

Role-play in coaching is ideal for eliciting the usage or non-usage of fundamental and simple tools of leadership. For example, if the manager fails to ask sufficient questions, to ensure that the given information reaches the right destination or to praise in an appropriate way, this tool can come in handy.

Role-play is one of those effective tools in the coach's toolbox that helps to develop the clients' communication and problem-solving skills. The coach has to provide a protective, receptive and safe environment and be able to offer instant feedback even about such rarely-encountered issues such as non-verbal communication and expressions used in a conflict as well as the manner in which the client talks about himself or herself or approaches others.

123. Sailing Ship

The 'Sailing Ship' is also a visual tool, but the coachee does not need any exceptional graphics talent. When clients start reviewing issues that may help them to make a decision and preparing themselves mentally for what is needed to carry them out, they very often leave out important factors. It helps them considerably to solicit support in order to tap into additional motivation when stuck. This 'Sailing Ship' helps coachees to assemble and arrange the motivators. Let us ask our client to draw a ship. (Does he or she draw a sail on it? Does he or she realize that a sail is also necessary?) While brainstorming, the client should organize the ideas into two groups, with tangible advantages at the bottom and intangible motivators at the top. The coach should make the client conscious that the ship also needs a sail, and that the body of the ship does not suffice, i.e. he or she should compile some other elements there too.

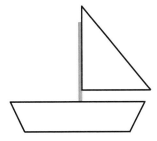

Most clients who create this drawing (because it is impossible to make all of them draw it) nicely fold this sheet of paper, keep it nearby, place it in their drawer or purse, and when they feel the need to change their course, take it out and remember by glancing at their long list of why they had to step out of their comfort zone.

124. List of Self-Limiting Beliefs

Richard David Carson *Taming Your Gremlin*'s book[125] is uniquely focused on how to get out of your own way in order to become more productive and achieve balance. This book is very well known in coaching circles. "The enemy in our head is much more dreadful than the one standing on the other side of the net" says Timothy Gallway in his guide *The Inner Game of Tennis,* which has become a classic. Helping clients to overcome internal obstacles is one of the coach's key roles. The majority of people - actually all of us- from time to time are limited by our negative beliefs. In most cases, we are not even aware of the negative effects of our thoughts. The coach's task is to help reveal the client's negative beliefs and have him or her realize their effect on him or her.

We ask our client to list the negative and positive thoughts to the SMART target and then modify the negative ones.

We can group these self- limiting beliefs as follows:
- Supposition: "I have to work a lot of overtime, otherwise I'll be terminated." "I'll surely not get a promotion if I ever go home earlier than my boss."
- Absolute: "I can't trust anyone.", "There is no free lunch.", "Life is hard."
- Unrealistic expectations from ourselves (i.e.. we would like to be the best in everything, we expect to be perfectionists)
- Self-limitation of alternative ideas (out of the box). He or she can only see two alternatives and does not even consider a third one. (Applying the Mercedes Symbol may be useful in such cases.)
- He or she cannot even hear the positive feedback or assumes that they are said out of interest, or are excuses that he or she was simply lucky. I once had a client who called to notify me that she had been given her annual evaluation and was to be definitely fired. She brought the report to our next, advanced session, and it turned out that she scored 90% on everything. However, she had skipped over that and had read one hundred times only about those areas that she should improve on.

Actually, this tool is a kind of straightforward list containing the self-limiting beliefs of the client (the client already knows about one part of it and writes it down; the coach notices another part of it, and the third part may come up by asking about them, or with the help of an outsider, such as a spouse or boss.

After exposing the negative beliefs, it is worth examining how deep-seated they are and how significant an effect they have on the client's life and the fulfillment of his or her goals. These should then be marked in the chart.

Upon preparation of the list, one more column containing the things that the client would like to change his or her beliefs for should be added. Some that do not have such a substantial impact can remain there, also deep-seated beliefs that they are not worth focusing on. (Some deep-seated issues are of such significance that is worth involving the services of a psychologist in the ongoing work.)

So, finally we have a chart of four columns, according to which the client can decide what he or she wishes to work on in order to reach the set goal.

It would also be useful to create a retrospective list, i.e. to catalog all his or her fears throughout the course of their lives and state, upon reflection, to what extent they were real. How did the client overcome them? It is always easier to determine later whether our fears were justified; however, it is beneficial to look back and realize that they were, for the most part, unreal.

This is also a useful tool to build self-confidence.

125. Drama Triangle[8]

This tool is associated with Stephen Karpman. Its premise is that we must be vigilant to avoid getting caught up useless games. The drama triangle helps us recognize if we are in such a game and also shows us how to extricate ourselves from it.

By the time we reach the Key Obstacles stage, hopefully we have a very open and honest relationship so that when the coach realizes that the conversation is heading in a wrong direction, he or she can genuinely point it out and can use the drawing below to illustrate it.

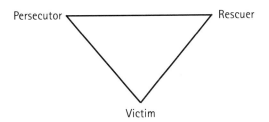

These three roles may surface before the Key Obstacles stage (i.e. at the Route stage) but most often they manifest themselves when the client has made a decision, implements it, and brings a pile of excuses to the following session. The coach should be aware that these excuses are not directed at him or her. It is difficult for the coachee to step out of the comfort zone; he or she would rather play the role of the 'Victim'. A skilled coach recognizes that this is a classic opportunity to play a game and exits; or unaware of this, assumes the role of the 'Rescuer' and tries to offer the coachee some good advice.

At this point, the client might fall into the role of 'Persecutor' finding more excuses and rejecting all ideas.

It is advisable to remain alert when hearing the following 'Victim' statements from the client:
- "Yes, but…"
- "I can't help not being able to do it…"

The coach should pay attention to whether he or she is making 'Rescuer' statements such as:
- "I just want to do you good…"
- "I just want to help you…"

The coach's options are as follows:
- *Not participating in the game:* He or she does not take up the gauntlet, i.e. the client is provoking the coach in vain; the latter must not assume the role of 'Rescuer'.
- *Exits the game:* When the game has already begun, he or she may even change the topic or sign with assertive communication that he or she does not want to proceed in this manner.
- *Gets into the spirit of the game but has a different result:* Being that it is a substantial challenge, I only recommend it to experienced coaches.
- *Exposure:* The coach can reveal to the client that he or she has recognized the game, at which time they pinpoint the exact nature of the situation and discuss how to proceed.

126. Y Curve[9]

We can best apply this tool when the client feels a bit demotivated. The coach should not blame himself or herself when the client cancels the sessions at this stage, sulks or complains. The resistance is natural, as the client has to step out of his or her comfort zone. The coach's task is to motivate and urge the client to shorten the painful period. When the client fails to do something, he or she should not interpret is as a failure but welcome it because it indicates that he or she is in the territory of concrete change.

This tool aids with empowerment and encouragement, enabling the client to feel motivated again with respect to the completion of the process. It helps the coachee realize that he or she is not acting alone in view of the fact that this is a natural course, namely that is a challenge to step out of one's comfort zone.

It is worthwhile to ask the coachee the following questions:
• Have you ever changed anything before?
• How did you manage?
• Was it fast or slow?
• Were there any objects or people who helped this change?
• What can I do to help you?

Mick Cope demonstrated the process with the following charts in conjunction with time:

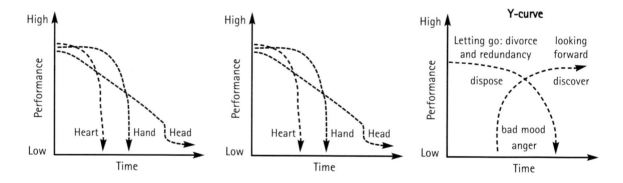

127. Cockpit Confirmation[10]

This tool is referred to by different names by many people. The name "Cockpit confirmation" was coined by Mick Cope. We instinctively try to avoid being measured, although all kinds of measurement could be useful when approached with a positive attitude. We can also learn from it even if something failed: 'What have we done, and what has happened? We have to determine what we are going to feel, think, and do if the change is successful and if it fails.'

Drafting an agreement at the beginning stating that the coaching should last until the client achieves his or her goals is advisable.

This tool assists the partner in measuring the results by observing them. It helps the coach refer to the correlation points that signal if the client starts to go wrong so that he or she could change in time.

180 TOOLFUL COACH

128. Deferring Games

This coaching tool helps us reveal the games that we play instead of looking into the mirror so that the coach could notice it in time and take the necessary steps.

The following games are most often played:
• *Cheating:* Unfortunately, the client often "cheats" and states that he or she has reached the goal in order to end the coaching process. At this point, the coach must draw a conclusion. A more serious problem is when the coach and the client both cheat, i.e. they mislead the client's manager. These are very grave ethical breaches that could undermine the coach's trustworthiness. Therefore, a fast billing is not worth the price for the coach as he or she may lose the honor.
• *Quick solution:* the client has achieved the goal once and it is no longer of importance afterwards. It might be that the coach and the coachee do not cheat deliberately but simply make the mistake of closing the coaching process when the client has already reached the target once. It might even end well, i.e. it is possible that the client will always act in accordance with the goal, but we must handle the situation cautiously.
• *"I forgot about it" and "I had no time":* - Beware of the client if he or she often relies upon this excuse because it suggests that the target is not important enough for him or her or there are other hidden issues.
• Setting a target that is too easy to reach.
• Too complicated; it takes more time to measure it than to achieve the goal.
• It is pointless to measure it.

Steps:
• What do we have to measure?
• What is the 'target-value'?
• Defining the system of collecting and analyzing data: 'Who, when and how measures'
• What steps to take when the measured values and target values are not equal?

129. Buckets and Balloons

This coaching tool is known by a multitude of names. The 'bucket and balloons' label is borrowed from Mick Cope's book.[11] This tool can be applied to identify those factors that resist change and result in durability. We apply this tool in the following manner:
We ask the client to develop a comprehensive list of their buckets and balloons.

Example:
• On the second day of time management training, the coachee is assigned an urgent task (bucket).
• A draft email written in advance that he or she has just arrived home, patience please...(balloon 1).
• Note to boss, and usual fire-brigade that the training is more important (balloon 2).

If the coachee is prepared for the potential buckets, it does not take him or her by surprise and can 'blow a balloon against it'.

130. eMAP (Russel)[12]

Mick Cope's book also contains this coaching tool, which can be utilized to help the client map his or her own emotions and then unfold the reasons for the movements between the shifts in emotions (they can signal with little arrows from which condition they got to another one). When the client notices that he or she is moving in the wrong direction, it is easier to change and avoid the stimuli triggering the wrong direction.

The client should jot down their feelings every 30 minutes:
– what impact the emotions have (pleasant or unpleasant);
– what the level of intensity is.

There are more than two thousand words expressing emotions that guide the clients in identifying theirs. When it is difficult to describe an emotion, it is sufficient to indicate which quarter it falls in and what level of intensity it manifests. We can observe the stages the client completed and what moved them along. If the clients create this type of chart, they can visualize how their feelings impact their performance. With the coach's assistance, they can elaborate on preventive and individual technical strategies during the disclosure process.

When the coachee begins proceeding towards the 'Stressed' zone, he and the coach should try the following- listen to music, read jokes or mantras or any customized solution.

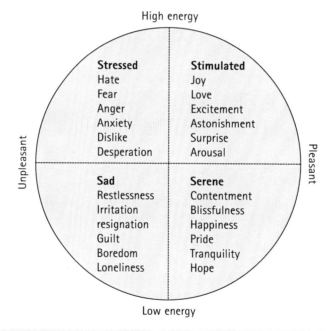

CASE STUDY (EXCERPT)

My client, the director of a large multinational company, had already participated in 'presentation-technique' training and media-training. Her video-recorded performances were analyzed with the help of a specialist. They had tried nearly everything.

Nevertheless, she was stressed before her presentations, and whether she was to give a lecture in the media or before hundreds of guests at the company, she always had a shot. Things were under control for quite a long time. She only requested a meeting when she felt she should have two shots instead of one. The reason she decided to contact a coach was that her father died of liver cancer, and she didn't want the same thing to happen to her.

We discussed the process: why she was stressed, what could be done, what she could do to be well-prepared. We discovered that she was already using all the state-of-the-art techniques and that the preparatory stage could not be any better. I introduced eMap to her, explaining its utility and how to use it. Although she was a bit skeptical, she said it would be worth exploring. She had recorded her emotions and their level of strength for an entire day prior to the presentation. After this test it became evident that even during the day when the presentation came to mind, her emotions were a bit unsettled, but the real issue was addressed in the five minutes preceding her lecture. When was asked to define her wishes from afar, she replied as follows:
– She wished that someone would distract her, i.e. she could forget about being stressed for five minutes.
– If someone were praising her, it would give her hope.

We killed two birds with one stone. When she felt that she needed her shot, she called me. I was cognizant of the fact that my task had doubled, namely to keep talking to her, using only positive reinforcement. We tried it twice, and it worked. On the third occasion I suggested to her that she should call someone else- not because I felt this task to be burdensome, but because it was in her interest not to become dependent on me with a twenty-year career still ahead of her. She asked for the opportunity to call me and thought of the person, other than me, to choose for the task. On the fourth occasion, she called her mother, who, having survived her husband's alcoholism, was more than willing to help her daughter.

In general, doubt and isolation trigger stress and fear. Therefore, if we can diminish the client's insecurity to a minimum level by teaching him or her how to be well-prepared, we simply have to focus on reducing feeling of isolation This can be achieved temporarily with the support of a coach, and later with a trusted friend, spouse, or colleague who can assume this role.

Notes
1 http://thinkexist.com/quotes/democritus/
2 Paulo Coelho: *The Alchemist*
3 Ibid.
4 Peter Szabo – Daniel Meier: *Coaching Plain and Simple, Solution-focused Brief Coaching Essentials.* W.W. Norton&Company, Inc., 2008
5 www.marshallgoldsmithlibrary.com/…/Peer-Coaching-Overview.pdf
6 László Fodor: *Psychodrama in Practice I.* Trans. Zita Delevic. Animula, 2000
7 Jonathan Passmore: *Excellence in coaching.* Kogan Page, 2006
8 S. Karpman: Fairy Tales and Script drama analysis. *Transactional Analysis Bulletin*, 1968
9 Mick Cope: *The Seven Cs of Coaching.* Pearson, 2004
10 Ibid.
11 Ibid.
12 Ibid.

VI. TOOLS OF THE LEVERAGE STAGE

> *"Plans are only good intentions unless they immediately degenerate into hard work."*
> Peter F. Drucker[1]

> *"Do not wait: the time will never be 'just right'. Start where you stand, and work whatever tools you may have at your command and better tools will be found as you go along."*
> Napoleon Hill[2]

In this phase coaches support their clients taming self-defeating behaviors. There are plenty of useful tricks and tools to utilize when clients start thinking about giving up but there is no excuse they have to go on if they want to reach their desired outcome.

131. Grades of Transfer[3]

Vogelauer also writes that while every client decides to implement his or her plans-those defined during coaching- into practice, not everyone succeeds. The original authors of this tool are Prochaska, Norcors, and DiClemente.

This tool is useful when we sense a client's insecurity ('I'll try it later!'), when he or she talks very vaguely about when and what steps are planned; or when he or she has not even begun the process and is already engaging in excuses ('I would prefer to wait for the result of that decision or what my boss says...', 'this is too fast for me, I need some more time').

For the coach it is important to be clear about the grades of transfer and discuss them with the client if necessary:

1. **Averting**
Typically, the client's sentences in this case are:
– "The aim that I fix isn't so important"
– "There are so many advantages to the unchanging situation."
– The coach's main task here is to confront the coachee with the inconsistencies.
2. **Making the client conscious.**
The client is conscious of his or her goal but is still insecure about performance.
3. **Preparation.**
The client begins planning the concrete steps. The more concrete the plan is, the greater the likelihood for success. Therefore, the coach must strive to encourage his or her client to set forth a more definite plan.
4. **Action.**
The coach's key task here is to encourage the coachee to act.

5. Continuation/stamina

Anyone may reel and crane. At this juncture, the coach must work on reinforcing the positive experiences, that is to say, that the client should not view failures and negative observations as a tragedy but rather as life experiences.

6. Stabilization.

It may take a very long time for past behavior to transform into a completely new behavior, and a considerable amount of patience is necessary for this.

132. Ready - Stepping Ahead – Obstruction - New Challenge

I am grateful to one of my client for this tool because it is his invention. It helped him in the Leverage stage. He is a head of department, and being an engineer, likes new structures and the well-organized life. Therefore, he also appreciates coaching when it can be well-structured. He arrived at every session with his own small printed chart on which he labeled where he was with his issues. He was always delighted to be able to include material in the categories 'Ready' and 'Moving Ahead'. Thus, he had no qualms about including items in the categories 'Obstruction' and 'New Challenge'. This tool has assisted others as well.

133. Behavioral Tests[4]

Cognitive therapy often applies the method of behavioral tests. There are two types- 'in vitro' and 'in vivo'. We also employ this tool quite often in coaching. First, we test the new behaviors with the clients in a protected area ('in vitro') and later ask them to consciously identify circumstances in life where they can practice the new behaviors. We often apply it when learning how to offer positive feedback and to engage in 'assertive communication'. You might wonder how it is possible to make top managers role-play different situations? According to my experiences, coaches should not fear engaging leaders in games, for they are often very willing participants in the latter. They can also feel that they should experiment with the new behavior and its consequences in a protected environment, and stepping out of their comfort zone helps them to effectuate real change.

CASE STUDY (EXCERPT)

The CEO of a sizeable industrial company contacted me with the issue of an extraordinary high staff turnover in one of his departments compared to the others. As he was a man of numbers, he did not want to rely on emotions but asked the HR department to make a statistical report about the staff turnover at the six departments during the past five years. The statistics confirmed his beliefs, i.e. he had employed the Financial Director three years ago and the staff turnover which had been below 10 % before had since exceeded 30 % each year- which was considered to be a critical level.

The CEO asked me to coach the Financial Director. It was imperative that the Finance director sign up for this since she too, not simply the CEO, needed to understand the value of a decrease in staff turnover. Fortunately, the Financial Director really welcomed the change for she too was frustrated about spending a lot of time on the following issues:

- Attempting to make employees reconsider when they announce their resignation and convincing them to stay (with no result thus far),
- conducting job interviews with the potential candidates,
- teaching new colleagues.

For the first homework, she created a list stating the reasons for subordinates' resignations during the past three years. The subordinates cited two main reasons: 1) the lack of sufficient positive feedback and 2) the impression that they were not a team but robots working beside one another. The latter reason caught my attention, because when the Financial Director cited as a third reason, the ample time spent 'teaching new colleagues' due to staff turnover, she did not even refer to the task of helping colleagues adapt to the team, although this would be as critical as the colleagues mastering their tasks professionally. Therefore, her two main tasks were team-building and delivering positive feedback. We began with the latter issue. We engaged in considerable brainstorming about what should be the first step. I also shared some approaches that my clients had adopted. She also came up with good ideas from inside the company, so the list became quite long. As a first step, she chose to extend the staff's weekly one-hour meeting by half an hour and brought a cake in (that she had baked the previous night to make the team feel the importance of the situation and her commitment). Her plan was to serve her staff some cake and praise everyone publicly for something. I thought that it was a well-built scenario, and it could not really be enhanced any further. I did not want to waste time by asking her what exactly she intended to tell everyone. However, it was a mistake on my part to think that I would save the client the cost of one coaching session.

Two days later, the Financial Director called me to say that 'the task is checked off' and asked me the date of our next meeting. Although her phrase assailed my ear, I did not consider it so important at that moment. The following day, the CEO called me to provide feedback about my work. He stated as follows: "I'm very pleased that you are the executive coach for our Financial Director. It has already produced a tangible result. Just imagine that she baked a cake and that not only her staff but also I had a piece. I was really content. By the same token, one of her employees said that while he was very happy to be praised on an individual basis (I am certain that it was also your suggestion), the coachee continued ranting and criticizing everyone: '... what I don't like about you..,...you should improve your...' i.e. she could not offer solely positive feedback to her staff.."

I was very much surprised. At the following session, I did not want to abuse the information relating to my client, so I asked the coachee to share with me exactly what she had told everyone. I listened to her and stayed silent. I sensed that she was awaiting my praise regarding her performance, but I could not do so. With the guidance of two questions, she realized that she had made a mistake by mixing the two kinds of feedback. She realized this on her own and decided to deliver only praise next time. Upon doing so, she called me in ecstasy, and instead of using the phrase 'task checked off', she remarked: "This was excellent! They were so pleased, and the entire meeting was so upbeat that they immediately provided positive feedback to me as well (and only positive). They can already see the change in me, namely that I want the team to be a solid one, and this also motivates me to continue the coaching. Believe it or not, they were not even grumbling about having to stay longer hours because of the monthly closing, although they usually do!"

The coaching ended successfully in that the CEO, my client, and the staff were all satisfied. Although I had made a mistake, we rectified it (my integrity prompted me to credit them for one lesson). I learned that if people are planning to praise their colleagues, and it is something that they had not previously done, I should not let them go without performing a 'behavioral test', i.e. they should tell me verbatim what they plan to say.

134. Positive Self-Talk[5]

This is a cognitive therapy tool to apply with clients who lack self-confidence. Often, clients are not accorded positive feedback directly, either because there is no one to deliver it (as they are on the top of the hierarchy) or because it is not common practice among managers. To boost her clients' confidence, the coach usually recommends that they list between two sessions actions on their part that were successful or merit acknowledgment. We would probably associate this tool with the Situation stage in the SPARKLE Model in the sense that it helps the client see clearly and become conscious of his or her abilities. However, it mainly arises in connection with concrete work when the goals are clear (i.e. reinforcing self-confidence). In this way, this tool could be linked to the Key Obstacles stage.

135. Distracting and Refocusing Attention[6]

This cognitive therapy tool helps most when a client has to focus on a particular work to accomplish a specific task. Here, the coach and the coachee try to assemble those tools that helped the coachee in the past or may help distract his or her attention in the present. In my opinion, this tool is worth applying in cases which are on the border of coaching and therapy. Only those coaches take on such cases and only under specified circumstances, with the understanding that they have the capacity to address them with the help of their competence.

Case Study (Excerpt)

A European manager was asked to be a lecturer at an international conference in Switzerland. This journey was very important for him but he dreaded tunnels. He knew that he had to pass through several tunnels to reach his destination, so he asked his coach to help him with it. Due to the financial crisis they would be traveling by car but he would not be the one driving. As distraction, they identified two effective tools: music and sleep. As refocusing, he always had to glance at his name, among the other lecturers, on the invitation to the conference, which was a great honor as no leader from his country had ever delivered a speech there. Owing to these protective measures, the client called his coach from Switzerland with a sense of relief and to the satisfaction of both of them.

136. Confrontational, Provocative Coaching

In my opinion, this is only one of hundreds of tools that we can apply. The most important task of the coach is to guide his or her client towards attainment of his or her objective, and this particular tool can come in handy in some cases.

I trust that a competent coach is strives for healthy balance. It is said a coach must have two body parts- a heart and backbone, i.e. we should have a heart, empathy, and understanding if the client is facing difficulties, but we should also have backbone, i.e. we should not let the client change his or her course with multiple excuses. A good coach should sometimes engage in provocative conversations in favor of his or her client.

If we simply listened to our clients without interruption, the coaching sessions could be lengthy. Therefore, should ask them directly about what we hear, asking powerful questions that help us see the topic more clearly and share how we feel and what we know from our experiences.
- Let us pay attention to what is unspoken about what we feel is missing.
- Let us ask what moves something inside us, or what is suspicious, contradictory.

The coach guides the client to the point, so he or she should not let the client deflect.

It is also worth implementing provocative coaching when the client would like to hone his or her negotiation, communication, or conflicts-management skills. If the coachee learns how to handle unnerving questions, he or she will not feel the need to fudge in real situations and negotiations.

Provocative coaching cannot only be applied in sharpening communication skills, it is independent from the topic of coaching. The external helper, the coach, may also ask challenging questions, and if the answer is too immediate or we have not even scratched the surface, we must ask them again: 'Are you where you are intended to be? Does what you are doing relate to who you are and is it propelling you forward? Are you able to accept loss and take risks? To what extent do you fear your level of power?'

While this tool may be very useful, we must also exercise caution when implementing it, so that we do not overstep our aim and the coach does more harm than good. Without any confrontation, the coach might become the client's paid supporter and does not help him or her achieve the balance sought.

Case Study (excerpt)

In the case of many corporate leaders, the coach can be the only objective, external support who usually helps them via the confrontation tool to not let it slip away and lose the sense of reality. One of my clients chose me for the above-mentioned reason. After being introduced to two coaches, he made the following remark:

"I was afraid that if I had chosen the other coach, I would not have gotten the exact things I was looking for in a coach. I felt at our first meeting that he wanted this work so much (for financial reasons) that he would never be honest to me or dare to say something to me that would jeopardize his source of income for a moment. And what I need now is honesty because I'm surrounded by opportunists, and I do not want to pay any more for that. You told me you would not accept just any client, and that if you felt that you could not help, you will refuse the assignment because truthfulness is very important to you. So, I was very curious as to whether you could see the potential in me and take me under your wings to help me so that I could become a better leader."

Yes, he needed this. However, our work over the course of six months did not consist of provoking him every day, but only when it was effective. In fact, as we clarified the rules right from the outset, I started with an easy topic: I asked him to discard his plastic, disposable pens and purchase one that is worthy of a CEO.

Provocative coaching has multiple levels and different grades. Sometimes a simple, clarifying question may also help a lot, i.e..:
P: - I am considering resigning from my job.
C: - Are you contemplating it or have you decided?
P: - You are right, it is unnecessary to change jobs, I have already made my decision.

The coach had also behaved provocatively with her offer of help.

Case Study (excerpt)

One of my coaching colleague's clients had been suffering from Work-Life-Balance. This woman was once a leading sportswoman and is currently a successful businesswoman now who seriously misses athletics and she feels that it is not good. Her homework assignment consisted of attending an aerobics lesson between two coaching sessions. She called the fitness room, registered for the class, packed up her sportswear, drove to the destination and stayed in her car. She spent the hour of aerobics in the car and shared with sadness the situation with her coach. She felt so sorry for the client that, in spite of being in the sixth month of pregnancy with her fourth child, she offered to accompany her to aerobics so that she would get out of her car. At the next coaching session, the client discussed the situation in a lively manner. She explained that she had since gone to aerobics three times, and that she had even bought a monthly pass. She felt very ashamed that her coach, who was six month pregnant at the time, proposed to join her. My colleague did not want to provoke her. Still, it was a provocation and it bore fruit. Therefore, a simple impulse was enough, and as she did not resort to the coach's guidance, the risk of dependence was not an issue (that she would only go to the fitness club with the coach and would not do so when the coach cannot accompany her).

Maintaining a healthy balance is very important, i.e. the coach may provoke his or her client with questions or statements, but the client must be aware of the fact that it is not for the coach's sake. It is a topic that needs to be covered at the very first meeting where the coach and the client co-create the coaching. However, the end goal is achieving success with a particular client. If this happens, the client will be grateful later on for having been challenged and slightly provoked.

Case Study (excerpt)

At a large, multinational company, my client was appointed regional manager. Her former secretary, a good friend placed a card of congratulations on her new desk in her new office in the new building. (A paper postcard, so, she did not send it electronically). My client was extremely touched (so much that her eyes welled up with tears as she was telling me the story), but when I asked her if she thanked her secretary, her answer was an embarrassed 'not at all'. We met two weeks after receipt of the postcard, and she promised herself as homework to spend 5 minutes with this issue (regardless of how busy she was in her new position) because their friendship was at stake. Two more weeks passed by, and we met again.
 – How are you?
 – Not well.
 – Why?
 – Because I miss my friend with whom I used to have lunch and talked to every day.
 – And why don't you now?
 – Because my secretary thinks that it's degrading for me to meet her.
 – Why does she think so?
 – Because I haven't even called her since. I haven't even thanked her for the postcard.

– Why not?
– I know it wouldn't hinge on those five minutes. I could have made time, it's not an excuse, but I felt it so inappropriate after two weeks and now after four weeks...
– Do you still want to meet her? Do you want to remain friends with her?
– Yes, I do.
– Are you calling her now?
– No, I'm not.
– Should it be your homework again?
– Yes.
– Do you plan to do it over the next two weeks?
– No, I don't.
– Do you want to come to our session feeling frustrated in two weeks' time again?
– No, I don't.
– Do you want to call her now?
– No, I don't.
– If you were her, would you be angry?
– Yes, I would.
– If you were her, would you forgive her if she called you even though after four weeks?
– Yes, I would.
– Do you want to call her?
– She won't answer the phone because she knows my number.
– Do you want to call her on *my* cell?
– Yes, I do.

That day, one part of my coaching fee was to cover the cell phone charges because they spoke for a long time. A friendship was rescued, which is even more important at such a high level of leadership.

137. Punishment

No, this is not corporal punishment, and it is not aimed at diminishing the coach's tension, but there are clients for whom and cases for which this tool can be applied.

Naturally, the usage of this tool also has its limits, conditions and rules such as the following:

– We must clarify in advance and not after it occurred what type of case should be followed by punishment.
– We must think of individual rather than collective punishment; that is the punishment that is appropriate for the particular client and the particular challenge.
– The punishment should be proportional as in the Civil Code and the Criminal Code, i.e. the punishment should not be disproportionately serious or petty because then it would lose its motivational force.
– It also serves the target, i.e. two steps instead of one.

Case Study (excerpt)

A small business owner contacted me to help her restore her work-life balance. Several weeks and months went by, but the balance always swayed. When her young son was sick or when Santa Claus visited kindergarten, Mom was always working. She was working but with constant remorse, which did not have a positive impact on anyone- neither the staff at her business nor the coachee. We were having the following conversation at our last session before Christmas:

- I feel that we are making no headway. You can see the target: a balanced mother who is doing her best at her workplace, and she is also a good mother. Nevertheless, I can't see us moving closer to the target. We have tried several coaching tools (Coat-of-Arms, Positive Visualization, Role-play, Free Association…), we are doing good with the first five stages of the SPARKLE Model, but the Leverage is inconsistent. How do you think I could help you the most?

- If you blackmailed me.

- If I blackmailed you?

- Yes, if you said you wouldn't coach me on whether I completed my homework well.

- I see, so you need an outside motivator in addition to reaching your goal.

- Yes, because it seems that my fear of becoming a bad mother and being left by my husband isn't compelling enough. I need something else to be stressed about. I don't understand myself either, but I feel that something needs to be dropped on the scales to tip the balance and make me come to my senses.

- I think it would be unethical to fry the fat out of you. Christmas is approaching. I wouldn't like to sit under the tree knowing that I let you down, but I understand what you are saying, let's figure out something together. What if you had a punishment that we agree to in advance and that is individually-tailored, generally suits your present challenge, and is proportional?

- That sounds great! Yes, I need something like that. Have you ever had such a client?

- Yes, I have. What worked for him was that, if he hadn't made one step, he had to make two. A trivial example is that if he didn't praise his wife in two weeks, he should praise his mother-in-law.

- That's funny, but it could possibly work for me too. What if I don't leave the office at 6:00 p.m. one day, arrive by 10:00 a.m. next day, and take my son to kindergarten later, but telling him a story first because he loves this so much.

- OK. This is really individualized and also supports your target because you are going to spend time with your son. What else disturbs you and your family most?

- When I answer the phone after 7 p.m. But I don't know whether it's important or not.

- You mean after work?

- No, just if such a person is calling me.

- But you can see that on the caller ID.

- Yes, but I'm always enlightened when I can see who it is.

- I see, so your husband's problem isn't your answering the phone but answering a phone call from your workplace.

- Yes. If I had a telephone only for business calls, and one for personal contacts (my parents, husband, etc.).

- I see, so your problem would be solved if you had two cell phones, a one for personal and another for business use.

- Hello! How come I have not realized this before? It's regrettable that I wasn't able see the forest from the trees. I have just been given a new cell phone, something terrific to try it out. I'll give that number to those five people whose call I would answer after 7 p.m., and I'll turn off my business phone. With regards

to this issue, I should be doled out the punishment to still answer the phone and offer my husband a back-massage in exchange.
- You can try it tonight, and if you answer the phone at 7:02 p.m., are you immediately going to give him a massage?
- Yes, and I would like to submit myself to a third punishment as well.
- You are really set in your ways! I won't stop you!
- If I don't have lunch, I'll make dinner for my husband! So, it's good for everybody! He likes it when I cook, and so do I, because I can enjoy a hot meal. Furthermore, our child also likes it because I am home on time if I have to cook.

All of us (client, her husband, her child, and her coach) spent a more enjoyable Christmas without having to be subjected to the punishment of coaching her any longer.

138. Reactive/Proactive Conditioning

Reactive conditioning: to an external stimulus (hearing the manager's footsteps —clicking to another website). Proactive conditioning: someone does something automatically for an expected consequence, potential reward, not thinking consciously about the cause-effect relationship.

Everyone has such habits, actions that they do not engage in consciously, but as a response to a kind of stimulus or for an expected consequence. The coach, as an external observer, may question the client's actions which he or she does routinely. To raise clients' awareness about their actions, 'Shadow Coaching' is the most useful tool because some significant elements may be omitted from the client's identification with the circumstances or scenarios.

CASE STUDY (EXCERPT)

An expert at a large multinational company had been in the same position for a long period of time. He had set his sights on becoming a manager and mistakenly thought that he could not say 'no' to a task for fear of not obtaining a promotion. He was wrong because his boss entrusted me with teaching him to say 'no', because if he juggled with many balls, more would then fall. He faced his erroneous pre-conception just in time- before an important ball fell that would have closed the door upon his promotion.

139. Pause Point Model[7]

This tool is also borrowed from Mick Cope's book. The 'Pause Point Model' can be applied to every spiraling problem in order to be aware of the process and plan the pause of those unforeseen events that might wind their way up. We must examine the moment giving rise to feelings, thoughts, and actions, and describe it in detail- how to do it in a different way, how to prevent the distortion of the events, and how an effective strategy can be mapped out that will confer a positive explanation upon the principal cause.

The coach's tasks are as follows:
• To recognize if the problem is spiraling out of control.

- To understand the stimulus.
- To map the process and show which level the coachee attains.
- To make sense of the spiral steps.
- To encourage the client to reflect upon the story, then draw and decide where he or she wants to test the limits next time. It is enough if he or she pushes it at the fourth stage, then gradually sooner.
- Planning and experimenting with a pause button as homework.

Questions:
- What would be the benefit of pushing the pause button sooner?
- Are you going to be able to push the pause button?
- With what do you expect the coach to help you?

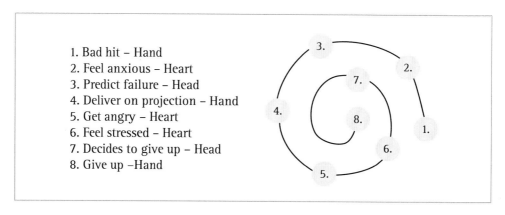

1. Bad hit – Hand
2. Feel anxious – Heart
3. Predict failure – Head
4. Deliver on projection – Hand
5. Get angry – Heart
6. Feel stressed – Heart
7. Decides to give up – Head
8. Give up – Hand

Examples:

Spiral: Crying child – mother reacting angrily. Pause button: grandparents/girlfriend/babysitter, asking for help

Spiral: Quarreling couple. Pause button: taking a walk.

Spiral: In case of a conflicted relationship: ringing cell phone with the partner's name on the display – stomach cramps, conversation starting from a frustrating situation. Pause button: the client does not answer the telephone immediately but calls the other party back later when it is most convenient for him in order to reduce the level of stress from where the conversation will start.

The 'Pause Point Model':

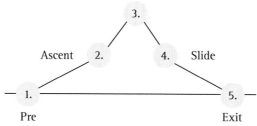

140. CHANGE Framework[8]

This tool, which is also borrowed from Mick Cope's, reveals the level of control that the coach can apply.

If the coachee has decided what and how to change, then they promised but failed to follow through, we must allow him or her to draw the conclusions.

If the client holds the key of motivation, achieving success may be slower, but it will be attributed to his or her own success and not depend on the coach. If the latter holds the key, change will be unavoidable but it is not certain if it will be long-lasting.

The client should make a choice: Is he or she seeking a quick-fix or long-lasting solution?

The level may also fluctuate during the coaching process and depends on the client's needs and budget	Command	The coach handles the change	The coach jogs to the running track with the client
	Heim		The coach calls the client to remind him or her to get up, that it's 7 o'clock.
	Agree		The client has to call the coach after every training to provide the latter with a progress report
	Nudge		Occasional progress checks
	Guide		The coach remains in the background
	Empathy	The coachee handles the change	The coach is 'there' for the client when issues arise

I like this tool very much. Which letter of CHANGE is relevant depends on the following factors:
- the coach's personality (to what extent he or she is direct or indirect);
- the client's personality and expectations;
- the topic of the coaching (in relation to the coach's and client's knowledge; i.e.. the coach may teach the client the process of effective delegation because the latter is motivated but lacks some knowledge);
- the coach's professional background;
- the actual stage of coaching, previous experience in coaching: whether the client takes the steps alone;
- the time limit of coaching, i.e. does the client want a quick solution (because it's a crisis), or is not constrained by time limits, so that he or she can think about a classical coaching process and the result will be more durable because the client feels that the result is exclusively his or her;
- the scope of the budget for coaching, i.e. how much time the coach can spend with the client.

Examples:

- The scope of the budget is decisive because in case the client lacks the funds for coaching, he or she stands a small chance that the coach will accompany him or her in jogging to the running track (there will not be shadow coaching).
- The coach may not have any business background. In such cases, the variation in empathy will certainly be an issue if the client has to figure out some organizational changes.
- Depending on the topic, a coachee's lack of relevant knowledge in the area in question is also a key factor, i.e. he or she is unfamiliar with the tools of an effective presentation or is unable to use the projector.
- The stage of coaching: the effect of prior experiences on the level of support – if the client fails to do the homework regularly, he or she will likely have to change the level of support, i.e. interfere more or even stop.
- The coach cannot be a crusader because if he or she follows the steps that the client should make, it will result in dependence.

CASE STUDY (EXCERPT)

The client should be aware of the options of quicker or slower but long-lasting solutions.

The director of a large insurance company could not really articulate what he desired; he only felt that something was wrong. The auto damage specialists, whose duty it was to meet with the clients and appraise the extent of the damage, were authorized to issue a reimbursement of up to about $5,000. Increasingly, these specialists would include a note on their form (where the amount in question was $5,000 dollars) stating that they could not make a determination and asked for their supervisor's - the 'damage controller's' - decision. In a short period of time, the controllers became so exhausted that although they were authorized to decide payments up to $15,000, several cases landed on the desk of my client, a director, which were below their 15,000 dollars limit. My client shared this situation with me in the Situation stage, and I reasoned as follows: 'What can be the reason? Lack of competence? Lack of regulating processes? Fear of responsibility?' I asked my client a lot of questions, but he was unable to answer them because he did not know most of his employees personally in view of the fact that they worked in the countryside and traveled to the nation's capital only once a year. Moreover, because of the high staff-turnover, he did not even meet some of them as they resigned within a year. This case was seeping out of many wounds. My client asked me to organize a team-coaching for this department because he feared that the employees would not divulge the real reasons and would not be honest with him. At this point, I had to ask him the following:

– "I can certainly holding a team coaching for the department. But do you really want this? I agree that we can have a quicker result this way because at the conclusion of the team-coaching, ideally we would have a list of the issues and might close with an action plan. But is time truly of the essence? Do you really need a quick solution and should I start working with your team? Or, as it has been an ongoing situation for many years, two-three months of waiting would be preferable while the two of us are collaborating as part of your coaching engagement? You will then be able to hold this one-day workshop before Christmas with the same result but as a long-term solution. You will benefit so much more this way."

The director assumed the responsibility as it was his team. He felt it was best for him to identify the cause of the problem himself, as he was in the best position to help his team resolve it.

Notes
1 www.quotationspage.com
2 www.quotationspage.com
3 Werner Vogelauer: *Methoden-ABC im Coaching.* Luchterhand Verlag GmbH, 2011
4 K. Mórotz – D. Perczel Forintos: *Cognitive Behavior Therapy.* Budapest, Hungary, Medicina, 2005
5 www.marshallgoldsmithlibrary.com/.../Peer-Coaching-Overview.pdf
6 K. Mórotz – D. Perczel Forintos: *Cognitive Behavior Therapy.* Budapest, Hungary, Medicina, 2005
7 Mick Cope: *The Seven Cs of Coaching.* Pearson, 2004
8 Ibid.

VII. TOOLS OF THE EVALUATION STAGE

> "What is rewarded is repeated.
> What is repeated becomes a habit."
> Anonymous[1]

The target of coaching is simply for the old habit to be replaced by the new one; this stage is critical. Change is always inconvenient as we have to step out of our comfort zone. Because habit is stronger than knowledge, people often return to their old habits when they fail to obtain some kind of positive feedback or reward. Knowing something is inadequate; it must become habitual, and we must not overlook rewards, praises, or celebrations.

141. Summary Pattern

If the client's manager and coachee are not the same person (in the case of most corporate assignments), a summary must be made for the former at the conclusion of the coaching process. This summary should contain the following information:
- the identification data of the coachee;
- the beginning and the conclusion of the process;
- the purpose of the assignment;
- the execution of the goals

Where a more detailed summary is called for, it should also contain:
- the exact date of the sessions;
- the syllabus or topics for each session;
- homeworks;
- the coaching tools.

I also find it very useful to add the following:
- additional areas that have been revealed during the coaching process and necessitate development; some suggestions;
- If only partial success was reached with the goals, what would the coach suggest?
- the coachee's opinion about the coach and the coaching process.

What follows is a real summary pattern. Granted, it is true that every coach has his or her own summary. The one enclosed below is simply only one option. They can also vary significantly in the number of pages; I have seen a wide spectrum from the one-page summary to the twenty-page one.

Pattern for Summarizing Coaching

Summary
Principal: Test Electronic
Client (name, position): Mr. Alec Test – HR manager
Coach: Ms. Maria Coach
Period: 02.12.2008.-19.03.2009.
Goal established: Delivering presentations so that the coachee feels successful and receives positive feedback.

Syllabus

Introductory session: Presenting the SPARKLE model to the client to make the client aware of what he can expect as a result.

Session 1. Situation, Positioning
  - Discussing former presentation experiences.
  - Defining what a presentational situation means for the client, what the elements of a successful one are such as Free Association and Positive Visualization.
  - Observing presentations from external aspect through Role-play.
  - Filling out presentational personality test.
    Homework: Reading 'The ten criteria of a good lecture'. Choosing those factors that can be met or with little effort (Alternatives).
Session 2. Route
  - Reading stories using the momentary and the expected presentational technique.
  - Rehearsing a presentation in front of the coach under normal and aggravating circumstances.
  - Evaluating Role-play.
    Homework: Rehearsing the presentation in front of her team (nine people).
Session 3. Key Obstacles
  - Rehearsing the presentation in a large hall.
    Homework: Lecture at local university
Session 4. Leverage
  - Discussing the experiences of the lecture at the University of Budapest, drawing conclusions (business attire).
    Homework: Preparing for the conference.
Session 5. Shadow Coaching. Evaluation, Celebration.

Applied techniques

  - Recommending professional books: 'The ten criteria of a good lecturer'; 'The golden rules of creating slide strips'; 'The ten criteria of a good lecture'
  - Shadow Coaching, Specification.
  - Free Association.
  - Positive Visualization.

- Role-play.
- Presentation. Self-assessment test.

Achievements: Successful lecture at local University and at the National Coach Conference.

Further suggestions for development: providing constructive (negative) feedback.

The coachee's comments:" I didn't believe I could achieve my goal of not panicking before a conference. It felt rewarding that many people congratulated me afterwards. Now I am brave enough to accept other performances as well. Thank you; I look forward to the next coaching process where I will learn how to cope with offering constructive feedback."

Due to the privileged nature of our communications for my client's sake, I am not allowed to disclose anything discussed at our sessions to the client's manager either. Therefore, this summary was recorded in conjunction with the client.

142. Controlling the Client's Prosperity

The coach must ensure the client's independent prosperity although, financially, it is preferable for the coach that the client remain a little "dependent". Needless to say, however, coaches must bring the assignment to a closure in due time. I adapted a chart for the SPARKLE Model which corresponds to Mick Cope's 7Cs model:[2]

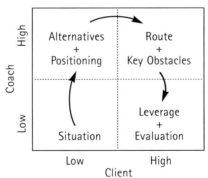

One can clearly observe in this chart that the level of dependence gradually fluctuates during the coaching process. In the Route stage, when the coach meets the client and they expose the situation, the dependence level is low. If the coaching process is successful, the dependence level alters from one stage to the next. At the conclusion of the process and subsequent to the Evaluation, the coach is able to let go of the client's hand.

There may be several ways such as Shadow Coaching, to ensure the client's 'flying solo'. For instance, the coach may listen to the client's presentation at a conference. He or she may also re-test the client with a scenario created by the coach: how they behave under stress, in a conflict or in a situation which was the target of the coaching process.

143. Drawing Conclusions

Global management consulting companies have 'lessons learned workshops'. They regularly organize a meeting at the completion of an assignment to look back and learn from the experience: what they should do differently next time. Similarly to consulting, looking back and reviewing the whole process is also important at the conclusion of the coaching.

The following questions must be answered:
- What was our target?
- What is the result?
- What helped and what set us back?
- What is the conclusion?
- What will we do differently next time?

Exercising candor in this stage is in the common interest of both the client and the coach. They should clarify whether there were any sub-targets that they were not reached and the potential explanation for the latter. If the coaching process was successful overall, such a clarification could be undertaken. This is also a condition of long-term thinking. Furthermore, if the coaching process was successful as a whole, our client might face another challenge when he or she is offered a promotion. In such an event, the client should contact the coach to ensure that he or she is well-prepared for the new challenges.

144. Celebration

We have to learn how to celebrate. Typical cases calling for a celebration are, for instance, when the coach accompanies his or her client successfully through the first six stages of the SPARKLE model but the Evaluation stage is cancelled, or they only create a summary but fail to celebrate the successes.

Celebration, which has an extremely positive effect on all three participants of the coaching process, should not be underestimated:
- The client's manager makes sure that they have not wasted money (e.g. they calculate the Return on Investment – ROI).
- Celebration also instills confidence in the coachee confident for having achieved success.
- Obtaining positive feedback at the conclusion of the process is essential for the coach because it helps the latter to start his or her new task with a higher level of motivation.

Celebration is interpreted in numerous ways. I once had a client who asked me to sit in the car with him and listen to "*We are the champions*" by Queen played at maximum volume. Other coaches spend some time with their clients as they partake in their hobby, i.e. play golf. Still others offer souvenirs to their clients to remind them of himself or herself: ex. a book. There was a case in which a client, who honed his decision-making skills was offered a dice as a memento. The coach may even order champagne so that they can toast to success. As can be seen, Celebration not bound by any rules.

Notes
1 www.quotationspage.com
2 Mick Cope: *The Seven Cs of Coaching.* Pearson, 2004

VIII. TOOLS OF QUESTIONING TECHNIQUES AND ACTIVE LISTENING

"He who does not understand your silence will probably not understand your words."
Elbert Hubbard[1]

"True friendship comes when the silence between two people is comfortable."
Dave Tyson Gentry[2]

In this book, I have devoted a separate chapter to questioning techniques and active listening because coaches have quite contrasting opinions about this topic. According to one group of coaches, coaching is nothing more than a questioning technique, and therefore, the tools and models in this chapter are completely purposeless. The other group of coaches holds that those belonging to the first group are not sufficiently qualified and well-trained, and therefore lack tools and only defend themselves without any supporting arguments. Perhaps the reader should have the last word here.

Active listening is one of the most critical coaching tools.

What is the attitude of a good coach?

– The coach does not want to solve the problems for the client; rather, the client must work on them it and clarify to whom the problems belong.
– The coach does not simply ask the client questions to satisfy his or her curiosity; does not only utilize probing sentences but asks real questions.
– The coach's guidance is based on honesty, with no ulterior motive.
– The coach avoids asking: "How is it possible that you can't solve it?" i.e. what is not a problem for the coach might be an issue for the client. Generally-speaking, coaches have advanced problem-solving skills; therefore, we must not judge the clients or underestimate their problems put in a nutshell: A skilled coach should not primarily think about the solution but rather encourage the client to find his or her own answers and solutions to their problems.

What does a coach not do?

– does not give orders.
– does not indoctrinate.
– does not label.
– does not spoon feed answers to the client.
– isn't preoccupied with his or her own thoughts.

We must be prudent not to rush to judgment and formulate a hypothesis, which may lead to closed or leading questions. We must avoid this.

What does a coach do?

- encourages the client.
- agrees with the client.
- accepts the client unconditionally because the latter wishes to avoid criticism. He or she uses self-messages.
- grants the coachee some time to reply.
- honestly reflects, summarizes.

How does the coach accomplish this?

- tries and wants to understand the client's message, feelings and needs.
- defines them with his or her own words.
- And then makes the coachee confirm it.

With Andrea Szabados, we developed a model for active listening, which is a mosaic word: ATTENTION[3]
Alertness: concentrating on the client at all times.
Target-focused questioning.
Time investment for the topic/person
Eye- contact.
Navigating the conversation.
Thanking for listening, acknowledgment for attention.
Interpreting the client's answers, giving constant feedback.
Observing the communication as a whole: concentration.
Neutralizing our emotions.

Active listening is not limited to sitting and remaining silent.
Listening is comprised of five different levels according to Liz Allen Fey.[4] She describes it the following way.

Level 5—Not Listening

Tuning someone out, thinking about something else, not paying attention. The "I'm sorry, what did you say?" syndrome.

Level 4—Listening to Tell your Story

Not really listening to what the other person is saying; instead, taking that time to prepare your remarks. The intent is to share how your story relates to the other person's for your own self satisfaction, not for their understand and learning. The "you think you had it bad, let me tell you what happened to me" syndrome.

Level 3—Listening for Judgment

Making assumptions and conclusions before you hear the whole story. Once you reach a "judgment" you no longer listen. The" here's your problem" syndrome.

Level 2—Listening for Application

Being able to listen to understand what you might take away from another's comments. Requires the suspension of assumptions and judgment. Requires us to listen harder. Very useful in groups gathering to learn from each other.

Level 1—Listening to Understand

Listening to just understand. Not to judge or apply, rather to understand the "what's it is like to walk in your shoes". And appreciating that by that active listening, not only is the other person heard, we as listeners are improved. This one takes practice, practice, practice.

The meta communication of the attentive coach

- Sitting back.
- Waiting pose; while the coach is sitting back, the other party can speak.
- When the client stops talking, the coach nods a few more times, remains silent, and the client resumes speaking.
- He or she holds a pen as a pointing tool.
- Hand pose: palms should be upward- as an encouraging gesture.
- His or her speaking tempo should mirror that of the client (the speaking speed reflects the speed of processing information in the brains)

Three pertinent quotations from André Louf's book[5] come to mind:

"Accepting someone without reservation does not mean approval at the same time. It's possible to accept someone by defining reservations about their behavior. 'Let him hate sin and love the brethren', said Saint Benedict (Rule, 64,11). The conversation must not be approved or judged, it can only be accepted."

"This behavior of accepting someone or something without reservation is called *empathy* by a new school of psychology. It presumes a bit more than benevolent neutrality."

"Listening with empathy is more than neutral listening. It can never be as neutral as some people would like it."

145. Meta-Model

Meta-Model in NLP is a pragmatic communications model used to communicate information in a speaker's language. In coaching, this framework may help the coach to get to the relevant details of the client's language. This questioning technique helps the coach refine the imprecise statements, situations and words with multiple meaning.

CASE STUDY (EXCERPT)

What follows are excerpts of specific cases that illustrate the significance of this questioning technique (i.e. we focus on a topic until its meaning becomes clear to both parties):

- My life is very stressful.
- What do you mean by stress? How do you know she us stressful? How do you define stress?

- My boss is very condescending to me.
- What do you mean by condescending? How does your boss behave when you feel that he is condescending? What does the adjective condescending to you?

Although the meaning of the words may be found in the dictionary, we may accord a different interpretation to a word. Because the coach may associate different thoughts and feelings than the client, that's why it's worth analyzing it in-depth.

A managing director at a building-trade company asked his managers at the first leadership meeting to make their employees replace the word 'rival' with 'competitor'. Some of the leaders immediately understood the reason, but those who did not have make negative associations with the word 'rival' did not.

My first leader ask us to use the words 'task' or 'challenge' instead of 'problem'.

146. Repetition

Evidently, a CD can also offer a literal repetition if we record the coaching session. Revision does not mean that when the coachee forms a sentence, the coach simply repeats it automatically. The coachee may utilize sentences that the coach spots because there is something interesting in it. That 'something' can be a lot of things. The coach may repeat it simply to bring it to the coachee's attention and make him or her aware of his or her own words. The coach can repeat it word for word, and sometimes the coachee might remark "Alright, I didn't mean it literally, but..."

In this manner, the picture becomes a bit more different. Repetition can also be useful in that the coachee can hear a third person echo his or her words, and sometimes it is easier to notice the optional solutions. It is also purposeful when the coach does not at first understand what the coachee meant, and therefore, he orshe repeats it again. The coachee then realizes: 'How would the coach understand if these details were not disclosed to him or her?'.

Furthermore, the tone of the client's voice and the wide spectrum of emotions may bring some new information.

Partner: I like Peter as a leader.
Coach: I see, so you like Peter as a leader. (The coach repeats the coachee's words verbatim. Although the coach did not ask a question, the client still feels that he or she should add something to it.)
Partner: Not only do I like him, but I also find him to be a great leader.
Coach: I see. So, you like Peter and also find him a great leader. (The coach again repeats the words of the coachee verbatim, refrains from asking questions, thus leading the coachee to feel that he or she should add something to the statement)
Partner: Moreover, Peter is my ideal leader!

What a significant difference there is between 'I like him', 'He is a great leader', and 'He is my ideal leader'. (The coach did nothing else simply repeated the client's words.

147. Summary

A summary is not only utilized as a tool at the end of the sessions or the coaching process, but also when the coachee engages a long monologue. In this case, we can offer feedback about what we heard the client say. Furthermore, it could also lead the coachee to recognize that the most important thoughts could be summed up in one sentence.

I once had a client with whom I had to apply this tool quite frequently because she was very talkative. I am not a quiet type myself, but she was chattier. She added so much information to her speech that would have led us very far. This tool is very useful with clients who are very talkative because we can reassure them that we are paying attention to them while at the same time providing them with a synopsis. Naturally it is also beneficial to us to have less information in our head.

148. Describing With Other Words

Stating the same sentences using different words may be an alternative of 'Repetition' allowing the coachee to make modifications, add new information, or clarify the facts.

The essence of this tool is that every word holds a slightly different meaning to each individual because we all look at the world through different lenses. If the coach describes the question using different words, the picture may expand, and such new dimensions that did not previously enter the client's mind or that are in a new context might open. This process may inspire clients to form new ideas. Both the coach and the coachee can be the describer. To the latter one I'm presenting here a short example, and a longer case study to illustrate when the coach is the describer.

Coach: How did you feel when your colleague said 'no'?
Coachee: Bad.
Coach: How could you describe this bad feeling?

CASE STUDY (EXCERPT)

Principal: I'm looking for a coach for one of my employees. He often misses deadlines on important tasks and procrastinates with regards to the less important ones. He should learn to prioritize.

Coach: I see. So, your employee holds a different opinion about the importance of tasks than you. That's why he misses deadlines.

Principal: Yes, he has a different opinion about the importance of tasks. But, based on what grounds? I'm the boss. He has to do the tasks in the order that I tell him.

Coach: I see. Your employee is acting defiantly. Although you instruct him on the order that he is expected to perform the tasks, he does not follow your orders.

Principal: He doesn't act defy; he simply doesn't do so.

Coach: He doesn't defy, he simply doesn't complete the tasks in the order you tell him.

Principal: What do you mean' as I tell him'?

Coach: If I understand it well, you think that the tasks should be performed in a specific order, and he doesn't do so.

Principal: Should I tell him the order I expect him to perform them?

Coach: If I understand it well, you are raising the question whether you should tell him the order.
Principal: Has the question been raised? Is it possible that it isn't him who needs a coach, but me?
Coach: If I can hear it correctly, you raised a new question. Who knows the answer?
Principal: I see. Rather than him, I am the one who needs a coach so that I could communicate my expectations in a more transparent manner to him, namely when and in what order I would like him to perform the tasks. It isn't going to be simple because he is quite hard-headed. You should coach me, rather than him as I can also make headway in this regard. Thank you for offering me a lead by simply repeating what I stated.

149. Silence

There is definitely more Silence in psychoanalysis than in coaching. While a coach cannot remain silent for one hour, sometimes 'Silence' is a very effective tool. Novice coaches often dislike using this tool. They argue that the client is not paying for the coachee to remain silent. They are right, the client is not paying for the minutes spent in silence but to obtain guidance in setting and achieving his or her goals, and this often requires some silence.

Silence might be present after the coachee's lengthy monologue in responding to a question. The coach then takes a pause so that the coachee's sentences can make sense. However, Silence can occur immediately following the question. In such cases, an inexperienced coach may consider it to be an irrelevant question. Notwithstanding the fact that the original question was pertinent, he or she might also add something or repeat it utilizing different words. This is a very effective approach in view of the fact that perhaps no one had ever asked the coachee such a question, thus forcing him or her to think it over. However, the coachee may also have been asked that question numerous times before, but he or she was reticent to provide the standard reply that he or she usually gives everyone. If the relationship is well-established and confidential enough between the coach and the coachee, the latter will answer by not an automatic reply but with courage and candor.

Silence indicates that the client is thinking and is thus not providing us with a ready-made answer. This is the world of the inaudible, intensive occurrences. What the coach experiences as endless seconds, the coachee usually does not because he or she is searching for his or her own real answers and engages in introspection.

In order not to feel uncomfortable, experience the urge of asking questions or to panic in such 'Silences' and to have the capacity to utilize the latter as a tool, the coach needs experience and professional confidence.

150. Good, Better, the Best Question

In Timothy Gallway's book, *The Inner Game of Tennis*,[6] the author raises a point about to the tennis coach's question in a whole chapter. However, this kind of train of thought is equally applicable to coaching.

When the tennis coach asks the player: 'Are you watching the ball?', the tennis player's reaction can be the following:

– he or she either responds explains in detail why he or she is not doing so or

- gives a routine answer or lies: 'Yes!' or
- retorts: 'Why should I watch the ball?'

This type of reaction is certainly not the first question that is asked in a positive, productive, developing conversation.

The problem can be exacerbated when the question is posed negatively: 'Why aren't you watching the ball?' The tennis player cannot have an adequate reply answer to the latter. He or she may even receive more negative answers to it and even stronger counter, or explanations.

However, if the coach propounds such questions as 'Which direction did the ball spin? How many times had the ball spin before it touched the net? Did it spin faster or slower than on the previous strike?', the tennis coach will not censure the player but encourage him or her to watch the ball even more attentively.

The professional coach's task is similar. Our purpose is not to clash with or scold our client when he or she fails to follow the established track, but to motivate the latter to find it.

All sorts of questions have their place in coaching, although we prefer 'wh' questions that provide descriptive answers to 'yes-no' questions that cannot furnish us with details that will elucidate the situation. Still, a 'yes-no' question is preferable to a qualifying, judging question such as "Why aren't you watching the ball?" An effective question by the coach could be descriptive, not judgmental and 'wh', not yes-no. Examples include " What problems are you occupied with nowadays?" Even more effective are questions such as "Which aspects of work are you occupied with nowadays?" since the word 'problem' does not negatively impact the coachee.

We, in Europe, often like to discuss 'problems'. At my previous company, we rattled our American boss's nerves when we went into his office stating that 'We have a problem'. Instead of waiting for us to tell him what it was, he immediately asked: 'Do you mean that you are facing a challenge?' Even one word can make a difference. It might be more effective to ask 'What kind of challenges do you currently experience as a leader?'

We find several groupings of questions in the topic titled 'Questioning Techniques'.

The method of questioning can be very sophisticated. We can apply probing (seeking more details) – leading (influencing) – reflective – and contextual (thinking together) questions. We must ensure to present different types of questions consecutively, as opposed to the same kind. We should mostly use probing and reflective questions, even though they might render the coaching a bit serious in tone. These question-groups are applied in the European model-based supervision and supervision-based coaching.

According to another grouping, our questions can be open, closed or leading techniques. Clearly, during a coaching session, mainly open questions should be presented because multi-word answers can be given in response to them. The coach is most able to guide the client's reflection with this question type.

There is no secret recipe in this area in that we must compile individual questions tailored to the client's unique needs. Most significantly, we should not formulate 'yes-no' questions but rather 'what' questions. When we spend our time contemplating which questions to ask during the session, we overlook one important aspect –listening with understanding.

Here is a tip: When we feel that we are losing our grip and are at a loss as what to ask our client, we should consider introducing the following 'wild card': "What would you ask yourself now?' Our partner will surely know the next question...

Notes

1 http://www.brainyquote.com/quotes/authors/e/elbert_hubbard_2.html
2 http://thinkexist.com/quotes/david_tyson_gentry/
3 Laura Komócsin – Andrea Szabados, www.toolfulcoach.com
4 http://tn.gov/dohr/learning/pdf/CoachesCorner/FiveLevelsOfListening.pdf
5 André Louf: *Grace Can Do More: Spiritual Companionship & Spiritual Growth*. Cistercian Publications, 2002
6 Timothy Gallway: *The Inner Game of Tennis*. Bantam Books, 1982

C) Sample Questions of the SPARKLE Model

As illustrated in the book, the coach is able to assist the coachee through a wide array of tools. Many coaches, especially rookies, like to have a set of concrete questions at their disposal. What follows are some powerful questions along with the SPARKLE Model.

The question-list has a dual purpose:
1. It may help the coach in the initial practice, i.e. he or she may navigate the sessions along those lines and may select questions stretching from the Situation the Evaluation stage.
2. Clients could also be asked to answer some of these questions in writing between the introductory session and the first session as part of the intake process.

The client does not necessarily have to know the answer to all the questions by the first session, but at least we will know for certainty that the answers he or she is not familiar with need clarification. Therefore, it is worth focusing on these issues. Another advantage is that the coach may ascertain the coachee's intention to proceed along this path, knowing that he or she did not seek out a coach simply because it was trendy. This will attest to the determination of entering into a coaching relationship or conversely, if he will skip the first homework.

Lists of questions:

In the Situation stage

- What has been on your mind recently?
- What is the biggest challenge you are facing right now?
- Why do you need a coach?
- Why right now?
- Why did you choose this coach?
- In which way can the coach serve you that you are not presently able to do alone?
- Are you ready to deal with this topic seriously or do you need a coach to place the problem on someone else's shoulders?
- What do you expect the coach to contribute to the solution?
- What is the present situation that you would like to change? Explain in details!
- How are you feeling in this situation? In which other situations did you experience similar emotions?
- What steps have you taken thus far to solve the situation? What was its outcome?
- What is at stake with change?

In the Positioning stage

- What results would you like to achieve by the end of the coaching process? How would you be fulfilled?
- What is the desired outcome?
- What kind of changes would you like to effectuate, and how would it improve your situation?
- To what extent can you influence the results?
- How do you know that there is a problem? What evidence do you have?
- How will you know that the issue is resolved?
- Do you have any undisclosed ideas about a solution? Are you willing to examine any alternative solutions?
- What must occur for you to feel that we have reached the goal?
- Have you ever thought of what an optimal solution would be like?
- What would be the ideal solution?
- What is required to achieve this ideal solution?

Many clients already hold a preconceived notion about the solution when they meet the coach for the first time. They may not tell the coach at the first meeting, but they have the idea in their minds. For example: 'I'm unhappy' (a potential solution being "I have to buy a villa in Spain.") or "I'm too overweight." (a possible solution being "I have to go on a diet.")

In the Alternatives stage

- How can the present situation be satisfactorily addressed?
- And how else? And how else? (T-model: Expand questions)
- What would you suggest to your friend if he or she turned to you with a similar problem?
- What would an ideal person or celebrity suggest to you?
- What would you do if you had more time?
- What would you do if the budget was unlimited?
- What would you do if you were the leader/owner?
- What would you do if you could start on a clean slate?
- What would you do if you had no engagements? (Family, loans...)
- And what else? (It is useful to take a short pause after this question because generally, the automatic answer is that nothing else is coming to their mind. The coach also gains some time during the pause to find such further alternatives that the coachee has not even considered.)

In the Route stage

- According to what criteria would you like to make a decision?
- If you decide so, what consequences does it have on you and others?
- What are the advantages and the disadvantages of the alternatives?
- What are the risks?
- What can you gain or lose if you select this alternative?
- From which alternative can we expect the best solution?
- Which alternative do you prefer? To which one can you commit?
- What steps are you going to take and when? What is your action plan?

– How can you split your tasks into smaller parts?
– What will be your first step?

In the Key Obstacles stage

– What are your key obstacles, saboteurs?
– What do you need to do as the first step?
– How can the coach support you to get out of your comfort zone?
– What may cause difficulty in changes?
– What causes the most important obstacle in carrying out your decision?
– What are you going to do to prevent or overcome objections?
– How can the coach help you overcome difficulties?
– Have you ever tried it before? Have you ever failed? If so, why were you not successful consistently?
– What factors made you return to your earlier habits?

In the Leverage stage

– Congratulation: Once you succeed! How can you reach to have it as a habit and not only a one time occasion?
– Who and how can support you to keep focus on and keep going on?
– How can you leverage this into other areas?
– From 1 to 10, how would you rate your level of commitment to 'doing what you had planned' in the future as well? If not a 10, what do you have to do for 10?

In the Evaluation stage

– What has changed in comparison to the period preceding coaching?
– How would you summaries the coaching process for someone else?
– What did you learn from the process?
– What are you going to do in a different way according to this new learning?
– To what extent did you manage the change?
– How would you celebrate the progress to make sure you will remember that?

If the client thinks over these questions before meeting with the coach, it is clearly showing that he or she aspires to real change. A piece of good advice to the client: 'Take yourself seriously, and consequently, then the coach will also do so.'

D) Reconstruction of a Real Business Coaching Conversation

The following re-enacted conversation confirms the utility of the questioning techniques as a tool.

P (partner): Hello!
C (coach): Hello! Are you ready for the coaching session?
P: Yes, I am. I've just finished selecting these data. Let's begin.
C: I suggest that we go to the meeting room that you booked in advance. We can talk there uninterruptedly. We won't be disturbed by any phone calls and the sight of pedestrians. Is it alright?
  P: Alright. Would you like a glass of water?
  C: Yes, please. (*They enter the meeting room, close the door, sit down at a table, at right angles.*)
  C: When we first met, we were discussing your objective with these coaching sessions. You have also mentioned to me that a month ago, you were appointed group leader of the Call Center. Your boss asked for the coach's support so that you could achieve the 55% activity of your employees in three months. At our previous session, we discussed your alternative options to motivate your colleagues. As homework, you and your colleagues were asked to rank 10 items on the form, with '1' representing what motivated your colleagues most and '10' symbolizing what motivated them the least.
  P: Yes, here they are. I've already done it with eleven out of twenty individuals, and we liked it so much that this week I'm going to do it with the rest of them.
  C: I'm happy you enjoyed the task! How did you select those eleven people?
  P: I selected them from the best and weakest performers. They enjoyed it very much! They greatly appreciated it!
  C: ... *(silence, waiting)*
  P: It felt great for them to know that someone asked what motivated them at the workplace. It has never happened to them before... And fantastic conversations were initiated this way. You know, a lot of our colleagues are transferred from 'Work Centers'. Many of them can't cope with the stress and resign in a few months. Many students among them also have a part-time job during the year, and then leave in the summer. So, I can say that there were such people in the group whose names I didn't even know because I never spoke to them. I also get on well with those colleagues with whom I go out to for a drink. We have quite a good team there.

C: What did you learn from this homework on motivation?

P: The first thing is how much my colleagues enjoy talking. I've decided to do it more regularly in the future, although I don't know yet what the reason will be ...Never before did I think that we would have the time for such things. We are always so busy, with a lot of telephone calls, preparing for meetings, trainings, and interviews. Therefore, I'm always submerged under a pile of work. (*the coach may write down: time-management, submerged under a pile of work*). I don't even know how I managed to do it... I was able to map out the work very well. I talked to my colleagues for half an hour or forty-five minutes each; I had time for one or two conversations per day. I could sense that they too lightened up a bit, you know when the gossiping began: 'what is it?', and things like that.

C: Am I accurately sensing that this homework was a real success for you?

P: Yes, absolutely. It was also refreshing for me to be engaged in something different than the daily routine for a while. I enjoy partaking in diverse activities; however, I lack the tools to do so.

C: Let's get back to the consequences of the task. You've mentioned before that your colleagues enjoy talking and you regularly grant them this opportunity. What else did you learn through the task?

P: (*thinking*)... I was astonished to see that in most cases I thought that my colleagues were mostly motivated by money; this task showed me otherwise. Some of them are motivated by a secure workplace, while others, by the opportunity of obtaining a promotion.

C: Let's see a concrete example.

P: Here is this guy Peter, for example.

C: What is he like?

P: His performance is quite poor; that's why I chose him. I was definitely interested in learning about his motivations. I assumed it was money. Instead, he ranked 'daily acknowledgment for his work' in first place, a 'secure workplace' in second place, followed by money...

C: Let's do the following: Calculate the difference between the two columns and then add them... (*the partner is working*) What can you see?

P: There is quite a big difference... I guess, the larger the difference, the less I know my colleagues' motivation.

C: Yes. That's right.

P: Well...(*thinking*) It's clear that I hardly ever speak to this guy...(*thinking*) I should speak to him more often...

C: Why do you think it's so important?

P: In order to understand his motivations better, and it doesn't need much time. Sometimes, we sit down for half an hour; it's convenient and should be accorded time in the daily workload because it's great.

C: Thank you for saying it. It's really useful when there's a regular conversation between the leader and the colleagues... When are you planning to have a talk with him again?

P: If I talk to someone every other day, everyone is up every second month - as we are 20 in the team. I don't think I could fit one person in my schedule every other day, rather one or two people per week. So, I'll talk to him in three months' time.

C: Alright. Are you writing it in your diary?

P: (*she is writing in her diary*)

C: You were thinking about the reason for such a meeting.

P: Yes. And for what occasion will I organize such a meeting?

C: For which occasion would you organize it?

P: I don't know.

C: Let's think together!... (*silence, waiting*)

P: Maybe we shouldn't over-complicate this issue. In three months, there will be a team-building trip to a wine country, which will be a great opportunity for a half an hour conversation. I'll ask him about his expectations about team-building and the types of programs he would like, etc.

C: Alright, that sounds good. Let's get back to the motivational task. You've mentioned that your chosen person, Peter, placed daily acknowledgment for his work in first place, with a secure workplace in second, followed by money. What are you going to do with this information?

P: I'll present it to him.

C: Alright. What are you going to do actually?

P: I'm going to approach him and thank him for his great work.

C: Why is acknowledgment more than a simple 'thank you'?

P: *(thinking)* I don't know…*(she thinks, the coach is waiting patiently; silence).* I could acknowledge him for what he does.

C: Yeah. I'll draw it. *(she takes a sheet of paper and draws a circle)* We can acknowledge him for what he does. And what else?

P: For his professional demeanor.

C: *(she draws an outer, concentric circle)* Yes. Is this kind of acknowledgement long-lasting?

P: Maybe not. A handsome guy often hears such remarks- that he looks nice- so, that he will be unaffected by them.

C: I think so, too. It's much more long-lasting if you acknowledge his performance, and even more durable to cite one of his positive characteristics and tell him what exactly he had done to earn your acknowledgement *(she draws a circle inside and adds: What is he like?)*. All right, I'm asking you now to describe to me such an acknowledgement as if I were your colleague!

P: Peter, you are very precise. You handed in your schedule for next week in a timely manner.

C: Great! When are you going to approach him to tell him?

P: This afternoon!

C: Fine! Let's see your next colleague. Why have you chosen her?…*(they look at the activities in connection with the other colleagues, elaborating an action plan for each of them- when and what to do)*

C: Thank you very much for doing your homework so conscientiously. I'm very pleased that it made you feel so successful. What else do you think we should address today?

P: I don't know…. These days, I'm constantly thinking about whether I could achieve this 55% activity if I were my employees.

C: *(she's silent)*

P: When I was making telephone calls, I usually succeeded, but not always. And I used to be among the better performers, …that's why I'm the team-leader now.

C: What would you do to achieve the 55% activity?

P: You simply have to put your shoulder to the wheel and make one call after the other. I used to not feel like doing it because some days I was not in a good mood and it was more difficult. At that time, I needed my boss to motivate me. It was really useful to obtain the statistics from him about my performance, namely my activity, the number of products sold, and how many minutes I spent talking on the phone. All the data is in our computer system; it's easy to retrieve them.

C: You've mentioned two things- regular control and following statistics. From what you're saying, leaders impact their team's performance.

P: Yes, definitely. I can feel it stronger and stronger that it also depends on me.

C: According to your experiences, what do you think you could do as leader to increase the team members' sense of responsibility?

P: I'll also try to send them the statistics of the previous day... And if my colleagues slack off during the day, I'll speak to them personally and ask what happened.

C: When are you going to start?

P: Tomorrow morning.

C: Can we agree to it?

P: Yes, we can.

C: I would like for you to bring for our next session the totalized performance divided into days. How much is the average activity? What's the number of the products sold? How long is an average telephone call?

P: Alright.

C: By the way, what connection can you see between activity and the number of products sold?

P: The more active the colleagues are, the more products they sell.

C: And what else does the number of products sold depend on?

P: Well, it also depends on the client they call... We should select clients according to certain criteria. (*brief pause, she thinks*) The phrases that my colleagues employ when making a phone call make a difference too. They are allowed to use a pattern sentence, but when they are handling excuses, they must also use their heads. So, I can say that the number of products sold also depends on their technique of handling excuses.

C: So, this number depends both on selecting clients and to what extent your colleagues are good at handling excuses. And what's the number you would consider great?

P: Six in a six-hour shift. Approximately one per hour.

C: You operate as a profit-center. What do you get your bonus for?

P: Naturally, for the products sold. As we speak, I'm starting to realize that I don't know why we are measuring activity when we are much more interested in the number of products sold per hour. I simply 'inherited' it because it used to be so.

C: There's a management guru named Peter Drucker who says: ' We can manage only what we measure.' How does this saying fit in here?

P: Really! Gosh! How is it possible that I haven't thought of this! It also means that it matters a lot what we measure. I've been focusing on activity thus far, instead of paying attention to the number of products sold. However, the latter depends on several elements; it can be measured accurately, so it can be managed very well too. I've been focusing on the time my colleagues spend on in addition to the telephone, but I haven't been observing their performance.

P: How can you get a picture of it?

C: I regularly listen to the conversations, either immediately or post-recording. That way, I can hear their manner of handling excuses. I myself carry out the selection of clients; they are not involved in that aspect.

C: Alright. Next time would you like us to listen to some telephone calls so that we could hear how well your colleagues manage to handle excuses?

P: Yes, I would love to do that!

C: What lessons did you learn from our conversation today?

P: Two very important things. If we had talked about these earlier, I probably wouldn't be here now. I learned two significant management lessons. One of them is that, instead of guessing what motivates my colleagues I should ask them. I consider that these conversations should be undertaken on a regular basis. I'm glad that I wrote down the date of the next discussion in my diary! The other thing is the importance of daily acknowledgment, which should be more than a simple 'thank you'. Moreover, it doesn't cost anything. Thank you very much! And it is also fantastic that we've just realized that we should focus on the number of sold products instead of on the activity. The new target is to sell one product per hour.

C: This sounds great! Congratulations on being open; collaborating in this manner could be fruitful. If you regularly have a discussion with your colleagues, if you know their motivations, and often acknowledge them, how do all these elements contribute towards attainment of your target, namely to sell one product per hour?

P: It appears to be quite clear. How to motivate them to sell more products used to be one of my main problems. If I help them understand why it is rewarding to them – as I am aware of their motivation – I create a positive, empowering working environment and their productivity will surely grow. This will contribute towards achievement of their goals.

C: Great work today! Let's see your homework for the next two weeks.

P: I'll have to acknowledge my colleagues' work and examine the statistics every day. I'll bring them along with some recorded telephone conversations. My most important task consists of modifying the performance assessment so that achievements could be measured according to actual sales rates instead of activity. I would like you to help me review a concrete action plan for this issue at the following session.

C: Sounds good, we will do that. See you in two weeks! Enjoy the work!

References

Graham, Alexander and Renshaw, Ben: *Super Coaching.* Random House Business Books, 2005.
Axelrod, Mitchell: *The New Game of Business.* Mitchell Axelrod, 2004.
Bono, see de Bono
Buzan, Tony: *The Mind Map Book.* Penguin Books, 1996.
Cameron, Julia: *The Artist's Way.* Penguin Group, 2002.
Cope, Mick: *The Seven Cs of Coaching: The Definitive Guide to Collaborative Coaching.* Financial Times Management, 2004.
Carson, Richard David: *Taming Your Gremlin: A Surprisingly Simple Method for Getting Out of Your Own Way.* Quill, 2003.
de Bono, Edward: *Six Thinking Hats.* Penguin Books, 2002.
de Vries, Manfred Kets: *Sex, Money, Happiness and Death: The Quest for Authenticity.* Palgrave Macmillan, 2009.
de Vries, Manfred Kets: *The Happiness Equation.* Vermilion. 2002
de Vries, Manfred Kets; Korotov, Konstantin, and Treacey, Elizabeth Florent: *Coach and Couch: The Psychology of Making Better Leaders.* INSEAD Business Press, 2007.
Downey, Myles: *Effective Coaching.* Texere Publishing, 2003.
Drucker, Peter Ferdinand: *Innovation and Entrepreneurship.* HarperCollins, 1985.
Drucker, Peter Ferdinand: *The Effective Executive.* Butterworth-Heinemann, 2007.
Ellis, Keith: *The Magic Lamp: Goal Setting for People Who Hate Setting Goals.* Three Rivers Press, 1998.
Gallway, Timothy*: The Inner Game of Tennis: The Classic Guide to the Mental Side of Peak Performance.* Random House Trade Paperbacks, 1997.
Dr. Gordon, Thomas: *Leader Effectiveness Training (L.E.T.).* Perigee Trade, 2001.
Hawkins, Peterand Shohet, Robin: *Supervision in the Helping Profession.* Open University Press, 1989.
Kaplan, Robert Samuel and Norton, David P.: *Balanced Scorecard – Measures that Drive Performance.* Harvard Business Review, 2005. Vol. 83.
Karpman, Stephen: 'Fairy Tales and Script drama analysis'. Transactional Analysis Bulletin, 1968.
Kimsey-House, Karen; Kimsey-House, and Henry; Sandahl, Phillip: *Co-Active Coaching: Changing Business, Transforming Lives.* Nicholas Brealey Publishing, 2011.
Lee, Graham: *Leadership Coaching.* Chartered Institute of Personnel and Development, 2003.
Leonard, Thomas: http://www.surpassyourdreams.com/CoachingModels.pdf
Louf, André: *Grace Can Do More: Spiritual Companionship & Spiritual Growth.* Cistercian Publications, 2002.
Michalko, Michael: *Thinkertoys.* Ten Speed Press, 2006.
Mórotz, Kenéz and Perczel Forintos, Dóra: *Cognitive Behavior Therapy,* trans. Zita Delevic. Budapest, Hungary: Medicina, 2005.
Passmore, Jonathan: *Excellence in Coaching: The Industry Guide,* Kogan Page, 2010.
Rifenbary, Jay: *No Excuse!* Possibility Press, 2007.

Savage, Grant, Nix, Timothy, Whitehead, Carlton, and Blair, John: *Strategies for Assessing and Managing Organizational Stakeholders.* Academy of Management Executive, 1991.

Szabo, Peter and Meier, Daniel: *Coaching Plain & Simple: Solution-focused Brief Coaching Essentials.* W.W. Norton & Company, 2009.

Vogelauer, Werner: *Methoden-ABC im Coaching,* Luchterhand Verlag GmbH, 2011.

Vries, see de Vries

Vries, Korotov and Tracey see de Vries, Korotov and Tracey

Ward, Lynn I: *4 Keys to Being a Million Dollar Dreamer.* 2005.
http://www.powerfull-living.biz/4KeystoBeingaMillionDollarDreamer.pdf

Whitmore, John: *Coaching for Performance: GROWing Human Potential and Purpose - The Principles and Practice of Coaching and Leadership,* Nicholas Brealey Publishing, 2009.

About the Author

Laura Komócsin - ICF accredited coach

After graduating as an economist in 1998, Laura started to work at Accenture (previously Andersen Consulting), where she had been working for 6 years as a Management Consultant. She worked in the Netherlands, England and Malaysia, for such multinational companies as SHELL, TESCO and BAT. She has been involved in the coaching field since 2003.

Laura was the founder President of the Hungarian Chapter of the International Coach Federation between 2008 and 2010. She also teaches at the Executive Coach and Mentor Academy at the KPMG-BME Academy (a management school, established by KPMG in Hungary and the Budapest University of Technology and Economics/BME) a curriculum that Laura developed herself . The subjects in her course include the basics and methodology of coaching, coaching tools, and the marketing of coaching.

As an Executive Coach she has successfully supported executives and senior executives of several large companies such as AMEX, UPC, Vodafone, TESCO, Kraft, Deutsche Telekom, Telenor, Erste Bank, TNT, MTV,etc.

Laura regularly gives lectures as a guest speaker at several universities and colleges and she had been interviewed over the past few years with almost every major business related newspaper and radio station in Hungary. She believes in the power of coaching and this belief motivated Laura to pass her knowledge on to as wide an audience as possible.

Her books published in Hungarian became bestsellers. Besides the two methodological handbooks (the English edition of the first volume that you hold in your hands and the other volume, which covers 21 classical coaching techniques with tools and tips) Laura is also the author of another coaching book, in which she shares 77 stories with coaches and executives.

She was included in the list of the "25 Most Important Hungarian Women in 2010". In 2011, she was awarded the title of the best known Hungarian Coach, and the Business Coach LLC lead by her is the best known coaching company in Hungary.

She lives with her husband and two children in Budapest, Hungary.

About the Coach Editor

Zita Delevic, PhD

Zita is an Executive Coach and Human Resources Consultant based in Miami, FL. She has been involved in the coaching field since 2005, graduated from The Coaches Training Institute (CTI) in London and New York and continues to study with the Center for Right Relationships (CRR). Her signature 3-step *New Leader Success Acceleration Programs* help executives moving into a new position to become effective and successful from Day 1. Her passion is working with high achieving leaders and their teams to maximize their personal and professional potential. Earlier in her career Zita served as Human Resources Manager for General Electric where she was responsible for change management and organizational development projects.

In addition to working as a coach, Zita is also a certified Senior Professional in Human Resources (SPHR), member of the Society for Human Resource Management (Greater Miami Chapter) and the International Coach Federation (ICF). She is a licensed provider of the Quantum Endeavor corporate coaching programs. Besides running her business, PebbleJam Leadership Coaching and Consulting (www.pebblejam.com), Zita currently serves as the President of the South Florida Charter Chapter of the International Coach Federation. She can be reached at zita@pebblejam.com.